To Ian,

An excellent friend!

Jake Beaty

Winter's Comin'

Jake Beaty and Jim Beaty

Tunari Press
GERMANTOWN, TENNESSEE

Jake Beaty/Tunari Press
3630 Crestwyn Drive
Germantown, Tennessee 38138
http://www.jakebeatyauthor.com

Publisher's Note: This is a memoir. Every attempt has been made to be as accurate as possible, including interviews with people who know the story and searching *The Lake Chelan Mirror*, the local newspaper. Some names have been changed to protect the guilty.

Book Layout ©2013 BookDesignTemplates.com
Book Cover by Sarah Loehr: http://www.thesarahco.com

Ordering Information:
Quantity sales. Special discounts are available on quantity purchases by corporations, associations, and others. For details, contact the "Special Sales Department" at the address above.

Winter's Comin'/ Jake Beaty. -- 1st ed.
ISBN 978-0-9972938-0-7

This book is dedicated to our children.

{ Prologue }

I WASN'T GOING TO SAY, "I wish I had."

I left work that afternoon, and when I arrived at home, I said to my wife, "It's time."

"Okay," she said, "We're as ready as we're ever going to be. Let's go."

I called my mom, breathless. "Hi, Mom. It's time!' We're moving to eastern Washington and building ourselves a log house."

"Oh, Jimmy, I don't like this," Mom said. "Are you really sure you should? It's silly and dangerous. What makes you think you can build a house by yourself, anyway?"

"Mom, Thea and I took Skip's class. Thea's going to help. We'll be fine, the babies will be fine. If it doesn't work out, we can always move back. We're not going to die over there, Ma! I'll have at least tried and not just wished I had."

"Oh, Jimmy. You should see the people in Europe, my cousins in Hungary. They have to go out in the street to get their water. The mom and dad live there with their two daughters and their two families—all living in the same house! They have one bathroom in a three-bedroom house. Why would you do that? Why would you move away from civilization?"

"Adventure, Mom! It's going to be okay. It's something I have to do."

Thea called her dad to share the news. He was no more encouraging.

"What are you going to do for work when you get there?" he demanded.

"We'll find jobs."

"You can't do that!"

"Yes, we can, Dad. You'll see."

After the call, Thea told me, "You know, my mom told my dad *no* all the time. 'No, you can't start your own business.' 'No, you can't build a house.' 'No, you can't have that car.' I listened to it all the time, and my dad never said a word. He just...lamented. I decided I'd never do that to my husband."

This move was a long time coming, and now the pieces had all come together.

{ 1 }

YEARS EARLIER, IN 1970, during my first year of college at the Burnley School of Professional Art in Seattle, a friend of mine knew some administrators at the University of Washington with a job offer. They had purchased a large thirteen-bedroom lodge in north central Washington.

The lodge had been vandalized and used as a party house by local youth in winters past, and we were to live there over the winter in order to prevent it from happening again. There were going to be eight of us: me, Debbie, Dave and Becky, Rick and Sue, and Charlie and Rosa. Watching the lodge wasn't a paying job, but we'd have a place to stay rent-free, without utility bills.

The lodge sat in the nearly eight hundred acres of the Diamond Bell Ranch in Wauconda, Washington. Lake Walker, about forty acres itself, stretched away from the lodge into a thick forest of tall ponderosa pine trees. In the lodge, an immense rock chimney towered over the four hundred eighty square foot living room. The fireplace itself was five feet wide, three feet tall. Wide stairways marched up both sides of the living room to the three-sided balcony of bedrooms above. Thirty people could sit in the dining room, served by a kitchen any chef would envy.

We had arrived in late June, after classes had let out for the summer, and there was still a chill in the air at night. The lodge was about four thousand feet above sea level and only a few miles south of the Canadian border in the heart of the North Cascades. The hottest day in July didn't hit eighty degrees. We explored the surrounding acres, finding several crumbling log cabins and small dilapidated board-and-batten houses—evidence of shattered homestead dreams over a hundred years before.

None of us had a regular paying job. Though we qualified for food stamps, there were other things we needed to buy that we couldn't purchase with food stamps. Charlie's parents in California needed their house painted, and they were willing to pay three of us a hundred dollars each for the job. Debbie, Charlie, Rosa, Dave, Becky and I loaded the truck with our gear and headed south in early September. We'd be back to the ranch when we had some cash.

Rosa had a great dog named Santo, and Charlie and I decided we wanted dogs, too. Charlie wanted a Malamute and I was interested in a Samoyed. I found a newspaper ad offering Samoyeds in Redmond, which was on our way south. We arrived to see several little white puff balls scurrying around the living room.

One caught my eye. She was smaller than the rest and ducked under the couch when we came into the house. I decided she was the one for me. I named her Clowd for obvious reasons, though I spelled it differently—that's just how I am. She was the runt of the litter and never did get very big, but she sure was smart. She and I spent every minute together—we became fast friends.

We painted the house, and during that time in California, I celebrated my 21st birthday. I wanted to get back home for a while before returning to the Diamond Bell Ranch. Debbie decided not to return. The others wanted to stay down south a few more weeks, so I loaded my pack, stuck out my thumb, and Clowd and I headed north. Our first ride took us from San Mateo to Napa, just north of the Golden Gate Bridge.

It was still early afternoon, so I stuck out my thumb again. A family in a VW bus stopped and gave me and my dog a ride up the coast. We went a long way north, to the town of Fort Bragg, arriving at their home way after dark. They put us up for the night and shared their breakfast. They had a dog, too and shared some food with Clowd.

Next morning, they took us back to the highway.

I stuck out my thumb and headed north.

We walked for hours. There were few cars on the road, and none stopped. We walked all day and passed only a few houses. We must have walked twenty miles when we came to a solitary little grocery store. I tied Clowd to the stair railing and stepped inside to buy something for us to eat.

"Why is it so slow out there?" I asked the fellow behind the counter. "There's not much traffic. We're trying to get to Seattle, and it's hard to get a ride with no cars."

"It's pretty quiet during the week this far north," he said. "Weekends are much busier."

I had no intention of waiting until the weekend.

"We'll just keep walking, Clowd," I said as I sat on the steps to share a snack with her. "We'll find a place along the road to spend the night. We'll keep each other warm." She cocked her head to listen, and I think she understood. It was the end of September, but we were still in California.

While we were sitting on the steps, a man in a station wagon came rolling in. He was a younger guy in a plaid shirt. He hopped out and went into the store. Minutes later, he came back out.

"You headed north?" I asked him.

"I sure am," he said. "You need a ride?"

"Yes, please!" What a relief we didn't have to walk the rest of the way to Seattle! We loaded up our stuff and away we went.

"Thanks for the ride," I said. "I'm glad for any miles we don't have to walk. How far are you going?"

"I just got off my boat," he said. "I'm a fisherman headed back to Corvallis, Oregon."

What luck! That's hundreds of miles closer to Seattle. We talked about a lot of things and it was a very pleasant time. He seemed like a regular guy.

We must have driven nearly four hundred miles when he finally turned off the highway and headed west. As the sky darkened he explained, "We'll be staying with some friends of mine out in the country, west of Corvallis." The narrow two-lane road wound through the hills toward the coast, into darkness.

He turned off the paved road onto gravel, and drove a few more miles. We approached a corner and he began to slow down, but he didn't turn. I couldn't see anything in the dark. We dropped off the gravel road down onto a two-track path that led out into a field.

My heart raced. *Oh man, where are we going?* I wondered. *Was this a bad decision? This might not end well.* We slowed to a stop and his headlights shone on a giant blackberry patch the size of a house. I braced myself. *What have I done?*

He honked the horn. A golden light blinked on from within the middle of the blackberry patch. "We're here!" he said. I could make out the silhouette of a woman in a long dress, waving in our direction. Then a guy behind her, waving too. There's a house in there, I realized, completely covered by that heap of blackberries. And people living in it!

I let out a sigh of relief. I hadn't till then realized I'd been holding my breath.

We found our way to the door and went inside. It was an old house that had been rebuilt. Warm and homey inside, it smelled of grain and seeds and incense and patchouli. They welcomed me as if we'd been friends for years. They made me a bed and served tea. We talked into the night.

Next morning, the fisherman offered us a ride back to the freeway, which was now many miles away to the east. I accepted and he delivered us to the northbound on-ramp of I-5 at Corvallis.

"Thanks for the long ride north, and for getting us back out to the freeway," I said.

"You're welcome," he said, and drove off.

While waiting, thumb out, I saw a very large beaver in the drainage ditch down near the freeway that disappeared into the culvert. Clowd saw it, too. Her ears perked and she whined and chattered, wanting to go after it. She was still very young, so I told her, "No. Who knows what a beaver could do to my best friend?"

Not five minutes later, a Chinese man with a heavy accent pulled up next to us and asked, "Ride?"

"Seattle?" I answered.

He smiled big, nodded his head, and waved me in. I put my pack in the back seat and slid in up front, Clowd on the seat next to me. His car was a mint 1961 Chevy Bel Air.

"Nice car you've got, here," I said. "It's in great condition." He smiled big and nodded. "I learned to drive in a '62 Impala," I said. He smiled the same big smile and nodded again. "You must have no idea what I'm saying," I said. He smiled and nodded. I smiled back and looked out the window.

I dozed off, awakening only as we crossed into Washington. A couple of hours later we were passing through Seattle and approaching the University district, my destination. I waved to the right and said, "Let me out here." He smiled and took the exit. I motioned to the right, but he stayed left and turned across the freeway on 45th, heading west, the wrong way.

"Okay, pal, just let me out anywhere along here," I said.

He kept going. *How do I get this guy to stop?*

"STOP!" I yelled.

He flinched and yanked the steering wheel. The car veered to the right and he sideswiped two parked cars, busting off his own mirror. He kept driving! I grabbed the door handle and started to pull—I wanted out! He stopped in the middle of the street, and I bailed out.

"Let me grab my pack!" I said, afraid he'd drive off with it.

I opened the back door and snatched my pack as he pulled away. "Thanks," I hollered after him. He grinned from ear to ear as he disappeared up the hill.

Several people were witness to the sideswiping and looked at me as if I were somehow responsible. "I don't even know that guy. He just gave me a ride." I was just glad Clowd and I were safe in Seattle with all our gear.

We walked back down the hill toward the U-district, and made our way over to the 'Ave' where a friend of mine worked. She was glad to see me and loved my little puppy. She gave me a ride to my mom's house in Edmonds as I shared my recent experiences.

"Oh, Jimmy, I'm so glad you're home," said my mom as she hugged me tight. "I just worry about you so much when you're with those friends of yours. Oh, and who is this?" she asked, seeing my dog.

"This is Clowd. I spell it C-L-O-W-D. Clowd, meet my mom."

Mom extended her arms straight out to take the dog, and Clowd seemed happy to go, wagging her tail and licking mom's hand. "Oh, she's so sweet!"

"We're only going to stay for a week, Mom, and then we're headed back to the Diamond Bell."

"I wish you could stay longer. You just got back."

"I know, mom, but there's a ton of work for us to do to get ready for winter. Winter's coming, whether we're ready or not."

"Yes, Jimmy. Well, I hope you find what you're looking for so you can get this out of your system and come back home soon—to stay. Your mom needs you, you know."

"Yeah, Mom, I know."

The week passed quickly, and Mom drove me to the bus station, trying once more to get me to reconsider. I waved goodbye as I walked to the bus.

This was it!

{ 2 }

CLOWD AND I STEPPED OFF THE GREYHOUND, in Tonasket to be greeted by Charlie and Rosa in the truck. I threw my pack in the back, and Clowd sat on my lap as we drove to the ranch daydreaming aloud about the adventure ahead.

The nights of late September were cold and we woke up to thick frost every morning.

"I see you've cut some firewood, Dave," I said.

"Yeah, but it sure isn't enough for the whole winter. The woodshed will hold ten times what I've cut so far. It's a big fireplace and the wood burns up fast. Let's cut down that big tree on the north side of the lake. I bet it would last us the whole winter," he said.

The tree was massive—maybe four feet through at the bottom. "Yeah, it's close, and we wouldn't need to cut down any other trees. Let's do it!"

We brought out the bow saw first. I held it up to the tree and Dave and I both laughed—it looked miniature next to the huge trunk. "We're going to have to do this the old fashioned way," I said.

"Like Paul Bunyan," he said, holding up a double-bladed axe with a smile.

There were two axes, so we set to work.

My axe bit into the tree. It felt good. I swung again at a different angle and I liberated a little wedge of bark and

{ 11 }

wood. "This is great," I said to Dave. "I'll make an under-cut on the side toward the lodge, and if you chop on the backside, we can meet in the middle."

Dave agreed and set to work on the backside. We chopped and chopped from opposite sides, settling into a steady rhythm, sometimes matching each other stroke for stroke. I liked the sound, as if the axes were talking—one thud, then another, back and forth, thud, thud, thud, thud. Hours later, it was getting dark and satisfaction had turned to exhaustion. We stepped back to look at our notches in the tree—we'd barely made a dent!

"We can probably finish the job tomorrow," Dave said.

"Yeah, let's get started in the morning," I replied.

The next morning, we both woke up aching and stiff all over.

"I didn't realize how out of shape I was," said Dave.

"We might have bitten off more than we can chew," I said.

We ate our breakfast and trudged back to the tree, axes slung over our aching shoulders.

Dave wondered out loud, "How did the pioneers *do* this?" We whacked away for several more hours and finally gave up for the day at lunchtime. We were making some progress, but still had a long way to go.

"So, how'd you do?" Charlie asked back at the house.

"Not so good," Dave said.

"Once you chop the tree down," Charlie asked, "how are you going to cut it into lengths?"

Dave and I looked at one another. "Hadn't thought that far ahead," Dave said. "We'll think it through tomorrow. It'll be easier to work with, once it's on the ground."

"You know," I said. "It would go a lot faster if we had some help from you two guys. Winter's coming, and we're not even close to ready. What are you guys even doing, anyway? Sitting up here at the house all day—listening to music?"

Charlie looked smug, but didn't say anything. Rick acted as if he hadn't heard me.

The next day, our hands ached, our backs ached, our shoulders were sore, and other muscles we didn't even know we had cried out. We were determined to get the job done, though, so we chopped and swung and hacked and worked at that giant tree through the cold morning hours.

"Man, this was a bad idea," Dave said. "We're not even a quarter of the way through this tree, and we still have to cut it up before we can even hope to move it."

"We might have to split them first," I said. "Even the rounds will be too heavy to move. We need a chainsaw."

"Should we give up on this?" Dave asked. "Maybe there's another way to keep warm."

In the back of my mind, I worried for the first time this wasn't going to work out. The ladies were doing their part at the house and kept us well fed, but the other two guys wouldn't lift a finger.

Rosa made tortillas from scratch. She hand-rolled the corn flour masa balls, and squished them flat in her battered wooden tortilla press. She'd toss one in a hot frying pan, and when it puffed up like a balloon, flip it over barehanded. She'd wait, then snatch it away and cast in the next. She topped her fresh, hot tortillas with shredded beef, diced avocado, a squeeze of lime and chopped cilantro.

She made a stew of cubed pork, slow-cooked in a sweet red chile sauce. Heaped in the bowl like a tumble of bricks, spoons could cut the pork. The savory aromas welcomed us back to the lodge and set our mouths watering. Rosa had learned from her mom. Becky had not, so she watched Rosa. Becky prepared chicken enchiladas one night, and was worried no one would like them.

"No, really, Becky, they're great. You're a good cook."

We returned to the house just before one o'clock in the afternoon and Charlie was still in bed! It would be dark in a few more hours. I was disappointed to think this adventure, this commune experience, was bound to fail because some appoint themselves as leaders and then expect the others to do the work. I spent the next couple days trying to figure out how we could make it work, but it was getting too late in the year. I was pretty sure we'd already missed our chance.

One morning, we woke to snow on the ground. The sky was blue and the sun bright, but the air was frigid. Clowd was getting bigger, but was still a puppy. She and Santo, Rosa's dog, were outside in the front of the house. I had let her out and gone back to my room to get ready for the day.

I looked out my window to see Clowd and Santo playing together down below. It was like Santo was the teacher and Clowd was the student. They sat side by side and Santo would look over at Clowd. He'd take off at full speed through the snow, dodging bushes, circling trees, running back and forth across the yard then sliding to a stop next to Clowd, his tongue hanging out, panting. He'd look at Clowd as if to say, "Now you go!"

She had stayed sitting, and watched intently as Santo ran his course. She'd tear off and follow his track exactly, returning to the start where Santo waited, watching to make sure she had not missed any turns. I watched, delighted as they shared the fun.

That morning Dave and I took the truck for a supply run. We started at Vern and Irene's general store. They had one gas pump and ran the Wauconda post office out the back. Vern and Irene didn't have all we needed, so we drove a few miles north to another tiny store at the south end of Lake Bonaparte. They didn't have everything we needed either, so we drove to Tonasket, about twenty-five miles west.

When we returned to the lodge, there was a station wagon parked out front. We came in through the back door and could hear a conversation in the dining room. We found four young men, wearing cowboy hats, sitting and talking to the rest of them. They wondered who we were, where we'd come from. We told them the story.

"So, are you guys hippies?" one of them asked with a creepy grin.

"Well, not really. We do want to get back to the land and be self-sufficient."

The same guy had been eyeing the girls and he asked, "Are you into free love and all that?"

"No, we're not."

"C'mon, what kind of hippies are you, then?" He lunged for Loraine and yanked her onto his lap. His friends laughed nervously. Rosa's eyes had a panicked look as she struggled.

Dave, Charlie, Rick and I all stood up and shouted at once.

"Turn her loose!"

"Get your hands off her!"

"Let her go!"

"Get out!"

Rosa broke free and ran across the room. The four of us faced the four of them, and they stood to leave. We followed them out and watched them pile into their car and drive away.

"These must be those cowboys from the valley we heard about," I said. "The guys who'd get drunk and bust up the lodge."

"Are you okay, Rosa?" I asked.

"Yeah, I'm just a little shook up. I sure didn't expect that!"

"Man, I'm glad they didn't start a fight," Dave said.

Charlie said, "I hope they just stay away and leave us alone."

Hours later, after dark, we had all gone upstairs to get ready for bed when we heard the faint drone of a vehicle approaching the house. Headlights flashed through the trees. The station wagon. They pulled up to the front of the house and opened their doors, laughing. Drunk.

Three or four stayed at the car as one of them clomped across the porch to the front door. He banged on the door, groped the knob. "We want in!" he yelled. "We just want to talk! Let us in!"

Dave hollered down, "Go away! We've all gone to bed!"

"That's okay! We just want to talk to your women!" he slurred. The guys by the car were laughing and egging him on.

I lifted up my window, and I yelled, "Go away, we don't want any trouble. If you don't leave, we're gonna call the sheriff."

"Go ahead," they said, "He's a long way from here tonight!"

The guy continued to bang on the door and the front windows. His buddies continued to laugh.

I grabbed my bolt-action .270 Winchester rifle and chambered a round. I aimed the rifle high and yelled, "Get out of here!" I pulled the trigger. Boom!

The guys at the car swore and yelled.

The guy on the porch scrambled back to the car in a flurry of whirling legs and arms. The driver started the car and peeled away, spraying dirt and snow, while the last guy was still closing his door.

"Wow, Jim, I'm sure glad you had that gun!" said Dave.

"Yeah, I think I scared them pretty good."

"I was so scared," Rosa said. "Who knows what might have happened if you didn't have that rifle?"

"I bet they stay away for good this time," said Charlie. "That should be the last we see of them."

The next time Dave and I went shopping at Vern and Irene's, we told them what had happened.

"I bet I know who they were," said Irene.

"Should we report it to the sheriff?" I asked.

"You can if you want to, but there are only a few deputies in the whole county and these boys are in trouble all the time. Sounds like you scared them and they probably won't bother you anymore. Otherwise, how you guys doing up there on the Diamond Bell? Are you ready for winter?"

"Nowhere near," I said.

"We were trying to chop down this big tree to use for firewood," Dave said, "but we gave up after a couple days. It was just too huge."

"That was a green tree," Vern said, "and wouldn't have been dry enough to burn this year anyway."

"Hadn't thought of that," I said. "The others are moving into Tonasket. They're going to rent a place to wait out the winter and start up again come spring."

"Good idea," said Irene." Winter can be pretty tough around here."

I was disappointed we had failed and I wasn't about to hole up in Tonasket for the winter. How could they afford to rent a place for five or six months, anyway?

"Becky and I are going to Canada," Dave said. "I don't want to be drafted and go to Viet Nam."

"I'm going back to Edmonds," I said. "I can't get drafted because of my surgeries—I already tried to enlist. I'll figure out how to follow my dream, but I'll do it on my terms. And no one else is going to interfere and mess it up."

"Good luck, Jim. This was fun while it lasted. Nice to get to know you."

"You too, Dave, Becky. Good luck."

Those who moved to town only lasted a month. They returned to California by the first of November.

{ 3 }

CLOWD AND I TOOK THE GREYHOUND BACK to Seattle and moved in with my mom until I could get settled. She was glad I was back sooner than she'd expected. But she figured wrong if she thought living in the woods was something I'd gotten out of my system. Someday I'd go back, and do it right, but that time was still a few years away.

In the meantime, casting about for my future, shunning the deadlines and rejections of a career in commercial art, I signed up for a course at Montana State University in farrier science—horse shoeing. I had always loved horses, and this way I could get paid to work with them every day.

I took Clowd with me to Bozeman, Montana and we secured a room at the Kester Hotel at the east end of town. Mr. Kester, the owner, was a tall, thin, older guy who reminded me of Ichabod Crane of Sleepy Hollow fame.

That first weekend, before class started, Mr. Kester said, "I own an RV park at West Yellowstone called the O-Bar-L Guest Ranch. How'd you like to earn a week's rent, helping me clear some snow? I need to get ready for the spring visitors."

"Absolutely!" I said.

We drove past immense herds of elk and even a few moose on our way to the O-Bar-L.

The snow was thigh-deep at his RV park.

"Here's the plan," Kester said, "We need to find the water, power, and septic hook-ups at each site. There are twenty-four sites under all this snow. I have a map of all the hook-ups, and I know right where they are."

He handed me a shovel. "I'll just step these off and you dig where I stop."

He backed up against the office wall and stomped through the snow, his lanky legs covering the ground. He counted out loud with each step, "One, two, three, four,..."

He turned to face me. "Dig here!" he said.

I dug, I found gravel. "No hook-ups here, Mr. Kester," I said.

"Move over this way just a bit," he said. "It's gotta be right here somewhere."

I dug again. More gravel.

He went back to the office wall again and strode out in a different direction, counting out loud. "Dig here!"

Again I dug. Gravel. We repeated this process for hours. We found four hook-ups.

"Well, that will do for today," he said, "but I do want to get that snow off the office roof."

"Hi, Mr. Kester." A young guy said as he walked up. "You need any help?"

"Hi, Andy. Yes we do. We're going to get the snow off the office roof."

We leaned a tall ladder against the edge of the roof and climbed up. It had an upstairs loft, so we were about fourteen feet off the ground.

"We'll get this front side if you'll start on the back," Mr. Kester told me.

I hiked over the peak to the other side, starting near the bottom, and chopped into the snow on my downhill side. I worked across the roof parallel to the edge. After about fifteen feet, a big chunk of snow broke loose and fell with a muffled thud. "This isn't going to be so bad," I thought.

Half an hour later, I started my final pass across the roof's peak. I looked over to check the progress of Andy and Mr. Kester. They were standing on top of the chunk they were working on, down near the eave. It was a big piece and they had started at the top and worked their way down the roof.

Man, that must have been a lot of work to throw the snow over the patch below them, I thought. Then I saw their perilous position.

Andy chopped away the last connection holding up the snow they were both standing on. The chunk broke free, and slid down the roof. Kester and Andy rode it over the edge, disappearing in a puff of whirling snow.

I walked down their side of the roof. When the cloud of snow cleared, I saw arms and legs and the kid's stocking cap in a huge pile of snow.

I almost laughed out loud, but I also knew it could be serious. I saw movement. Andy and Kester were emerging from the pile.

"Are you all right?" I hollered.

Mr. Kester looked up at me and nodded.

"I'll finish this in a few minutes," I said, "so you guys can stay down there."

I worked another ten minutes to push down the last big chunk of snow, then crawled down the ladder. Mr. Kester had a fire roaring in the office's tin stove. Kester turned around to warm his back and squatted down to catch heat.

That's awful close, I thought, when the entire back of his nylon quilted jacket melted into a wad.

"Look out!" I yelled.

He leapt away and pulled off his jacket. "Oh, no, look what I've done now!" he said, seeing the melted mess that had been his jacket. "Let's get back to Bozeman," he said, looking embarrassed and exhausted.

◥◣◢◤

I started class Monday. We learned corrective shoeing and blacksmithing. We made shoes from a flat bar using a forge and anvil just like the smithies in the old west. Local farmers brought in their horses and we shoed them under the watchful eye of our master farrier and teacher, Scott Simpson, for a dollar each.

One time, a local farmer brought in a matched pair of Percherons. Their feet were bigger than dinner plates. They only needed a trim and not shoes, so Scott assigned each of the eight of us a foot to trim.

I got the left front foot of one of those massive horses. His head alone was as big as my torso. I cleaned out his sole, then placed his hoof on my knee to finish trimming.

He pushed down with a hoof twice as wide as my leg and stood up on my knee. I dropped his foot and scolded him for his behavior. I picked his foot up again and placed it on my knee, and again he stood, his full weight on my scrawny little knee.

"Stop it," I yelled.

Scott came over to see what was up.

"He keeps standing up on me when I go to trim his foot."

"Well, boys," he announced. "It's time you all learned how to throw a horse!"

He led the horse outside and we all gathered around. He instructed us to first hobble the front feet together with a stout rope, then tie another rope below the fetlock of each hind foot and run the loose ends up between the front feet. Two of us on each rope would pull the slack and the horse would gather his balance, and with each pull get his hind feet closer to the front. His feet were nearly together, but he still didn't go down!

Scott called to the rest of the guys to give this horse a shove so he'd go down to his side, where we could finish the job of trimming his feet. All eight of us pushed like a football team to get that big old horse to go down. The horse grunted when he hit the ground. We bound his feet together and I went back to finish what I'd started a half hour earlier.

That giant horse struggled to free himself. The ropes were just loose enough for his right hind leg to slip through the binding and punch me square in the chest. I flew ten feet and landed with a thud on my back. A couple of guys jumped on top of the horse to keep him down and Scott came over to ask if I was all right.

"I don't think I'm hurt," I said. "The hoof was so big, it's like he pushed me."

"Well then, get back over here and finish this up." he said. We re-tied the feet and finally got all four feet done.

In addition to technical knowledge, we learned the physiology of horses' legs and feet. Our class even had a chance to trim the feet of a herd of steers. We ran them into a shoot next to a table and bound them to it with heavy straps. Then we tipped the table flat so the steer was on its side and we trimmed the feet at our waist level. We trimmed dozens of them. It was fascinating and I learned a lot, graduating second out of eight.

Back in Edmonds, I tried to build my own farrier business. I bought an anvil, hammers, nippers, clinchers, pullers, cutters, rasps, knives, hoof picks, and made a leather apron. I printed some business cards and set up columns in my ledger to track income and expenses. I walked into a large tack store, expecting to be able to leave a stack of my business cards near the register.

"We don't have enough room for all you guys to be leaving your business cards. Just write your name on the farrier list over there," the cashier said, pointing to a bulletin board. The first sheet of notebook paper had a name and phone number filling every line. I lifted the first sheet and I saw the first open line two-thirds of the way down the second sheet.

"There are that many farriers in Snohomish County?" I asked.

She nodded her head.

I hadn't seen that coming.

The calls trickled in, apparently from owners who had called down the list one farrier at a time, being repeatedly refused due to the nastiness of their horses. Unsuspecting at first, I agreed to the jobs. The horses bit, kicked, jumped, reared, spun, or refused to stand still. After three bites on my shoulder, and two close calls with hooves striking past my face, I rethought the whole thing. It might have been lucrative, someday, but I didn't want to get hurt in the process. I figured when I finally got my own horses, at least I could do all the trimming and shoeing myself.

{ 4 }

I HAD ALWAYS BEEN INTRIGUED by mechanical things. As a kid, I took everything apart. I could always get them put back together again and even made repairs if needed. I took my bike apart many times and understood its workings pretty well. Hearing of a job at a bicycle shop nearby, I applied for a mechanics' position. After a short interview, I was hired. I repaired, adjusted and assembled new bikes. It was a good job and I enjoyed the work, but it didn't pay very well.

Not long after, I had a chance to double my pay, taking a job in Shelton with Simpson Timber. I had logged for ITT Rainier in Gray's Harbor after graduating high school, so I knew what I was getting into. I worked as a choker setter for a few months, which means I placed a noose of cable around each tree that choked tighter the harder it was pulled. It was grueling work to climb over and under and around the massive logs, lying like pick-up sticks, with an armload of heavy chokers, but my body adapted, and thanks to all that work, I was in the best shape ever.

I worked in the woods all winter. I set many chokers, but also spent time setting up spar trees. We had to find a tree at least a hundred and twenty feet tall, and maneuver it along the winding logging roads with a bulldozer on both ends. At the site, the rig-up lead would select a dozen stumps for us to notch in a two-hundred foot circle around the spar tree. Eight stumps were for the main guys, to keep the spar upright, and four stumps were for the buckle-guys, which prevented the spar from buckling when the yarder pulled especially hard.

We had our own personal axes, which we guarded closely and sharpened to a razors edge. We'd test the edge by shaving our arm hair. The sharp edge made a hard job a little easier. We had to chop deep notches to prevent the guy lines from slipping over the stump and letting the spar tree fall under load.

The steep hills made standing and swinging an axe difficult on the best day. The stump edge on the uphill side might be two feet from the ground, while the edge on the downhill side might tower eight feet above the ground.

Once, we were notching guy stumps in ten inches of fresh snow. I was chopping away with my razor sharp axe when my foot slipped. The axe glanced off the stump and sliced through my left boot at the root of my big toe. My feet were numb, so I couldn't tell whether I'd cut my foot. I peeled back the cut leather and didn't see any blood, but I needed to know for sure. I found a place to sit and pulled off my boot.

The axe had cut through my leather boot and completely though my heavy wool sock, but it hadn't touched my skin. I lucked out, but doggone it if I didn't have to work all day in ten inches of snow with a big hole in my boot, soaking my foot. Somehow I managed to avoid frostbite. The local cobbler repaired my boot the same day we returned to town. I wasn't the first logger to cut up his boots.

Hauling the heavy guy line cables involved first using a smaller wire, about three-eighths inch diameter, called haywire. We climbed up the bank carrying the haywire and pulled it around the stump notched for the guy line. Then we hauled it back to the landing through the snow to reach the stump directly behind the spar tree, a hundred feet away.

Three of us struggled to pull the wire up the hill. I was at the bank's edge, thirty feet above the landing, the other two guys behind me. The cable reached me coated in a layer of ice. We used cotton gloves for safety, so my hands and fingers quickly went numb.

The guy behind me yelled, "Pull harder down there! I'm doing all the work here, you lazy SOB!" He yelled more and cussed me out. The guy behind him never said a word. I was doing the best I could, and I was near tears with the struggle to pull the wire up the hill. We finally got the haywire back to the landing and connected it to the guy line. The dozer winch then pulled the guy line up the bank and around the stump.

We connected three guy wires to the top of the spar tree, and then, using two bulldozers, pulled the wires through blocks chained to the stumps. Slowly the spar tree stood upright, the butt end resting in a shallow hole at the back of the landing. We wrapped the remaining guy lines around stumps to secure the spar before we slacked the first three, and then wrapped those around their own stumps. We spiked them with railroad spikes to the stump, made another coil, snugged it with the dozer, and spiked it again. We wrapped at least five times and spiked each layer to ensure it wouldn't come lose during the strain of logging.

I was involved in every phase of the process and even went up the tree with climbing spurs once. The tree swayed back and forth as I spiked in the J plates, which kept the guy lines from slipping down the tree, and then rigged the guy lines one at a time, hanging the bull block at the top of the spar tree.

I was also being trained to replace the line truck driver. The line truck was a modified old Kenworth with a bed-mounted, ten-foot diameter, PTO-driven cable spool. We loaded and carried both guy lines and main line to the landings when wear made replacement necessary.

The main line was one-and-an-eighth to one-and-a-quarter inch steel cable, depending on the length, and weighed around ten pounds a foot. Our longest cable was a mile long and that old truck handled it. That's fifty-two thousand pounds of cable.

The truck had two transmissions in line, so it had sixteen speeds. That took some getting used to. We called being in first gear on both transmissions "deep under first gear"—very low, very slow. We needed deep under first gear to climb the two miles to the landing with all that weight.

To replace the wire, we first attached the old main line to the truck and drove off down the road to pull it off the yarder. We used our load weight to pull the mile of cable off the yarder. Then we returned to reel off the new line. We connected the end of the wire to the yarder and it started to pull.

The line truck had a band brake that fit the outside of the ten-foot spool. A long lever with a foot pedal activated the brake. I had my foot on the brake as the yarder started taking the line onto its spool. The coil grew larger on the yarder. The coil grew smaller on the truck. The cable flew off faster and faster.

I had to keep tension with the brake to prevent the wire from spooling too fast and going slack, which would mess up the transfer. Soon I was standing with both feet on the brake pedal but still having trouble slowing it down.

Heat radiated off the spool, my face a foot away. It was burning hot with a quarter of the line still to go when the entire brake lining burst into flames—more than thirty feet of flaming brake lining.

The guys kept yelling, "Hold the tension!" so I rode the brake and leaned back until the last of the line was on the yarder.

We let the drum cool down, then drove back down the hill to load the worn line we had removed earlier. Once loaded, I drove the truck back to camp to end our day. We rounded a corner of the narrow road, and the road got steeper. We picked up speed.

My mentor Al said, "Downshift a couple gears and save the brakes. This hill is a mile long."

I tried to downshift, but couldn't find the gear. The gears are cut square for strength and don't shift easily. We picked up more speed. I tried again, pushing and shoving and grunting and sweating. We careened down the narrow winding dirt road with fifty thousand pounds of cable behind our heads, and I've managed to find neutral!

Al seemed unfazed, and that scared me even more. *Doesn't he understand what's going on? Shouldn't he be freaking out? We're about to die!*

Al calmly said, "Stay off the clutch and rev up the engine while you hold pressure against the gears."

I let out the clutch, revved up the engine and pushed on the gear shift. Sure enough, it slipped right into the gear we needed, and I regained control of that old Kenworth! I sure was glad when that day ended—I was frazzled.

CB&D

Simpson Timber had a seniority deal when it came to advancement. A ten-year mill worker had first dibs for a position in the woods over a guy with nine years of experience.

We needed a rigging slinger on our crew. He's the guy who's in charge at each logging show. He communicates with the yarder operator with a series of whistle toots that tell the operator what is happening out on the hill and what to do. The yarder operator, who controls the cables that yard the logs out of the forest onto the landing, cannot see what's going on in the forest, so he depends on the rigging slinger to tell him. The whistles also let everyone else know what he has chosen to do. A long-time mill worker had been promoted to rigging slinger, and by giving the wrong whistle signals, he almost killed me.

We had logged down the hill in the morning, and were working our way back up, getting the logs that had been under others on the way down. The return trip is called getting the cream, the easy logs. We tried to time it so we'd be close to the landing by the end of the day.

We were on our way up, getting the cream. The guys below me had set two chokers on three logs—one on one and one on two. They were spread out on both sides of the path the logs would make as they were hauled up the hill. I had a hold of the third choker and needed to have the rigging come ahead just a little bit so I could reach the easy set of two logs just a little bit up the hill from what I could reach.

I yelled over to the rigging slinger, "Come ahead easy!"

He tooted his whistle three times. But that tells the yarder, "Come ahead full."

I waited for the second set of three toots, but they never came.

The yarder spun up, and that big, powerful machine jerked the first three logs up the hill toward me. They were eighteen inches around and could have smeared me all the way to the landing. I leaped backwards and fell between the two logs I was going to set. Half a second later, the three logs already set skidded over me on their way up the hill, missing my nose and chest by inches.

I jumped up and called the stupid guy from the mill every foul word I knew as a logger. He looked sheepish, but didn't apologize.

I noticed the side-rod, the foreman for our section of the woods, standing a few hundred yards away.

I yelled over to him, "Did you see that?"

He yelled back, "Are you all right?"

I said, "Yeah, but maybe not next time! Why is a mill guy pulling rigging if he doesn't know the damn signals?"

The side-rod turned, got in his truck and drove away. When we got back to camp, I complained to the superintendent about what had happened. He said, "It's just how Simpson does it. Union rules, you know."

Well, screw that! I'd heard from the manager at the bike shop. He was going to open his own shop on the Olympic Peninsula, and he thought I'd make a good replacement manager for Alderwood Cycle in Lynnwood. The owner agreed, and offered me the job. I accepted.

છ౮

A pretty red Toyota Land Cruiser with a black vinyl top beckoned to me twice a day on my new commute to and from the bike shop. It was on the used car lot, but it looked brand new. My high school art teacher had one and had raved about it. I thought the FJ40 Land Cruisers looked so cool. I had collected advertising and brochures since high school.

Just for grins, I stopped by the car lot and inquired.

The salesman explained, "It was purchased about three months ago, but the buyer said he couldn't find any cool wheels that fit, so he brought it back."

I was flabbergasted. "So what are you asking?"

"Well, as you can see, it's virtually new, so the lowest we can go is thirty-two hundred."

I did a quick calculation. I was expecting something closer to four thousand dollars, the value of a new car.

"How much trade in would you give me for my Jeep pickup?" I asked.

The salesman looked the truck over, conferred with his boss, and came back with an offer: "We can give you eight hundred for your truck."

"Deal!"

I drove away in a gleaming red 1973 Toyota FJ40 Land Cruiser—almost too cool to be true!

⋘⋙

The bike craze was in full swing, and everyone wanted a ten speed. All the brands were selling well, but kids' bikes and accessories like bells, horns and handle bar streamers were not. To make room for more ten speeds, the owner pulled the slow items from the other seven stores he owned and foisted them on me. When I protested the clutter, he said with a shrug, "Figure it out."

My store was already stacked high with new bikes still in the box and many others in various stages of assembly. We sold bikes so fast our shop crew often had to stay late into the evening, assembling enough bikes to keep the floor full. We tripped over boxes of bells and streamers during our build parties, and still more useless trinkets came. I didn't want to deal with the frustration, and despite the danger, I did like being in the woods. It was time for me to go back to logging.

Back then, getting a job as a logger required only a pulse. I had experience in addition to a pulse, so Weyerhaeuser in North Bend hired me the same day I applied.

My new job in the woods required me to be up by 3:30 AM, eat, then drive for an hour to the yard. I'd climb on the crummy, the logging company crew bus, and ride another hour to the landing before my pay would start. Then at the end of the day it was another two hours before I'd get home at six. I'd have dinner and crawl in bed by seven. I was gone for twelve hours and only getting paid for eight, but it was good pay. I ate like a horse, yet still boasted a thirty-three inch waist.

I did have a problem, though—I hadn't met even one woman in the woods. I was getting up there in age, almost twenty-five, and I hadn't had a girlfriend for a while. One of my high school buddies was married to a nurse who worked at Northwest Hospital in North Seattle. Her name was Kitty.

{ 5 }

KITTY," I ASKED ONE DAY, "Do you know any single girls who might want to meet a handsome guy like me? The hospital's crawling with females—there must be a few who are single."

She chuckled. "I'll see what I can do, Jim."

Kitty was a good saleswoman. She lined up five prospects.

I met the first one at Kitty and Joel's place, and we had a pleasant conversation, but there were no sparks. I met the second at their house as well, and the moment our eyes met, we both knew. We didn't say much—didn't have to.

We planned a jeeping trip to Wallace Falls for the next weekend. Joel had a Jeep CJ and I had my Land Cruiser. We had invited two other couples, and Kitty's third prospect from the hospital was going to be my blind date for the day. We drove both rigs to pick her up at her house. She came out the door smiling and something happened inside my head. She moved toward the Jeep, but Kitty said, "No, you're riding with Jim in his Land Cruiser."

Kitty introduced us. "Hi, Jim," she said. She was all smiles and I was impressed.

"Hi," I managed lamely.

Riding with me were two other friends, Ray and Judy.

"Hey, Ray, what are you doing here?" Thea asked as she climbed in.

"Hi, Thea, I've known Jim since high school. This is my girlfriend, Judy."

"Hi, Judy," Thea said. "Ray, don't you live in the house next to Greg?"

"Sure do," he said. "We moved to Edmonds just before my senior year."

"You know Greg?" I asked Thea.

"Yeah, he was my old boyfriend," Thea replied. "For about three years."

"Greg and I used to work on cars together at Morris's Garage, next to Joel's house," I said. "Who else do you know?"

She started naming names, telling stories. She talked and smiled and talked all the way to Wallace Falls, easily a full hour. She and I had known the same people for five years, yet never met. Just as well—she had been straight-laced, and I might have been too wild for her tastes if we'd met earlier. We had both moved closer to the middle, and God knew this was the right time for us to meet.

We drove up the rutted muddy road until we reached the Wallace Lake parking area. We brought some pistols to shoot some targets. I noticed Thea plugged her ears and winced each time we shot.

"You got a problem with guns?" I asked.

"No, not at all. They're just really loud." she said.

Okay, then. She even fired a couple of shots. Another check in the plus column.

She talked the whole way back to her house from the falls, but I was able to get in a few words edgewise. I liked her. I stopped the Toyota outside her house, and reached across her lap to pop the door open for her.

"I had a fine time," I said. "And I hope you did too."

"Yes, I did," she said, and hopped out. She walked toward her house and turned at the last step. She smiled her beautiful smile and waved. I drove straight home and collapsed in bed. I needed the whole weekend to recover from my week of work and get ready for the next.

Our first date

I called her the next Friday. "Hi, Thea, it's Jim. How have you been?"

"I'm great. How are you? You didn't call. I thought maybe it hadn't gone well last week." It was more of a question.

"I work real long hours and come home bushed. I'm usually in bed by seven."

"Oh, I see. Well, I'm glad you called," she said.

It sounded to me like she meant it. "Would you like to go out next Saturday?" I asked. "We could meet with a friend of mine from the old neighborhood, along with his girlfriend." I'd been out of the dating scene for a while and didn't want it to turn awkward.

That next Saturday, we met my friend and his girlfriend at the tavern to play pool. Thea and I enjoyed easy conversation as late into the evening as my heavy eyelids would allow—past eight o'clock!

We met the next Saturday for our third date, and at the end of the evening, I stole my first kiss. I didn't want to rush. I was brought up to respect the ladies. She told me later she was relieved I had finally kissed her. So many other guys were so aggressive and pushy, acting as if the price of a burger and a movie entitled them to special favors. Thea was intrigued by my slower pace.

We had been seeing each other for only a month by Valentine's Day. I made a special card for her. On the front I drew a pretty good likeness of myself on my knees, praying. On the inside I wrote, "I thank God that I found you!" I meant every word. She loved the card.

Our Saturday dates became regular. Then one night, her mom invited me over for Sunday dinner. Thea didn't know, and invited one of her other boyfriends to dinner as well. He was there when I arrived. I glared at him in silence, and he glared back. Thea ran to her bedroom to hide. I folded my arms across my chest and stared, waiting him out. Thea came out of hiding and walked him to his car. She handed him a music tape.

He flung the tape into his car, flopped in after, slammed the door, and sped off.

"So, who was that?" I asked.

"Oh, that was Rick," she said. "I see him sometimes on Friday nights for dinner and a movie."

"Hmmm..." I might have been a little growly, but just for a minute. She became bubbly and talkative after he left.

Her mom served a great meal, and I polished off the first heaping plate in no time.

"There's more, there's more. Eat as much as you want!" her mom said.

"Well, I do get awful hungry working in the woods as hard as I do."

"Yes, of course, there's plenty, have as much as you want."

So I did. I piled my plate high a second time and cleaned it down to the shine.

I learned later Thea's mom had said to her dad, "Well, if she marries that one, she's going to have to buy a lot of groceries and do a lot of cooking!"

We dated from then on—Saturday nights, of course. "I'm going to live in a cabin in the woods," I declared one night, "and I might become a hermit. I figure I'm going to end up sitting in a creaky old rocker on the porch, shotgun across my lap, just enjoying the view."

"I could probably be a hermit's wife," she said, "as long as I can have hermit children. But he also has to believe in God. That's number one."

"I agree," I said. "Top of my list for a wife."

She started saying *no* to other guys on Friday nights. Her mom invited me over for Sunday dinner again, and there were no more surprises like the first time.

In early May, on the way to the tavern to play pool with Rick and Judy and Lenny and Chris, I asked Thea, "So, when you think about getting married, what kind of ring do you want?"

"Well, if it's just a band, then a really fancy yellow gold band. But if there are diamonds involved, just one—a single round one on a plain gold band with a plain wedding band."

"Huh, okay."

After a few rounds of pool, while we were sitting in a booth at the tavern, I leaned forward and asked, "Well? Will ya?"

"Will I what?"

"Will you marry me?"

We'd discussed our beliefs, plans for the future, and more, and agreed about most. I figured we were ready. She did, too.

"Yeah!" she said, flashing her beautiful smile.

It took until August to find the right ring. My mom was excited about it all and would frequent antique stores and hock shops looking for jewelry and fine glass.

"Look what I found today, Jimmy," said my mom one afternoon. It was a beautiful antique ring with a canary yellow diamond in a gold filigree setting.

I called Thea. "Can you come over for a few minutes?"

She greeted me at the door and gave me a kiss. Mom was there with us in the kitchen.

"Turn around," I said to Thea. "Put your hands behind you."

She seemed confused, but turned. I grabbed her left hand and slid the ring on her finger—a perfect fit.

"Oh, I love it!" she exclaimed, and hugged me tight.

Lenny and Chris were also engaged, and planned to be married in December, so we talked about January, but I didn't want to wait that long.

"Let's get married sooner," I said.

We set a date for November 30th. Our friends were surprised, yet could see this was meant to be. They knew if we'd met any sooner, it might not have worked out so well.

We looked all over for a good cake topper, but none of the plastic bride-and-groom figurines looked like us. The guys were all blonde or bald-faced, and I had dark hair and a beard. The girls didn't look anything like Thea. Since it was close to Thanksgiving, Thea found a little plastic turkey and we plunked that on top of the cake among the flowers of frosting.

Thea explained to my mom, "We couldn't find a topper we liked, and besides, he's marrying a turkey, and so am I." My mom was horrified. I think that made it more fun for me.

Jake Beaty

{ 6 }

WE MOVED TWICE IN THE FIRST MONTHS of our marriage, settling in a one-bedroom house in North Seattle, which we bought for $15,000. We searched the want ads for another Samoyed to serve as Clowd's companion. We found Danny, a big male owned by a girl leaving for college. He fit right in.

I saw an ad in a sportsman's magazine for cheap land in Idaho, so Thea and I loaded up the Land Cruiser for a little trip with Danny and Clowd. Six hours later we were outside St. Maries, Idaho, looking at hundreds of acres of clear-cut. The logging company had come and gone and all they'd left were stumps.

Cheap land is cheap for a reason, so we kept driving. We followed a two-lane road east along the Saint Joe River, whose headwaters were high in the Rocky Mountains. I was curious to see where it would go.

"It's getting dark," Thea said. "Don't you think we ought to set up camp?"

"Yeah, you're right," I said. "I'll look for a spot."

A little farther ahead, we spied a grassy field between the road and the river, and I pulled over. I lifted the top part of the tailgate and tied a rope to the handle. I staked the other end of the rope to the ground about ten feet away. I stretched a tarp over the rope and staked the sides to the ground, forming a little A-frame tent with no floor.

I spread another tarp on the ground to keep us off the dirt. If it rained, we'd stay dry.

Thea jostled me awake. "The dogs are growling," she said.

"Let's listen," I said. We strained, but couldn't hear anything. The dogs quieted, so we fell back asleep.

It was my turn to ask. "Did you feel that?"

"Yes!" Thea hissed. "Something ran across my legs!"

I flashed my light into the darkness. Nothing.

The dogs growled a few more times, and some cat-sized critters ran across our bodies a few more times in the night.

The rising sun brought answers.

"We camped on a field covered with gopher mounds!" I exclaimed to Thea. "Next time I'll stop while there's still daylight so we can see where we're setting up camp."

We continued driving east along the river, climbing the hill it flowed down. Hours from anywhere, we came upon a store having a going-out-of-business sale. We stopped to investigate. The place made me think of a general store from the old west, and it was jammed with a collection of the coolest items for homesteading—kerosene lamps, hand cranked grain grinders, massive two-man saws, and wrought iron candle chandeliers.

"We're selling everything," the owner said. "We've only been snow-free for two weeks, and it'll be back again in two more." (It was early August.) "Nobody drives this way anymore—they all take the interstate."

"As much as I'd love to take it all," I said, "We don't have the money or the room in our car. Sorry it hasn't worked out for you."

The river dwindled to a stream and the stream disappeared under a large patch of snow. Still, we climbed. The pavement gave way to gravel and the gravel gave way to parallel lines in the dirt. No one had come this way in a long time. The road stopped climbing, then descended. Two hours later, pavement reappeared. Through a gap in the trees, Thea spied a town at the bottom of the valley. It was another two hours before we reached the town. We pulled into the first gas station we found, and I asked the man at the pump, "Where are we?"

"Missoula, Montana," he said. "How much gas you want?"

"Missoula, Montana? Are you kidding? We drove over the Rocky Mountains on a dirt road! How cool is that!" I said.

"How much do you want?"

"Oh. Yeah. Fill 'er up, please."

We drove south and followed the highway back into Idaho and visited The Craters of the Moon National Monument. We continued west toward Sun Valley, camping on the shores of a little lake just off the road. Our sleeping bag was covered in frost when we awoke, and we could see our breath. The next day, we drove through McCall, Idaho and into Oregon, where we found a real campground called Target Meadows. The sign said it had been used as a US Army artillery range from the late 1880s through

1906. It was the middle of the week, so we had the place to ourselves. We enjoyed the solitude. The following day we returned home.

"Too bad we didn't find any property," I said to Thea, "but we saw some incredible country."

"Yes, we did," she said. "I think even the dogs enjoyed themselves."

Back in Seattle, we searched the want ads for months. "Hey, Thea, look at this. 'Forty Acres in the Okanogan' it says." I showed her the ad in the paper.

"That could be nice," she said. "Call the number. Let's go look."

"The property is in Oroville," I told Thea. "Up on the north end of Wannacut Lake, it's past the turn to the Diamond Belle Ranch, close to the Canadian border. I love that country up there." We drove over that weekend. My expectations had been too high.

"Hmm, it's all pretty steep," I said. "Not much flat land to build a house on. Look at the spines on this cactus—they could pierce a leather boot!"

"Yes, but we can see the lake," Thea said.

We walked around, looked from every angle, and imagined building a house here, or there. "I suppose we can make it work," I said.

"Let's buy it," Thea said.

We did. We were the proud owners of forty acres in the Okanogan. We invited several friends to come with us to the property on Memorial Day weekend—we took Kitty and Joel, Ray and Sheila, and Ted and Marylynne.

"Real nice over here," Ray said.

"The weather is great," said Sheila.

"You're really going to build a log house and live over here?" Ted asked.

"It's quiet and peaceful," Marylynne said. "It'd be a great place to visit."

"I love how it smells!" said Kitty.

"I bet the hunting is good over here—this is real mule deer country," Joel said.

Traffic jammed and slowed on the drive home. There had been no east-bound traffic since we crossed the pass. We slowed to a stop behind a line of cars on Highway 2 near the Ranger Station east of Skykomish. We were parked for three hours before we even started to move, and even then we crawled along at fifteen miles per hour all the way to Monroe. There had been a bad wreck in Monroe and the traffic was backed up for twenty or thirty miles.

"Let's never cross the mountains on a holiday weekend again!" I said.

Back at the hospital on Tuesday, Thea and a friend were talking about their holiday. "I'm from Oroville," Thea's friend said. "Good luck getting a job over there."

"What do you mean?" asked Thea.

"Why do you think I'm here in Seattle? I have the wrong last name. So do you. There are three or four families who own Oroville—the Scotts, the Jennings, the Wards. Good luck finding meaningful work if you're not one of them."

We went back to the property in October to go hunting with my cousin Jack. He took a picture of us sitting together by the campfire that became a family favorite. We didn't know it at the time, but our very first baby had just begun growing in Thea's belly. We had been trying for almost three years. We laughed and cried and hugged when we found out.

We didn't get a deer, the land was steep, job prospects in Oroville were intimidating, and Thea was pregnant. We went to visit the property owner at the hotel he ran on Aurora Avenue.

"Can we turn the property back over to you?" I asked. "We're thinking this maybe isn't the best timing for us right now."

The same ad we had seen earlier was back in the paper the next week.

⋘⋙

Thea and I were walking with Danny and Clowd around Green Lake on a sunny day in May. A little girl came running up to our friendly-looking dog, and I put out my hand and pushed her away.

"Don't you touch my daughter," her dad grumped at me.

"My dog doesn't like kids," I shot back. "Would you rather she got bit?"

The man and his daughter left and Thea asked me, "What if Clowd doesn't like the baby?"

"We'll give the baby back," I said.

Jacob was born at 9:50 AM on Saturday, June third, 1978. He was eight pounds even and twenty-one inches long. It was a tough delivery, and I worked hard helping Thea puff, puff, puff during labor. After they both fell asleep, I went home to get some rest.

When I returned the next morning, Thea asked, "What happened to you? Your pants are just hanging on you!"

I had cinched my belt three holes smaller. I'd lost twenty pounds the previous day—more than Thea.

Clowd had snarled and growled and snapped at kids before, so we were nervous when we brought Jacob home. We kept him bundled in his blankets at first, and presented him to her for a sniff. She seemed okay, so Thea sat down in a chair with him. Clowd was sniffing the whole time, but not growling or snarling.

Thea set Jacob on the floor, and Clowd sniffed his little body from head to toe, side to side. I was ready to jump if her manner changed at all. I needn't have worried. She laid down and curled around him. He was part of the pack. We didn't have to give the baby back.

ଔଞ୍ଚ

"Are you guys going to church anywhere?" our neighbor asked one day.

"No, we haven't found a place yet," I said.

"You ought to check out the Greenwood Church, on 81st and Fremont," he said. "They're good folks, non-denominational—the Bible is their only guide."

So we went for a visit. The people were friendly and warm. A welcoming committee came to our house later in the week and invited us to come back. We returned a second time. They remembered our names. A third time, and again, and then lost count. Greenwood became our church and the people became our companions.

One night during a home Bible study I was struck by some advice from Paul to the Thessalonians. "Live a quiet life and work with your hands."

Someday, that's what I'm going to do!

If a guy's not careful, *someday* can be a code word for *never.*

{ 7 }

I HAD TAKEN A NIGHT CLASS ON WELDING at the Junior College. I'd impressed the instructor with my brazing skills, so he recommended me for a job. I was hired as a silver solderer at Belshaw, a company that manufactured bakery equipment. I met Pete, an Albanian immigrant who had come to America in the mid-1950s. He was a master machinist and we would talk for hours. I was fifteen years younger than him, but we became friends.

"I'm thinking about buying some acreage," I mentioned to Pete once. "Build a log house and get back to the land."

"I once had a chance to buy some property on the Olympic Peninsula," he said. "But I never did. I was going to build a summer cabin over there, too, maybe near Bremerton. I wish I had, but it's too late now."

"Well, why didn't you?" I asked.

"Oh, you know—the wife. She said it was a waste of time and money, that I should be saving for our daughters' weddings instead."

He had pictures of his family on his tool box. Two daughters. "Yeah, how does an ugly guy like you get such pretty daughters?" I teased.

He laughed. "Must be the wife, I guess. You know, I wanted to do more bird hunting, too. I have this chocolate lab that was going to be my bird dog, but he's old now. I wish I'd gone hunting with him more often when we were both younger."

"Well, why don't we go hunting with him now?" I asked.

"Oh, I don't know."

"C'mon, Pete, the clock is ticking, let's do it! Where should we go?" I asked.

"I do know a place we could go," he said.

I showed up early the next Saturday. We loaded up the dog and our gear in the back of his truck. We were after brants—a black and white, short-billed, salt-water goose the size of a duck. We drove to the southern point of Whidbey Island. Our spot was a large cove between two points, on a gravel beach littered with driftwood. Gusts of wind shoved breaking waves onto the shore.

"Is this weather going to be a problem?" I asked Pete.

"No, this is the best weather for bird hunting. The brant can't sit still because the waves are too big, so they fly more on a day like this. I've hunted here before," he said. "Trust me."

On cue, a small flock of brants flew by, skimming the waves as they crossed the bay from point to point. They passed in front of us about thirty yards off the beach.

"We should hunker down in the driftwood to wait for the next group to come by," he said. Moments later he whispered, "Here come some now."

We rose up as they approached and led them by a few feet. We fired together. Boom! Boom!

The one I was after dropped into the waves, but his kept right on going.

"Go get 'em!" he said to his dog. His dog took off down the beach, eyes locked on the bird. That old dog dove right through big waves breaking over his head to get the bird I'd shot.

We hunted for hours and the birds kept coming. I used up an entire box of shells and missed only a few times. I shot seventeen birds. Pete got four.

"That was great fun," Pete said at the end of a long day. "You know the limit was twelve birds between the two of us, right?"

"Oh? No, I wasn't even thinking of that. Why didn't you say something?"

"Well, you and the dog were having such a good time, I didn't want to spoil it," he said, smiling. "I should have done more of this. I could have, but I didn't. I wish I had."

"Thea," I said later as I walked through the front door, "I don't want to say 'I wish I had'."

"What are you talking about?" she asked.

"It's all Pete ever says—'I wish I had.' I mean, he's a great guy, and I like spending time with him, but he has so many regrets. He wishes he'd bought some land, built a summer cabin, gone hunting more often, on and on. But he never did it and now he's too old. I don't want to have any regrets."

"Okay. So what do we need to do?"

"I've been thinking. The property situation still isn't sorted out. But even if it was, there's more to it. We're not going to have electricity, so I need to find a power source. We already have that beautiful Quaker fireplace insert, so we should be able to keep warm, but we still need a fridge and a cookstove."

"A propane fridge, like they're selling in Mother Earth News?"

"Yes, but those are all too small, or too pricey, or both. There has to be another option."

"I can look in the local want ads," Thea said, "and see what I can find."

One day, reading the local want ads, she stood up and bolted for the door. The car keys jingled as she grabbed them from the hook.

"Where are you going?"

She yanked the door open. "I found an ad for a Servel propane fridge for sale at the second hand store. I want to get there before anyone else does."

Half an hour later, the phone rang. It was Thea—she sounded excited. "There was already a couple looking at the fridge when I got here," she said. "They were trying to get the salesman to lower the price. I was in the next aisle, peering through stacks of dishes. The husband said to the salesman, 'Give us a second,' then turned away to whisper with his wife. I came out from behind the dishes and I said 'This fridge is sold—to me.'"

"You did what?"

"Yep. The couple and the salesman looked at me with their mouths open. I said, 'I'm paying full price. I'm buying this fridge.' The salesman said 'okay,' and I paid him for the fridge—it's ours to pick up! Can you come down with the truck?"

"I'm on my way!"

I arrived to find Thea standing proudly next to the perfect fridge. Over five feet tall and almost three feet wide, this was no camper fridge. It was made in the fifties and looked the part—clean white paint and "futuristic" rounded corners. The door opened to reveal three generous shelves, a good seal, and a nice little ice box up top. The door closed with a satisfying click. Ninety-nine dollars.

We started looking for a cookstove next. My great Aunt Elsie had cooked on one into the mid-sixties. She made it look easy. She talked about the old country as she cooked. She'd come to America in 1896. I was confident Thea would have no trouble adapting. We found a business near Bremerton whose owner refurbished and sold antique cookstoves and parlor heaters. He had a showroom filled with cookstoves, pot-bellied stoves, and parlor heaters between 60 and 150 years old. Fresh white enamel paint, solid black cast iron, and gleaming nickel plating—the old stoves looked brand new!

We fancied a beautiful Monarch cookstove that had been re-plated and repaired to new condition. It was three thousand dollars, the cost of a car at the time, but it was the one we had to have. We had purchased another stove previously that needed work, but it wasn't really what we wanted, especially after seeing what else was available. We traded it in for the magnificent Monarch.

⋘⋙

I hit a pay ceiling with Belshaw, and took a job with ELDEC, the Electro Development Company, working on aircraft instruments, close to our home. It was the graveyard shift, but I didn't have to commute into Seattle every morning. I hadn't been on the new job more than a few months when I hurt myself doing some yard work. I was lifting half an old railroad tie when I felt something snap deep inside my belly. I started feeling sick inside.

"You need to see a doctor," Thea said.

"Bah, I'll be fine."

"No, this is serious. It might be something related to the surgeries you had as a kid."

"Yeah, yeah," I said, but I knew she was right. I'd spent years of my childhood in and out of hospitals because I had Hirschprung's disease, a birth defect involving my intestines. I had already had seven major surgeries.

At the hospital the doctor said, "We think you've developed adhesions from your previous surgeries and your system is stopped up again."

"What would cause all that?" I asked.

"Back in the fifties," the doctor replied, "they had a different recovery philosophy than we do now. They'd operate and then leave you to lie down till you healed. By doing it that way, thicker scar tissue formed, and some of your incisions healed to each other. The organs grew, but the scar tissue didn't. At this point, some of your scar tissue has tightened enough to seal the intestine. We'll cut that out, sew you back together, and you will have an active recovery to limit the formation of more adhesions."

I wondered what 'active recovery' meant, but not for long. They had me sit up four hours after the operation, and start walking two hours after that.

"What did you do to me, doc?" I asked after the surgery. "I hurt from my hips to my armpits."

"There were a lot of adhesions," he said. "We had to get them all."

I missed six weeks-work, and had plenty of time to think. I had flat-lined twice on the operating table as a kid, and though this surgery went well, it *might* have gone wrong. There's no promise of tomorrow. Life can be short. I realized I needed to live it now, or I'd end up like old Pete, wishing I had. The thought of building my own log house was always on my mind and I never stopped planning for that day. It had been over two years since we'd sold the Oroville property. Time to start looking again.

∞

I wanted to look near Ellensburg. Once, when I was little, I'd gone with my mom to a horse ranch in Cle Elum, near Ellensburg, and I had warm memories of the experience and the place. I figured Ellensburg was the best of eastern Washington, the opposite of everything I disliked about the west side. It was warm and dry, not rainy and cold. Open spaces instead of constricting crowds. Few cars on the road, rather than gridlocked traffic. It was peaceful and quiet, not buzzing with noise. That's what I remembered, anyway.

What I didn't remember was the wind. Thea and I drove over the mountains one weekend to look at real estate listings in town. I stepped out of the car, and the wind tore at my hat. I jerked my hand up just in time. Seasonal banners mounted to light poles throbbed and snapped. We ducked into a diner for respite. An old codger sat at the counter sipping coffee.

"Sure is windy out there today," I said to him.

He turned on his stool. He looked me up and down. "It's windy out there every day," he said, returning to his coffee.

"Like this?" I asked, desperate. I looked at Thea.

"Like this," he said not turning around, "all the time."

So this was Ellensburg? Boo! I wanted wind for the windmill, but not all the time. No, thanks. We looked further north, we found a real estate agent in Wenatchee.

"There is some land for sale near Icicle Creek, a little beyond Leavenworth," she told us.

We drove west on Highway 2, past the turn for Icicle Creek, then twenty minutes farther up the highway, near the Nason Creek rest area. I opened the car door, and the hum of high power electrical lines overhead was so loud Thea and I looked at each other, and said, "No way" at the same time. I closed my door.

"Don't you even want to see the property?" asked the real estate agent.

"Nope," I said. "We don't want anything this close to power lines."

"There is another piece of land up the river from Entiat. It's near Ardenvoir, where the Mad River comes in. Would you like to see it?"

"I've always liked that area," I said, "let's go." We drove back down the highway the other direction, passed Wenatchee, and kept going. We arrived at the property to trudge through fields of high grass and brush that clawed at our legs. The agent's heels sank in the dirt. Her nylons ran. Her skirt snagged. She stopped at the edge of the river and pointed beyond.

"That's the house over there," she said. "You'll need to build a bridge to get to it."

"What? Build a bridge?" I looked at her. I looked at the little cabin in the distance, looked down the steep bank to the river—it was too deep and wide to cross even with my Land Cruiser.

She didn't even bother to reply. Her shoulders sagged.

"This isn't what you signed up for, is it?" I asked.

"Oh, no, it's fine," she said. "I'd like to help you find the property you're looking for."

"We really are looking for a place in the wilderness," I said. "The kind you wear hiking boots and jeans and a flannel shirt to see."

She looked down at the runs in her nylons.

I smiled at her. "It's okay, it really is. We can find someone else and you don't have to go on our expeditions with us."

"Well, there is another agent at the office, and he might be able to help you," she said, giving us his business card. We drove back home to continue our search some other time.

We had been looking for property for seven years, even before we were married in '74. We looked up the Nahahum Canyon outside Cashmere, we looked off Blewett Pass and Stevens Pass, we looked in Idaho, Oroville, Ellensburg. Now we had looked up the Entiat River, and we were still no closer. Would we ever find the right place?

{ 8 }

WHAT ABOUT LAKE CHELAN?" Thea asked me one day. "I've spent summers there since I was six months old. I love it!"

Thea's dad, Paul, and his friend, known to the family as "Uncle" Larry, had purchased a small house in Manson near the lake in the early sixties. Larry and his wife, "Auntie" Pat, lived in the house. Thea had visited them often over the years.

"There aren't any trees," I said. "It's just brown grass and brush."

"But the lake, dear—Lake Chelan! I think there are some trees up in the hills anyway. We could at least look."

"All right, I suppose we could look."

We drove three and a half hours across the Cascade Mountains on the weekend after Memorial Day, 1981. We walked into a real estate office in Chelan.

"We're looking for some land, about forty acres," I said.

"We have an agent who can help you."

"Hi, my name is Richard," the man said as he walked from his desk in the back. "I know of some land for sale in Union Valley."

There were two other couples also looking for land, and Richard packed them into his station wagon to go see the property.

"I'll follow you," I said.

Thea was irritated by the presence of the other two couples. "He's trying to play us off each other," she said as we drove behind.

"Let's just stay quiet and keep our cards close," I said. "We don't have to play."

We drove toward the north side of town, then climbed up and out past the hospital on a steep zigzag road in the bottom of a massive rocky washout. The road traveled flat and straight past the cemetery and rodeo grounds, then curved and climbed again. Flat, climb, flat, climb. The pavement ended before the last climb began, and two miles later we crested the ridge at 3,300 feet.

We dropped down the back side of the ridge, and followed the ups and downs and twists and turns of the dirt road for three more miles to the property. Ponderosa pine and Douglas fir blanketed the north slopes at altitude above Lake Chelan. Trees! This might be okay after all. The air was cool and fresh—an entirely different experience from downtown.

We emerged from a dense stand of Douglas fir and turned right onto an open meadow sloping gently southward, still green from the spring rains. The local wild sunflower, arrowleaf balsamroot, not all yet gone to seed, dotted the meadow with yellow. Purple lupines grew in the long shadows of scattered ponderosa pines. To the south, across a wide valley, a tree covered slope dominated our view, and distant in the east, the dark basalt rim of the Columbia River Gorge stood tall. Wheat fields stretched to the horizon on the Columbia plateau. Lake Chelan wasn't visible, but it was only twenty-five minutes away.

We stepped out of the Land Cruiser. I inhaled deeply. I felt a deep peace. I'm sure my blood pressure dropped and my heart rate slowed. Birds sang in the trees. A breeze rustled the grass. There were no other sounds except a surprising ringing in my ears.

Richard and the other couples walked down the hill toward the only man-made structure visible in any direction. Thea and I hung back to let them get ahead.

"Wow! This is it!" I whispered to her. We grinned at each other.

"I agree," she said. "But let's not say a word in front of any of them. We need to act like we're not interested." We moved down the hill toward the others.

"...they lived up here in an old school bus," Richard was saying." It was parked right close here so they could use the shed as part of the living area. I think the kitchen was in the shed and they slept in the bus. They sold the bus to Dan and Vicki, neighbors who live right over the hill there, to the north. I have a place of my own, right next to them."

"It is nice up here," I said.

"It's so far from town," one of the ladies murmured, her nose wrinkled.

"Thea, look at this," I said. "The shed was built from apple bins." It was three bin panels wide, and four bin panels long, making it twelve feet by sixteen feet. The

{ 67 }

roof sloped to the south at a shallow angle. It appeared solid and well-built.

"Now, how big is this piece?" one of the men asked.

"Twenty-five acres," Richard said. "Most pieces up here are twenty acres, but this one is a little bigger."

"And how much are they asking?" the same man asked.

"This property is a steal at ten thousand," Richard said.

"What's that?" I asked, pointing. I noticed a flat spot about two hundred feet west of the shed fenced off with stout poles.

"Oh, that's the corral," Richard said. "They had horses up here. There are miles of riding just past Dan and Vicki's."

I looked at Thea with a big goofy grin. She would have made a better spy than me—she pretended not to see.

"Do these roads have names?" I asked. I was thinking of how to give directions to our friends who might visit.

"They sure do. The main road is called the Union Valley Loop Road. The switchback turn down there," Richard said, pointing south, "is Sawmill Road, and this little road on top is School House Road."

"Was there was a school house up here?" Thea asked.

"There was a whole community up here back in the thirties and early forties. The school house was on the corner of this property, right over there." He was pointing toward where we had turned from Sawmill onto School House Road. "There was a post office and a store on the Loop Road where that tight turn is above the creek.

There were several families up here trying to make a living farming. Back then this place was covered with first growth fir. They built a saw mill a few miles farther north. It was a busy little place."

"What happened to everybody? Why did they leave?" I asked.

"I think there was a fire. All the wheat burned up along with the trees they hadn't cut. That was the end of the town of Union Valley."

The other couples looked bored.

"Everybody ready?" Richard asked.

They piled into the station wagon, we climbed into the Land Cruiser, and we made our way back to town.

"Don't you just love this view?" Thea said as we crested the last rise and began our long descent. Lake Chelan shone deep blue at the bottom of the valley, backed by a low mountain spine.

"Is that a fire lookout on the highest hill?" I wondered aloud. "There could be a repeat of the fire that wiped out the town the first time."

Richard parked his car around the corner from the real estate office. We parked next to him.

"Thank you for showing us the property," the first couple said. "But we're looking for a place a little closer to civilization."

"Yes, thank you. We'll be in touch," said the second couple.

"Did we see a fire lookout on that highest hill above town?" I asked Richard.

"Well, yes, and radio towers. There are hang gliding championships from that hill, it's called The Butte."

"So, are there a lot of fires around here?" I pressed.

"Oh, now and then, but they know what to do to control them. Don't worry."

I thought of the meadow, the views, the quiet, the breeze. Thea looked at me. I smiled and nodded.

Thea leaned in to Richard and said, "We'll meet you at the office to sign the papers."

It was finally happening! We'd looked all over eastern Washington and finally found the perfect spot—and on Jacob's third birthday, no less. Dinner at Uncle Larry and Auntie Pat's that night would be a double party. We burst in the door of Pat and Larry's, our words tumbling out before either had a chance to say hi.

"We found the greatest piece of land up in Union Valley!" I said.

"We signed the papers today!" said Thea.

"Call your dad." Larry said to Thea, interrupting.

"What about?" Thea asked. She looked at me nervously.

"Just call your dad," Larry said.

When her dad answered, he said "Call Gay,"and hung up.

"Hi Gay," Thea said, "Is everything okay?"

"No," my mom replied. "Wally died yesterday. He was in San Francisco for a coffee convention, and they found him dead in his hotel room."

"Oh, no! What happened?"

"It was a heart attack. Please come home."

Wally was my step-dad, only 56.

We ate cake to celebrate Jacob's birthday and buying the land, but it wasn't the same.

My father was a Squadron Commander in an Air Force bomber group stationed in South Korea. In April of 1952, he was to fly one last mission, then return to the States for re-assignment. He went missing-in-action with his replacement and a small crew. I was two and a half years old. My mom married Wally in 1967, my junior year of high school. Wally moved us into a majestic log home the summer before my senior year. I loved that log home. I had imagined I would live in one of my own when I finished school and settled down. We were finally making it happen, and Wally wouldn't be around to see it.

"You can't leave me now," Mom said when we returned from Chelan. "I really need you to stay."

My brother had come over to support Mom and be there for the funeral. "I know it's hard, but don't squash their dreams, mom," he said.

"Well, I don't want to be alone. I will have a hard time being alone." She was in tears.

I loved my mom, and staying home for her was not a hardship. She had known too much death in her time. Her father had died in 1920 when she was two years old—he scratched his ear with a rusty nail and died of blood poisoning. In 1939, when my mom was twenty-one, her mother had died. My older brother Patrick died in 1946 when he was three years old—he had a tummy ache and by the time they got to the hospital, it was too late. They never learned the cause. My own dad, her husband, went MIA in 1952. I flat-lined in surgery in 1954 when I was five years old, and again in 1961 just before I turned twelve. Now Wally was gone.

What had just seemed so close was now far away again. It was to be another season of waiting, but my dream had not died. It was only postponed.

{ 9 }

THEA AND I TALKED IN BURSTS on the drive back over the mountains. At times we could hardly contain our excitement for the beautiful property we'd found, and our words came in a flood. At other times, we were mindful of Wally's death and Gay's sadness, and our conversation would ebb.

We sold our house on 112th street for $72,000 in July. We had paid $39,000 three years before. The buyers could not get bank financing, so we carried the contract. They paid us five hundred dollars a month and we put all the money into an account for when we could move to our beautiful property across the mountains. My mom offered one of her rental homes to us, the little brown house on 203rd street, the last full acre in Shoreline. We paid a hundred dollars a month.

"We should stay at least one more year," I said to Thea.

"It's such a relief to have the property," Thea said. "Now we can save some money and plan for the move."

More than just a log home in eastern Washington, Thea and I also wanted a big family, a passel of kids. It had taken nearly three years for us to get pregnant with Jacob, and Jacob's third birthday had come and gone and number two still wasn't in the oven.

{ 73 }

"How did it go?" I asked when Thea came home from the OB/GYN in July.

"The doc said we're safe to have another baby."

"Say no more!" I said.

In October Thea gave me the news. "We're pregnant!" she said, smiling and crying. "We're due on June 29th."

"Thank you, God!" I said.

ᏣᏍᎤ

We had learned about an extension class offered by the University of Washington that taught how to build a log house, with Skip Ellsworth as the instructor. We signed up and drove out to Duvall the first weekend of November. Skip had built several log houses on his property in Duvall. As a youth, Skip had helped his father repair many log structures, and in the process learned which designs held up best to the elements.

"I'm going to show you a series of slides—examples of what *not* to do when you build your house," Skip said.

He clicked to the first slide. "Don't build your house directly on the dirt. See how the bottom log is rotted almost halfway through? I'm going to show you how to build the right foundation for your log home."

He clicked to the second slide. The class gasped. A half-finished log wall with a four foot hole was leaning kittywampus. "Don't cut your windows and doors as you go," Skip said. "Leave your logs alone until the shell is complete. I will show you how to add doors and windows."

He clicked to the third slide. A few groans. "Don't chink your logs with this ugly cheddar cheese yellow foam crap. It's ugly and will rot your logs. I'll show you how to do it with mortar," he said.

He clicked to the fourth slide. A wall half-finished was nine feet tall at one end and ten feet tall at the other. Skip said, "I'll show you how to keep your log walls level."

For three more hours Skip showed us those how-not-to slides. He followed through on his promises to show us the right way instead. He taught us how to lift our logs without heavy equipment or cranes. He explained how to obtain our logs and other building materials inexpensively—even free. He extolled the virtues of living free of the burden of a mortgage and gave us the confidence we could build our own homes.

Skip said, "Before you build your house with logs, build it with dowels. Make a model. Half an inch equals one foot. If you can build it with dowels, you can build it with logs."

We settled on one of the many floors plans I had drawn, and I began building my model. I made the 2 x 12 floor joists to scale on my table saw and glued them into place to see how they would all fit together. I made rafters out of smaller dowels and pin-nailed them into place. In the process, I discovered a few problems and was able to make changes on the small scale. I took my model back to Skip, and he pointed out another "don't do." I had planned a balcony to be accessible from the upstairs master bedroom, but to get there, I had cut the top log.

"Never cut the top log," Skip said. "Build stairs that go up and over the top log if you really want that balcony."

We decided to forgo the balcony, and leave the top log whole, as Skip recommended.

⊂⊃

"Let's go see the property in the snow," I said to Thea that January. "I'd like to know how much snow there is, what to expect for the winter."

"Let's get a hotel room instead of staying with Pat and Larry," Thea said.

"Okay."

We checked into the hotel, and the next morning I was raring to go.

Thea said, "I'm not feeling well. You and Jacob go see the snow. I'm going to stay here and rest."

"You sure you're okay?" I asked.

"Yeah, I'll be fine, you go see the snow."

Jacob and I drove up the hill into the bright, clean snow. The main road was plowed most of the way, but soon we were pushing through untracked snow. We turned into the shadow of pine trees flanking Sawmill Road and pushed up the slight grade that skirted one side of a small valley. We broke out of the trees as the road curved higher and steeper up the valley, and my tires spun in the deeper snow. I stepped out to lock my hubs— the snow was knee-deep. We moved forward again, though no more than two hundred yards before the road steepened even more.

Jacob's eyes widened as the Land Cruiser struggled through the deep snow and stopped.

"We're okay, bud," I said. "The snow is up to the bumper. We can walk from here."

The road there formed the south western boundary of the property, so I hoisted Jacob to my shoulders, and we trudged up the road to get higher on the hill before cutting into the field. The sun shone bright from a clear blue sky. The snow reflected the sun like a mirror. The pine trees were dark green against the sky and snow. Their trunks appeared almost black. The snow was about eighteen inches deep, enough to cover most of the bitterbrush, but not all. As we approached the corral where I planned to build, we looked east to see the distant Columbia Plateau covered in snow. I smiled and stopped to enjoy the view. My heartbeat was the only sound I could hear.

"I think we're going to be all right, bud," I said to Jacob. "There's a lot of snow, but we'll gather firewood all year long. We'll stay warm."

Jacob and I returned to the hotel to find Thea lying on the floor in front of the sliding glass door.

"Are you okay?" I said, rushing to her.

She opened her eyes. "I'm just enjoying the sun beating down on me," she said with a sleepy smile.

"You scared me," I said. "Jeez! Anyway, you should have seen the property. Oh, it was so beautiful! About eighteen inches of snow. I think we're going to be just fine up there."

Thea motioned for me to help her stand, and once on her feet, she shuffled to the bathroom.

Minutes later she came out wide eyed, fully awake. Her voice was high and strained. "We have to go. I'm bleeding! The baby!"

{ 10 }

RACING BACK OVER THE MOUNTAINS, we made the trip in three hours, a normal time for dry pavement, but fast in the snow.

We walked in the house and Thea strode directly to the phone.

"Doctor, I'm bleeding," she said.

We arrived at the doctor's office and he peppered Thea with questions.

"Okay, we'll do an ultrasound and see," he said.

He slathered her stomach with jelly and moved the probe around. At first there was no sound, then something for a second, but he lost it. He moved back, and found the sound again. Through the static and crackle I could make out a regular rhythm—a heartbeat. He listened for a while, moving the probe this way and that, and relaxed. Smiled.

"Well, the baby is fine," he said. "The heartbeat is fine. You did great. If anything like that happens again, come straight in."

We stayed on the west side of the Cascades for the rest of the pregnancy.

One of the dads in our Lamaze class was a big shot for Boeing. He gave tours to the visiting executives from Japan and spent some of his wage on accessories for his burly Ford Bronco. Among them were semi-truck snow chains he'd cut down to fit his tires, Armstrong 11.50 x 15 Tru-Tracks—the very same tires I had on my Land Cruiser. He sold me the chains for $40—a steal. I could only imagine then how useful they would end up being later.

Our second son was born four weeks premature at 10:10 AM on Monday, May 31st, 1982. He weighed five pounds, one-half ounce, and was seventeen inches long. His little buns fit right in the palm of my hand. We named him Lucas, after Lucas McCain, *The Rifleman*, a favorite Western TV show of mine when I was a kid.

⋇

One advantage to following Skip's advice about building a model house was knowing how many logs we would need to build our house. I counted seventy-five dowels. I would need three logs to be at least forty-two feet long, and seventy-two logs to be at least thirty-one feet long. I wanted minimum diameters of twelve inches on the big end, and nine inches on the small end.

We drove to the property in August. Tall straight trees abounded on the northern slope, but building our house would consume them all. We drove to nearby Purteman Gulch, but the trees were spindly and sporadic.

"I think I'm getting a migraine," Thea said.

I turned to look. Her face was pained. "Let's go back home. We can look for logs some other time," I said.
Thea stayed quiet as we drove home, but she became animated as we came to the top of Stevens Pass.

"He pooped!" she shouted with glee. "He pooped, he pooped! Pull over, he pooped!"

Luke was three months old and had gone three weeks without a BM.

Our friends Ted and Marylynne happened to be driving by and saw us pulled over. They stopped to see if we needed help. Luke had pooped all over Thea—her legs, her lap, her hands—and all over himself. When Ted and Marylynne arrived at the car they found Thea covered in poop laughing and giggling.

"What are you doing?" Marylynne asked, horrified. "It's all over you! How disgusting."

"Who cares if it's all over me!" Thea replied. "The baby pooped! He's going to be fine!"

"This is another reason why we're never having any children," Marylynne turned and said to Ted just loud enough to be heard.

"Jim had Hirschprung's disease," Thea said. "One symptom is constipation, and we were afraid Luke might have the disease." She looked down at Luke. "Oh, you're going to be okay!"

"Glad you're okay. See you guys later," Ted said and returned to their VW bus. Marylynne had turned to go without even saying goodbye.

Thea didn't notice. Our baby was healthy.

 glaring

Labor Day Weekend, despite my determination never to cross the mountains on a holiday weekend, we went back to Union Valley. We just couldn't stay away.

The meadow was dry and brown in early September, but hadn't lost its charm. The dried leaves of the wild sunflower crunched under our feet like tortilla chips. The air was warm and dry, not a hint of fall or winter, but I knew the truth.

A vehicle drove down our driveway less than five minutes after we arrived.

The guy stepped from his rig with a smile. "My name is Dan, this is my wife Roberta. We live over by Church Camp. You must be the folks who bought Stiles' place. I saw you go by."

"Yup, we are. I'm Jim, this is my wife, Thea, and our boys Jacob and Lucas. How many families live up here?"

"Well, let's see." Dan paused. "There are three or four folks who bought up here recently. They haven't had a chance to build yet. There's actually a party over at the Carlson's today. Most of Union Valley will be there, or are already. Would you like to go over and meet them?"

"That would be great!" I said. I looked at Thea and she nodded approvingly. We followed Dan back the way we had come, up Watson's Grade, past a log house on the right.

"That looks like a Skip Ellsworth house to me," I said.

"It sure does," Thea said. "I wonder if they'll be at the party."

{ 82 }

We pulled in to the Carlson's place. Parked cars and trucks lined the side of the road. Nearly twenty people gathered around a fire pit and a table covered with casseroles and salads.

"We don't have anything with us," Thea said to me as we walked toward the group.

Several turned and smiled as we approached.

"Hey, everybody," Dan said, "This is Jim and Thea. They bought the Stiles' place."

"Welcome to The Hill!"

"Hi, I'm Leif and this is my wife Mary. This is our place. Where are you from?"

"We live in Seattle, but not for long," Thea said.

An old fellow with a weathered face walked up. "Glad to meet you. I'm Tommy, this is my wife, Frankie, and my brother, Jay. That's my son Ray and his wife, Bonnie."

"Well, hello. We're glad to be here."

"We live near the bottom of the hill as you start up, down by the orchards," Tommy said. "You ever need anything, let me know. We'll be glad to help."

"Thanks!" I said. I turned to Thea and whispered, "I'm even more pleased you suggested Chelan. Good idea."

A tall young guy approached us. "Hi, I'm Dan Mathews, this is my wife Vicki. You bought Doug and Roberta Stiles' place? We have a place just beyond it to the north."

"Yes, we did. Richard told us about you guys. He has a place right next to yours." I said.

"Yup, that's us, glad to meet you," he replied.

"Glad to meet you," Vicki said.

We met another older fellow too. "Greetings," he said. "My name is Wayne Leatherman. My place is east of Ken West's place. I dug it into the hill. It's small, but cozy. You'll have to stop by sometime, I'm usually there. If you need anything, let me know."

We met Leif's brother, Hans, and their mom and dad. Colonel Richard Carlson and his wife had purchased the property a few years earlier and shared it with their children, so each of them had built a home on the twenty acres and they all lived there together. Their piece looked down on Lake Chelan far below and the little town of Manson tucked into the hill.

We heard a Jeep coming down the driveway. Everyone turned and Leif said, "It's Ken and Maryanne."

They parked and stepped out of their rig with a smile and waved to the group. "We made it," Ken said. Maryanne held a bowl of salad covered with clear wrap.

Mary announced, "Let's eat!"

Thea moved close to Mary and said, "We didn't know we needed to bring anything."

Leif overheard and said, "Don't worry about it, there's always more than enough for everyone. Help yourselves to the cooler, too."

We all mingled and swapped stories about who we were and what brought us here. The food was great.

Ken walked up with Maryanne and asked, "Which place did you buy?"

"The Stiles' place." I said, "You can see it from that log house as you start down Watson's Grade."

"That's our log house," Ken said. "You've got a nice piece of land. I heard Stiles wanted to be a screenwriter, so they moved back to California."

"We sure like it. We're excited to get started. Did you guys take Skip Ellsworth's log house building class?"

"Yes, we did. It's a great way to build."

"We did, too," I said. "Last fall. We sure learned a lot."

"If you need any help, let us know." Ken offered.

"Thanks, Ken."

We spent that night at Pat and Larry's. We missed the crush of cars returning to the west side by heading for the pass right after breakfast.

⊰⊱

We still needed logs, but I wasn't having much luck on my own. I found a logging company out of Leavenworth that would sell and deliver as many trees as we wanted. I paid $1,500 for the logs and the delivery. I thought this was a steal, but I didn't know how painful the delivery experience would turn out to be.

The logging company hired a father and son team from Cashmere to deliver the logs with their two trucks. We met at French Corral, up the Entiat River, and I handpicked the logs as they were loaded. I couldn't speak, as I had laryngitis, but I could point my finger or shake my head, so that was enough.

The father started his truck and put it into gear at an idle. The son fell in behind his dad. I pulled out of the loading yard and accelerated onto the Entiat River Road. I looked back to see them falling behind, so I slowed down. Moments later I checked again, and they were still falling behind, so I slowed down more. I found their sweet spot at five miles an hour. *What could be wrong?*

I drove on the shoulder the whole way. I stopped several times, just waiting for them to come into sight. I couldn't believe how slow they were going. We crawled the twenty-two miles to Chelan in four hours, and that was the easy part. We still had to climb 2,000 feet in eight miles on a dirt road.

Leaving town, we began the climb to the property. An hour and a half later, we'd gone seven miles and arrived at a part of the road we called the Roller Coaster. The road drops one hundred feet into a valley over the course of a quarter mile, rises and drops over a little hump about twenty feet high, and finally climbs fifty feet in the last tenth of a mile, about a ten percent grade. There are steeper streets in Seattle.

I drove to the top of the last hill and kept checking my rearview mirror for the lead truck. *I really should be able to see him by now.*

I stopped and waited. Nothing. I hopped out of my Land Cruiser and trotted back to the crest of the hill. I watched the lead truck trundle over the hump in the middle. He wasn't going fast enough.

"C'mon, man, grab another gear!"

He climbed a third of the way up the final rise when one of his tires spun. He stopped.

I squeaked at him, "You'll need to get a run at it!"

He backed down the hill to the bottom of the dip and climbed out. "This is as far as I'm going!" he yelled up at me.

I walked down the hill and whispered fiercely, "We're not there yet! You can see my place from right up there!"

He whirled around and leaned into my face. "I had no idea the road would be so steep!" he yelled. "I'm not about to ruin my truck trying to climb this horrible hill!"

"I've driven log trucks myself," I squeaked, "on roads steeper and rougher than this, lots of times. Just get up some speed, and you'll sail right up."

"It's true, dad," said his son. "A little run at it would do the trick."

The dad yelled again, "No. This is as far as I'm going!"

Then he turned to me and said, "And you owe me seven hundred dollars!"

"I've already paid for delivery, and you haven't delivered the logs to my property!" I was straining with every word.

"Dad, try again. We can make this hill."

He barked at his son. "Dump your load right there."

His son sighed dramatically. He slouched back to his truck and began unchaining his load. The father unloaded his load of logs by the side of the road at the bottom of the second dip, and a little behind, his son did the same.

"Um, dad? Now what are we going to do?"

"What do you mean?"

"Well, the road is too narrow to turn around, and I don't think I can back up that hill."

The father, having already dumped his logs, then surveyed the situation. He looked back the way they had come. He squinted. He looked toward the way I wanted them to go.

He stuck his arm out straight. "We go that way," he said, pointing ahead.

My jaw dropped.

He stalked away, climbed into his truck and started the engine. He put his truck in gear and motored up the very hill I had been begging him to climb.

I stared after him, my shoulders slumped. I turned to look at the son, but saw only his back. He started his rig and chugged up the hill behind his dad. Ten minutes later, they had turned around and were on their way back home. I waved my arms and gestured to the pile of logs that was my home as they drove by, but neither of them made eye contact.

The woods swallowed the sound of their engines, and I was alone in the quiet with my logs.

Well, now what am I going to do? I had planned to peel most of the logs while they were still fresh and easy to peel. I had no equipment to move these enormous logs and the next day, Saturday, was opening day of hunting season. I could imagine the hay day the hunters would have cutting up my house to use as fire wood in their camps.

I raced to the property and rummaged in the shed for a small piece of plywood to make a sign. It said: "These logs are my house, please do not cut." I nailed it to the pile and hoped for the best.

Jake Beaty

{ 11 }

I KNOW WHAT I'LL DO, *I'll visit Tommy Hill!*

"Hi Tommy," I squeaked through my laryngitis when he opened his door. "I'm Jim Beaty, we met about a month ago at the Labor Day party at the Carlson's?"

"Yes, I remember. How are you? Did you find any logs for your house yet?"

"Sure did," I said, "and that's why I'm here. The log truck just dumped them in the bottom of Roller Coaster, and I have no way of moving them. It's two trucks' worth, seventy-five logs over forty feet long. I wonder if you have any ideas?"

Tommy replied, "Well, let's see what we can do about this."

I was surprised by his response. He just dove in, like it was his problem too. "I have my bulldozer, my poppin' johnny tractor, and a heavy equipment trailer." He turned to his brother and son who were there listening, "Jay, Ray, let's hook the trailer up to the tractor and haul the dozer up to Roller Coaster. We've got some logs to move."

The poppin' johnny, so called because of the pop-pop, wait, pop-pop sound the powerful two-cylinder engine made, was a big farm tractor, the rear tires at least five feet tall, the hood six or seven feet high. It was as long as a pickup truck. It was strong enough to haul that bulldozer on the trailer all the way up to the top of Union Valley.

We arrived at the piles of my beautiful house logs and went to work. We chained the first log to the blade of the bulldozer. Tommy lifted the log and maneuvered to set it down on the equipment trailer. We unchained the log, and Tommy went back for another. Four logs maxed out the trailer, and Ray towed the trailer with the poppin' johnny to the property. Once there, we released the logs to roll off the trailer and into the field above the build site. We returned to the piles for the next load. That first round trip took about an hour and a half.

We loaded the trailer with four more logs and drove back to the property. We rolled the logs off the trailer into the field. We headed back for more. We worked until dusk, though we'd barely made a dent.

So much for peeling these logs while they're fresh. "Tommy, Ray, Jay," I said, "I am so sorry, but I have to get back to work or I might lose my job. Here's $40 to cover your fuel."

"No, keep your money," Tommy said. "Don't you worry—we won't quit till we get this job done."

I hustled back to Chelan the next weekend. I drove through Roller Coaster first. I couldn't believe my eyes. Not a single log was left. I continued to the property. All seventy-five logs were spread out like pick-up sticks on the hillside. While I'd been at work in Seattle, Tommy, Ray, and Jay had lifted, hauled, and dumped my logs for four or five more days.

I drove down the hill to Tommy's place. "Wow, Tommy, thank you so much! I have to pay you for your help." I said.

"No, thanks, Jim," Tommy said. "You just be sure to help someone who needs it in the future."

I expected winters in Union Valley would provide me with many opportunities to do just that.

⋘⋙

After returning home, I continued to amass my supplies for the build.

Skip had told us, "The best way to spike your logs together is to use half inch rebar in eighteen inch lengths. Drill through the top log, and pound the rebar through the top log and into the log below. Stagger the location for each layer of logs. When logs dry, they shrink. They will shrink to their own centers on the rebar, and the walls won't settle or drop."

I ordered a bundle of rebar to be delivered to our little brown house. I had borrowed a bolt cutter with thirty-six inch handles to cut the rebar. I straddled the first piece of rebar and bit it with the jaws of the bolt cutter, leaving eighteen inches sticking out. I squeezed the handles. Nothing. I squeezed as hard as I could. Nothing. I rotated the bolt cutter so one handle was on the ground. I gripped the upper handle with both hands. I pushed down. Nothing. I pressed down until my feet came up. I broke a sweat, but not the rebar. I bounced on the handle. It moved! I bounced again and the jaws bit a little closer.

{ 93 }

Third time—no charm. I bounced a fourth time and clipped off the first piece. Five minutes. I was breathing hard. "One down, one hundred and ninety-nine to go," I muttered to myself.

I worked in an aircraft instrument machine shop at the time, and one of the inspectors was called "Big Wally." He was six-five or six-six and must have weighed three hundred pounds. He was soft-spoken, a gentle giant. He didn't live far from me, so I talked to him the next day at work.

"Hey, Big Wally, would you be willing to give me a hand with something after work?" I asked.

"What do you need, Jim?"

"I'm having trouble trying to cut some rebar. I'm bouncing on this big bolt cutter, but I can't get the rebar to break. Would you be willing to come to my house and help me cut up a few pieces of rebar some night after work?"

"Sure thing, Jim," he said. "When should I come over?"

I hesitated. "Are you available tonight?" I asked.

He was. When he arrived, we set up a jig to keep the length consistent, and I fed him the first rod of rebar. He held the bolt cutter and crunched down. "Ping!" The first piece popped off. Big Wally didn't grunt or strain. He didn't rest one cutter handle on the ground. I pushed the rod forward. "Ping!"

Push. "Ping!" Push. "Ping!" Four pieces in less than a minute!

I had twenty sticks each twenty feet long. We made thirteen spikes from each long stick for a total of two hundred sixty spikes. It was a giant pile when we finished, and we were done in ninety minutes. Big Wally smiled the whole time. So did I.

"Big Wally, you just saved my life! I'd like to pay you for your time."

"No way," he said. "Help someone else when they need it." Just like Tommy Hill.

"I will. I promise. Thank you so much!"

ගෙන

In November we went to a reunion for our log house building class. "Reynolds Aluminum is closing out all of their metal roofing," a classmate told us. "They're selling it for half price in order to close out their supply, and they'll cut it to length."

We drove to Reynolds Aluminum in Kenmore that day. They still had many color choices, so I selected a nice olive green. We needed thirty-eight pieces cut to twenty-three feet for our project. They cut the roofing and delivered it, along with the ridge cap and edge trim, to our house in North Seattle for sixty-two cents per foot! Everything we'd looked at before had been nearly two dollars per foot. We spent less than six hundred dollars to roof our entire cabin in steel, rated to last a hundred years. Six cents a year is a good cost for a roof, no matter how you slice it.

"We still going out to dinner next week?" I asked Thea. It was our eighth wedding anniversary. We had promised each other when we married that no matter what, we'd go out to dinner for our anniversary. She was holding little Luke, a preemie, just six months old. She looked down at his sweet, sleeping face.

"I can't leave him, Jim," she said. "I can't leave him with a baby sitter, I just can't."

On the big day, Thea made us a pizza for dinner.

"Happy Anniversary, dear," I said.

∞

There was no electricity to our property in Chelan. It's an assumed convenience in the modern world, and life gets very difficult for the average suburbanite when a winter storm cuts the power for a few hours.

"How are you going to do it?" our friends asked, incredulous, especially of Thea.

I spoke up. "You forget that in thousands of years of human history, we've only had useable electrical power for a hundred. We're accustomed to its conveniences, but life, and a good life at that, is possible with limited to no electricity."

"Okay, Jim. Okay, okay."

I did want at least *some* electricity—enough for a radio, some lights, maybe a kitchen appliance or two—so I had been researching wind power. I selected a WINCO 12-volt wind generator which included a ten-foot four-leg tower—like an oil derrick. The blade was a precision-cut eight-foot long cedar 2 x 4. It was a long, skinny propeller against which the wind pushed, rather than the other way around, as on a plane. The power generator head was a cylinder the size of two basketballs, but the layers of copper coils hidden inside the blue painted steel shell made it weigh eighty pounds. It was a three-phase alternator rated to produce five hundred watts. A long tail fin extended from the back of the power head to keep the blade facing the wind. I knew the ten foot tower would not be tall enough, but I figured I'd come up with a taller tower once on site.

There was no water on our property in Chelan, either. We could live without electricity, but no one lives without water. We'd need to drill a well.

I'd seen the ads for the Deep Rock Hydra-Drill in the back of *Mechanics Illustrated* and was intrigued. Why pay a guy several thousand dollars to drill your well, when you can do it yourself for hundreds, and then sell the drill to someone else when you're done? That was the theory, anyway.

Many of our friends at church knew about our plan to build a log house in eastern Washington, and some of them were helpful both before and after the move. Russell Brown was one of those. He stopped me one Sunday after church. "How are you doing, Jim?" he asked. "Making progress getting ready for the move?"

"We sure are, Russell. We're filling our garage with all kinds of supplies and appliances and equipment."

"Well, I have something you might be able to use, not sure if you'd be interested..."

"Oh, yeah?"

"We have a nice camper we never use. I'll give it you free—just haul it away."

"Wow! Really?"

I called Thea's dad. "Hi, Paul. Can I borrow your truck this afternoon? A friend is giving us his camper."

I drove to my father-in-law's after church, then on to Russell's place. The camper was a deluxe model—propane stove, heater, and refrigerator, toilet and shower, big beds, storage space—it was primo.

"How can I begin to thank you?" I asked Russell.

"Just help someone else when you have the chance," he said. "God bless you."

"Yes, He does."

Back home with the camper, I said to Thea, "Doesn't it seem like God is really on our side in this whole process? I mean, the roofing was half price, Big Wally cut all that rebar for us, Tommy, Ray, and Jay moved all our logs for free, and now Russell gives us his camper!"

"Yes, I think we're supposed to do this," Thea said. "God is really showing us favor."

"We can park this camper next to the shed where the bus was parked. We can live in the camper and the shed while we build the house."

ELDEC, the company where I worked, started a round of lay-offs in the spring of '83. It was time. This was the opportunity to follow my dream. I could still hear Pete: "I wish I had..."

I approached my boss. "I want to volunteer to be laid off."

"Jim, no, you're too valuable. We're not going to lay you off. Anyway, why would you volunteer to be laid off?"

"I have a dream to build a log home in eastern Washington, and it's time to make it happen."

"We were going to lay off Roberto," my boss replied.

"No, Roberto is a hard worker. You should keep him. He's newly married with a brand new baby and really needs the job. If you lay me off, I can collect unemployment while I'm working on the cabin. This is something I really need to do."

"Okay, Jim," he sighed. "If you insist."

They laid me off and Roberto kept his job.

I drove home and said to Thea, "It's time."

"Okay," she said. "We're as ready as we're going to be. Let's go."

Our parents were not as supportive as we had hoped they'd be, but we weren't going to let them discourage us.

The people at Greenwood Church were sad to see us go, yet encouraged us. They even organized a going away party. We would miss them all for sure.

I rented the biggest moving truck Ryder had available, advertised as twenty-four feet long. We loaded the twenty-three foot long roofing in first, on the floor, and a foot of it stuck out the back. I scratched my head. I looked up into the box and saw the overhang above the cab. It was about two feet long—that must be it.

Friends from church and friends from years ago came to help us move. We loaded our five hundred-pound fireplace, our beautiful Monarch stove, our precious propane refrigerator, pedestal sink, claw-footed tub, windmill, well driller, wall tent, pieces of rebar, roto-tiller, draw knives, sledge hammers, tire chains, our recliners, kitchen table set, books on homesteading, boxes of clothes, and all the other material accumulations of our lives. I tied closed the door of the moving truck.

Thea's dad drove his pickup, hauling the camper and towing my four by ten foot trailer. Thea drove my Land Cruiser with Luke, the Samoyeds Danny and Clowd, and our cat, Sammy. Ted drove our Chevy van. I drove the big Ryder truck with Jacob as my co-pilot. Everything we owned was in these four rigs. Our little caravan left the little brown house on Thursday morning, April 28th, 1983, headed east.

We took Highway 522 from Shoreline to Monroe, then we followed Highway 2 through the whistle-stop towns of Sultan, Startup, Goldbar, Index, and Skykomish. We caught glimpses of the Skykomish River between gaps in the salmonberry brush and vine maples wearing beards of moss. The river raged with spring melt. We climbed out of the river valley and conifers with mossy trunks took over for the vine maple as we climbed to Stevens Pass.

Everything changed east of Stevens Pass. The sky became bluer. The clouds became light and white, relieved of their heavy grey burden on the hooks of the peaks. We could see farther because the trees spread out to share the reduced water. As we descended, the air warmed. We were really doing it! We passed the Fifty-Niner Diner and soon saw the Wenatchee River, tough in its own right, but no contender to the Skykomish. We drove through Leavenworth, Peshastin, and Cashmere, and skirted eastern Washington's version of a city, Wenatchee. We saw very few trees as we followed the Columbia River north, mostly grass and sagebrush. What was still green would soon fade to tan as the summer heat and drought set in. Then it would turn white with snow.

We drove through the town of Chelan and up the hill to the property. We set up the wall tent and an army tent borrowed from a friend of Thea's. Ted helped us unload the trucks, van and trailer into the tents. We hoped the tents wouldn't be holding our stuff for long. We were finally done Friday afternoon, but it was too late to return the moving truck.

I wanted to return the rental truck Saturday and the nearest dealer was an hour south back in Wenatchee. Thea's dad dropped off the camper and drove his truck down to Manson to spend the night with Pat and Larry. We entered Wenatchee from the north, dismayed at the knotted traffic. I didn't think it was such a big city. If this was normal, I was certainly glad to be living an hour away. We dropped off Ted at the bus station for the return trip across the mountains thanking him for his help.

I pushed into the snarl with the big rental truck, and Thea followed close behind in our van. We oozed like mud, bumper to bumper. The Ryder dealer was at the south end of town, only three miles away, yet it took us forty-five minutes, a jogging pace. We didn't get back to the property until dinner time.

We learned later the annual Apple Blossom parade had been rolling down the main street on the day we returned the Ryder, which explained the heavy traffic. It wasn't normal, only an annual event, yet I was happy to be living far away from a place with the potential for that much traffic. No, thanks.

Within the week I had started to prepare the building site. It was early May and the hills were green and dotted with flowers, but I'd learned my lesson at Wauconda—winter was coming, and it wasn't going to wait for me.

{ 12 }

SKIP HAD SHOWN US HOW TO CONSTRUCT a foundation of gigantic pier blocks.

"Make them four feet tall," he said. "The base should be three feet by four feet, and taper to one foot by two feet at the top. They'll each be twenty-four cubic feet of concrete, or just shy of a yard." The plans called for nine piers, so we would need one ten-yard capacity cement truck to pour the foundation. The going rate for a truck was five hundred dollars.

Thea and I took our drawings to the county to get a building permit. "Well, for a house that size," they said, "if it's going to be a permanent dwelling, you're going to need a continuous foundation."

Thea and I stepped away from the desk and whispered. "This will cost us the entire budget for our house!" I hissed. "A continuous foundation with wall and footing would be fifty yards of concrete. That's not including the cost of the forms or the work to get it done."

"What if we're just building a vacation home?" Thea asked.

"Ooh, great idea!"

Back at the desk I asked, "What if it was not a permanent dwelling and merely a vacation home?"

"Then the pier blocks would be fine," he replied. "The fee for the initial permit is two-fifty. We'll follow your

{ 103 }

progress, and the permit will need to be re-issued every six months till the project is complete."

Back in the car I said to Thea, "Like heck we're getting their stinking permit or pouring a continuous foundation! We're going to build it the way we planned. The house will outlast most stick houses anywhere."

"Yes, dear," she said.

I decided to build the house below the brow of the hill rather than at the very top because the winter winds would blow hard on a house up there. We had heard how severe the winters could be. I chose the flat ground of the corral for the building site.

"How are you doing at the corral?" Thea asked after my first day of work.

"Doug built that fence to last," I said. "He used eight-inch spikes and did it well."

"Yeah, I can hear the squealing of nails and your cussing all the way over here," Thea said.

I pried and cussed for another whole day to complete the job. I couldn't use the poles for any other projects, so I stashed them for firewood.

Skip had showed us the proper way to set up batter boards to establish our building's footprint, so I made the preliminary measurements. The inside dimension of the house was to be twenty-four feet by twenty-eight feet. The corral spot wasn't big enough for the whole building. I needed to have a little more land leveled to accommodate our house.

I had met a fellow downtown who owned a small tractor with a front loader, and I explained the job to him. "Do you think you can get the job done?" I asked.

"Of course," he replied. "Hundred bucks?"

"Great," I said. "See you tomorrow."

He drove his tractor up the next morning and started scooping. By noon he hadn't made much headway. His bucket was small and there was a lot of dirt to move. He pawed at the dirt into the evening, but it wasn't nearly enough.

"Thanks for your effort, but it looks like I'm going to need a bulldozer," I said. I paid him and he drove back down the hill.

I thought of our friend Tommy Hill and went to see him the next day.

"Tommy, I need to enlarge the building site for the house. I hired a guy with a tractor yesterday, but it wasn't enough. I think I need a bull dozer. Can you help? I'd pay for your time."

"Yeah, I'll help, Jim. Just refill my fuel tank?"

"Deal!"

He was on-site with his bulldozer within an hour.

"I need the site cut further into the bank so I won't be building on fill dirt," I explained to Tommy.

He made his first pass and revealed a series of decomposing granite ribs running down the slope. Some granite was not entirely decomposed. It resisted mightily. Tommy raked the blade across the ribs, banging and clanging. The rock surrendered with loud cracks. Tommy scraped and scratched. The rock crunched and groaned. The engine roared, and columns of black soot rose from the exhaust. The tracks squealed and clanked. The granite relented, yielding under Tommy's bashing and crashing. He grew the flat spot till it was big enough for the house, and then some.

At the end of the day Tommy asked me, "How do you plan to find water?"

"Well, actually, I don't know," I said.

"There is a method for finding water called 'witching,'" Tommy said. "Some people have trouble with the name, but I figure the good Lord gave us the ability to find water in places you wouldn't expect. So call it divining or witching or whatever you want, but I'll show you how it works."

I had my doubts. We were high on the hill, and the only evident water was a trickle in the creek bottom a half mile away.

Tommy said, "Some people got it and some don't. I happen to have the gift and maybe you do, too. We need to find some choke cherry branches to find out."

We looked, but couldn't find any so high on the hill. "These bushes here just might do," he said. Neither of us knew their name.

"You need something running with sap, not pitch, for the best results."

"What's the difference?" I asked.

"Sap is like fresh honey," he said, "thin and runny. Pitch is like old honey—thick and gooey."

Tommy found a trunk with a large branch. He broke the branch off a foot past its junction with the trunk. He stripped off the extra twigs leaving one toward the end and the tip eighteen inches long to form a Y with the main beam. He grasped the two legs of the Y with his thumbs down and palms out. He turned his palms down and twisted the main branch against his chest. He walked slowly across the building site. I walked beside him.

"I'm starting to feel something," he said as I watched the thick end of the branch pull away from his chest. The stick twisted farther with each step until it was pointing at the ground between his feet.

"There's where you'll find water" he said. "If you count your steps from when you first start to feel the pull, you can get pretty close to how deep it is down there. This one is pretty deep, but it's there. Here, you try."

He helped me hold the stick just right and I paced across the rest of the cleared area. "It's twisting!" I shouted. I tried to stop it. I gripped hard, but the bark peeled off in my hands and the stick continued to twist. Ten steps from where I first felt movement the stick pointed straight down in front of me.

"I can't believe it!" I exclaimed.

"It must be a big source to pull that hard," Tommy said.

I scraped an X on the ground with my boot heel.

"Now," he said, "come at it from over there to find where it crosses to be sure you've found the right spot. Get another stick, though. That one's used up."

I did it again and sure enough, I ended up back at the same place.

"I'd dig right there," Tommy said.

I marked the spot with a small pile of rocks so I could find it when the time came to drill our well.

But first, we needed to buy some lumber for the next series of projects. I needed 2 x 4's, plywood, and nails just to get started, and would need more for the rest of the build. I bought 2 x 12's, over five thousand board feet of 2 x 6 tongue and groove car decking, insulation, particle board and more.

"Can we have a ninety-day payment plan?" I asked at the lumberyard when our first total was tallied. It was over five thousand dollars.

"Just a minute," the cashier said. "I have to ask the boss."

An in-charge looking lady came out from the office area. "Where do you live?" the owner's wife Sharon asked.

"We live in Union Valley," I said.

"You mean 'Hippie Hill?'" she nearly spat. "We'll never get our money," she said to the cashier.

Thea bristled. "We've always paid our bills," she retorted.

"You have to make a payment every thirty days," Sharon said.

"And we will," said Thea.

"Thank you very much," I said, and hustled Thea out of there. "Let's go, dear." We needed to avoid burning this bridge.

Back up on the hill, my flat spot now plenty big enough for the house thanks to Tommy, I marked out the location for my batter boards. This step had to be taken before anything else in the build was even contemplated. The batter boards consisted of three wooden stakes driven into the ground with two horizontal boards affixed to the stakes to make an L just outside the building's dimensions. Each of the four corners had a set. Then I tied strings between the parallel horizontal boards at opposite corners. I slid the strings along the horizontal boards until they formed a perfect rectangle with square corners. The strings marked the inside dimensions of the house.

The noise and dust and smoke of Tommy's bulldozer work had broadcast a message to the residents of Union Valley. A few curious neighbors came to investigate. I was standing in the bottom of the first pier block hole I'd dug when they arrived, so I climbed out.

"Hey, Dan, Leif. How are you guys?"

"We're good. We heard the bulldozer and wanted to see how things were coming along."

Dan pointed west across Sawmill Road, and said, "I own that property right across the road from you. I buried a pipe up the draw connected to a seep and I put a valve at the bottom. You can use it to get water any time you like."

"Wow, thanks, great to know!"

"Those holes are for your foundation?" Dan asked.

"Yeah, I'm following the Skip Ellsworth method," I said. "The foundation will be nine giant pier blocks."

"You need any help?" Dan asked.

"The digging is going pretty well," I said. "Maybe when it comes time to install the forms and pour the cement?"

"I could round up some guys for Saturday," Dan offered.

"Wow, yeah, that'd be great," I said. "I'll have all the holes dug and the forms built. If you come this Saturday, we can place the forms, and I'll have the truck come in the afternoon."

"We'll be here," Dan said.

After Dan and Leif left, I realized I may have spoken too soon about the ease of digging the pier block holes. I dug the first six holes easily, but for the three near the bank on the north side, I had to swing a pick for hours to chip away the granite. I needed all the forms to be level. Only eighteen inches of the four foot pier would show above ground. I needed to locate them precisely to set the first logs forming the perimeter of the house. Twelve inches of rebar would extend above the top of the pier to secure the first logs and hold the building in place.

Just for fun, Thea took a picture of me in one of the holes holding one of Jacob's plastic beach shovels. We showed it to my mom later, and she was horrified.

"Did you really dig those holes with that plastic shovel?" she asked.

"It's the only one I could fit in the holes, Mom," I said.

"Oh, Jimmy!" We still laugh about that picture and story, decades later.

Dan returned that Saturday with Ken West and Chuck Caravue. I had the forms ready as promised, and they helped me lower their bulk into the holes I'd dug.

"Thanks, guys!" I said. "Can you come back next Saturday for the pour? The truck was all booked up this weekend."

"We'll be here," they said.

The concrete pour was a few days away, so I decided to try out my Deep Rock Hydra-Drill. We would need a well, and this was a good time to drill it.

The drill rig consisted of a frame that held a gasoline engine and twenty ten-foot sections of hollow drill rod. The rod had male threads on one end, female threads on the other. The drill bit was tipped with carbide and perforated to allow water under pressure to spew out, cooling the tip and clearing the way as it drilled down into the earth.

The intake of the gas-powered water pump was three inches in diameter to supply the large amount of water needed. I filled three fifty-five gallon drums with water from Dan's source in the valley, and hauled them up to the site.

I set the rig up. The drill bit plunged into the ground. I attached a second length, and it dove in after the first. The pump had already emptied one drum of water! I switched to the second drum. Grinning ear to ear, I started the third drill rod.

The bit stopped plunging. The silt coming out of the hole had changed color, and I figured I'd hit rock. I let the rig work and it did make progress, but I had to stop several times to refill my drums of water. The night was coming on fast, so I elected to shut down and continue the following day—big mistake.

When I came out to continue drilling the next morning, I found the hole had caved in around the drill bit. I didn't realize the consequences until later. I started the pump and spun up the drill, but I did not see any downward progress. I let it work for five minutes, but no water came up, and the pipe did not go any deeper. I added weight to the drill motor—still nothing. The upper section of pipe whipped a little as it turned and wallowed out the hole for a few feet down. I fiddled with it most of the day, and after trying to pull it back up out of the hole without success, I thought I'd try again another day. I unscrewed the last section of shaft and set it all aside for another attempt after the piers were poured.

It was Saturday, the day of the big cement pour, and our helpful neighbors had arrived at the site. We were off the beaten path, so I drove down the hill to meet the cement truck.

We filled the first pier to the brim and then some. We moved the second and did the same. No troubles until we came to the form front and center. The dirt there was the softest because it was closest to the front of the slope. More of the form showed than the others, though I had dug deep enough to hit solid ground. We started dumping concrete into the form and it burst open, spilling nearly a half yard of cement onto the ground. We frantically scooped up the wet cement and tried to repair the form. I sprinted for the shed and came back with a coil of wire. We wrapped that around the top and jammed in a small chunk of plywood to contain the concrete until it could cure. It didn't look very good, but it did the job and would be covered by the front porch when we were done.

"Thanks again for your help," I said. "I couldn't have done it without you. Let me know when I can help you, and I'll be there."

"You bet." "Will do." "No problem, Jim. Glad to help."

⊗⊗

I wanted the inside walls of the house to be plumb. The diameter of the logs varied over their length, and varied from log to log. I wanted the results of any variation in size to appear on the outside of the house. To make this happen, we would need to position lifting poles before lay-

{ 113 }

ing any logs. I needed to stand on end four poles, each five to six inches in diameter, and twenty-four feet long. There would be one pole in each corner, about a foot inside the dimension of the inside of the wall.

I had the holes dug, but Thea and I couldn't stand the poles up by ourselves and tie on the guy lines. Too heavy! We tried four times before giving up.

"Let's go to town for groceries," Thea said.

We descended into the heat. It was warm at the property, but oppressive in town. It was at least ten degrees cooler on the hill.

At the grocery store I thought I saw a familiar face from the coast. I hurried to the end of the aisle for a second look. It was Joel and Kitty with their eighteen month-old daughter. These were the folks who had introduced Thea and me on that first jeeping blind date a few years earlier.

"Hey, Joel!" I shouted.

He whirled around. "Jim!" he said.

"How are you doing?" I asked.

"We're good, Jim," he said. "We're in town for the holiday weekend with the whole family—my mom and dad and brothers and sisters and a sister's boyfriend. How are you guys?"

"We're doing great," I said. "Do you guys want to come up to our property and see what we're up to? I could actually use some help, too. I need a hand getting some tall, heavy poles into position."

"You bet, Jim. Lead the way."

They followed us up the hill and I described to them the general limits of the property. They were duly impressed. At the building site I showed them what I was trying to accomplish with the lifting poles. The pole we had been struggling with lay on the ground where we'd left it. We maneuvered the end into the hole, and, walking together up the length of the pole like raising the flag on Iwo Jima, managed to get it standing.

Boy, that felt good! We all stepped back to admire our work. No one was holding the pole or the guy lines. Augh! We ran to grab it before it fell and then tied off so it would stay. One down, three to go.

We carried the next one to its hole. We plunked in the end and walked up the length. This time, we all held on until it was tied off. We'd broken a sweat and were huffing and puffing, but all the poles went up without incident. I nailed two short 2 x 4's at a ninety-degree angle to an eight-foot 2 x 4 near the ends. I nailed those two short legs to the lifting pole so the eight-footer was exactly plumb on the line of the inside dimension of the house. I did this seven more times, once for each end of the four walls. This way, when we hoisted the logs into place, they would roll up against those 2 x 4's and form a nice plumb inside wall of the house.

೦೩౪౦

I was digging out the pier block form in the southeast corner when disaster struck. The concrete had cured for a few days, so I was shoveling away the dirt to unscrew and

{ 115 }

remove the plywood forms before backfilling so we could continue construction. Jacob was away at the shed messing around with something. Luke crawled, cooing and gurgling, toward mom in the opposite corner.

"Goo goo gah," Luke cooed.

"Tink." My shovel hit a rock.

"Whish." I pitched some more dirt onto the pile.

"Chink." My shovel bit again.

"Gah gah gee." His voice sounded small, muffled, like he was far away.

I looked up. Luke wasn't among the pier blocks. He wasn't with Thea.

"Where's Luke?" I shouted to Thea.

Her eyes darted left and right and she shrieked in panic, "He's down the well!"

I sprinted the fifty feet to the open well top and dove to the dirt. I gaped into the darkness.

{ 13 }

GOO GAH GAH." LUKE WAS STILL COOING calmly. I could see the top of his head, down in the dark hole. The hole was eighteen inches in diameter at the top and tapered down to six inches at about four or five feet. My eyes adjusted to the darkness and I could see both of his arms were above his head like he was reaching up for me.

"Oh, my God!" Thea screamed. "Can you see him? Is he okay?" She had run to the well and was pacing back and forth, spinning wildly from side to side. "Can you reach him? Oh, God, please, my baby! Please! Oh God, oh God, oh God!"

My mind was racing. *Can I reach him? Will I cave in the hole if I get too close? Maybe just a little bit further.*

I strained to push my right hand down to reach my baby boy. His fingertips wiggled against mine.

"Grab Daddy's hand, Luke," I said with forced calmness. "Reach up to Daddy." I jammed myself even farther into the hole.

My face pressed hard against the dirt. Handfuls of dust rained into the hole onto Luke's head. I worried the sides of the hole would cave in on him. I pinched his middle finger with my thumb and forefinger. I pulled. He budged. I gripped more of his tiny hand. Tenderly I pulled him up and out into the daylight.

Sobbing, Thea and I gathered him up between us, holding his breathing, living, precious little body.

"Thank you, thank you, thank you, God!" we both cried.

"Take him," I said to Thea.

I retrieved my shovel from the pier block and packed the well hole with rocks and dirt.

The next day was Luke's first birthday.

୦୫୫୦

We needed a phone. We had no way to call for help when Luke fell down the well. Our nearest neighbor was ten minutes away and they didn't have a phone, either. We did learn that with all the new folks moving into Union Valley, the phone company was making their way up the hill toward us.

Our neighbor Ken came to visit. He said, "Jim, we have a phone at our place now, and the installers are coming your way."

I drove down to the Loop Road to see where they were. I found them putting in the line and a junction box right in front of Buzz Hunter's place. They were on track to reach the bottom of Saw Mill Road in the next day or so.

I stopped my rig and got out to talk. "Hi, my name is Jim Beaty and I live with my family at the corner of Sawmill and School House Roads, about a half mile up. We'd like to get a phone at our place. What do I need to do to make that happen?"

{ 118 }

The lead man replied, "The first half mile is free, but you'll have to dig a ditch for us to bring it onto your property."

Ken had just put in his line the day before, so he still had the Ditch Witch he'd rented from Wenatchee. I drove to his place.

I asked him, "Ken, what do you say we split the cost on the Ditch Witch and you let me use it a few hours to dig my ditch?"

"That'll work fine, Jim. I rented it for two days. I didn't know how tough the ground would be."

The topsoil was soft and I dug the ditch in no time. It was about three hundred feet from the road to the house. Our plan was to bring the phone to the building site because that's where we spent most of the day. Even though the house wasn't built yet, we didn't want to have run all the way over to the shed to use the phone.

When the crew came up to lay wire, I asked, "Would you be willing to run the phone to the neighbor beyond us after you've finished up at our place? You know, since you're already up here."

The lead man asked me, "How much farther is it?"

"Well, it's a little farther than the free half mile by road from our box, but maybe you could cut them a break?"

The lead man counted his crew. "If your neighbor can bring us seven bottles of whiskey, we'll be happy to do it."

I ran over the hill and down through the woods to tell Vicki.

"Oh, yay!" She jumped in her truck and sped for town. She returned in forty-five minutes and handed out the gifts. "I'm just tickled to finally have a phone at our place!" she said.

The phone installer came up a couple of days later. "Where should I hook up the box for the phone?" he asked.

"Can you put it here?" I had built a small wooden box with a little roof on it and nailed it to a tree about thirty feet from the house site. It looked like a tall bird house without a front. The phone could sit in there and be out of the elements.

"We'll call it 'the phone tree.'"

"That *is* unusual. But I'll do it if that's what you want." he said.

"We live over there near the shed in the camper, but we're over here all day every day working on the house."

"I can reel off another bunch of wire so you can take the phone over there, too, if you want."

"Yes, please—that'd be great." And he did—at no extra charge.

We would take the phone to the camper with us at night, and hang it on the tree during the day. We heard later the phone company wouldn't install a phone any more unless it was inside four walls with a roof. We might have been the only people to have a phone on a tree in Chelan County.

I had considered putting in a driveway to the house right from Sawmill along the phone path to keep it short.

Nearly every afternoon the wind would come up out of the west. I noticed the dust would kick up and I thought about it blowing right into the house every time anyone came down the driveway. I decided to come in from the east instead, so the dust would blow away from the house instead of toward it.

We hired an excavator to dig a drain field to the east of the house and install a septic tank. He also dug a pond at the crown of the hill above the house with his bulldozer. I was going to fill it during the summer to have a few thousand gallons of water to fight any wildfires that might flare up. *We might even take a dip on those hot summer days.* While he had the dozer there, I had him cut in the driveway to curve around the hill from the gate at School House Road down to the house. That eliminated having to climb the hill in the snow. The previous owner had a road, but it came straight down the hill, and I was sure it would cause problems during the winter.

❦

Thea was doing her best to be a homesteading wife. She had planted a little garden between the shed and the camper. She started with tomatoes, peppers, lettuce, carrots, peas, and green beans. We were spending a lot of money on milk for our cereal, so Thea asked the neighbors what they did in this situation. Leif was using goats for milk, and before we bought our own goats, we decided to try some of his goats' milk.

Happy 5th Birthday Jacob, with Luke and Thea

We poured it on our cereal the first morning and Jacob gagged.

"Gross!" he yelled. "What is this?"

"It's goats' milk," Thea said. "It's good for you."

"I'm not eating it." He pushed his bowl away.

We couldn't get him to take a second bite, and he was our eater.

We tried it on oatmeal the next morning. Same reaction. I wasn't fond of it myself.

"It does taste weird," I said to Thea. "Tangy, but not like it's sour."

Thea made some chocolate pudding with it for that evening. We managed to get it down.

Leif asked us if we wanted more milk.

"It tastes different than we expected," I explained, trying to be gracious.

"Oh, yeah, well they eat the bitterbrush, and it has a strong taste. It took us a while to get used to it."

"Bitterbrush?"

"Yeah, you know, all the 'sage' brush growing all over the place? Well, it's actually called bitterbrush, and for good reason."

"Oh. Okay. Well, we're gonna pass, but thanks anyway."

 C3❧80

I'd finished removing the forms from the piers and had allowed them a few days to cure. Now the house was ready for the logs, but the logs weren't ready for the house. They needed to be peeled first. I fetched a log from the hill above the site and dragged it down with the Land Cruiser. I used a peavey to roll the log up onto some smaller logs so we could sit astride and peel. We had our best luck peeling the bark off with a drawknife.

Thea and I sat facing each other in the middle of the log. Straddling the log, we grasped the handles of the drawknife and pulled it toward ourselves. This shaved away a narrow strip of bark from the log. We sat in the same place, made a few passes to widen the strip, then scooted backwards to repeat the process.

The logs sat over the winter from the year before, so the bark wasn't soft and wet anymore. The job was much harder than it would have been if the logs were still fresh. Pull, shave, pull, shave, pull, shave, scoot. Repeat. Thea and I peeled two logs on that first day.

Hot and sweaty and tired, we walked back to the camper and shed. I showered in the breeze under the solar shower that never quite warmed up the water. I did some math in my head while I rinsed away the grime, teeth chattering. *If we peel two logs a day, and we have seventy-five logs to peel, that's thirty-eight days—almost six weeks. We need to pick up the pace if we're going to be ready for winter!*

We peeled two more logs the next day.

Next I drilled holes in the logs for the rebar. I had purchased a Troy-Bilt rototiller a few years earlier and fabricated a bracket to fit the tiller. I mounted a 110 volt generator I'd found in the J.C. Whitney catalog, and spun the generator with a belt from the eight horsepower tiller engine. The generator powered my giant drill. A few times the trigger stuck and the drill twisted away from me—about broke my wrist.

Four logs were peeled and drilled, so it was time to hoist them into place and set them on the foundation. The placement of these first logs was critical. They would establish positions for the rest of the logs and determine whether the house were square and in the right place. I measured and re-measured before I drilled those first holes in the logs. They needed to be right because the rebar was stuck in concrete and wasn't adjustable.

We strapped up the first log and hooked it to the come-a-longs hanging from the lifting poles. We cranked the handle, click, click, click. The log rose off the ground. We cranked the log over the tips of the rebar and lined up the holes, lowering the log onto the rebar.

The log settled onto the pier blocks with a quiet "thunk."

"Yes! It worked!" I was beside myself.

We lifted the second log into position.

"Thunk." It dropped into place. I grinned widely at Thea.

Logs three and four settled in, too. I checked for square—all good. I had only drawn this house on paper and built it as a model. I was thrilled to have the first four logs attached to the foundation.

Then I remembered the chimney footing—I hadn't poured the cement. I had a yard of concrete to mix and pour into a form in the middle of the house and a log perimeter right in my way.

A neighbor loaned me his giant cement mixer, so at least we didn't have to mix it all by hand. But the mixer was way too heavy for Thea and me to lift up and over the logs. We mixed the concrete outside, dumped it over the log into a wheel barrow, and rolled over to dump into the form. It took us three hours. It was four by six feet and twelve inches thick.

"Thea, if we ever do this again, let's pour the chimney footing *before* we build the wall."

I reversed the direction of the pinwheel of logs for the next layer. I crossed the corner joints below and spiked them together with a log above. I reversed the pinwheel again for the third layer, and so on. I never weakened the logs with notches, and I reinforced the corner joints at every step with horizontal spikes. It was a bullet-proof design.

Stacking each successive layer was tricky because the butt of a log is thicker than its tip. The top of the logs would get out of level very quickly if I didn't measure and match the logs as I went. Opposite corners of the building will each have two log butts together, one bumped into the side of the other and spiked into place, then the alternating two tips together at that corner on the next layer. Each two layers of logs would bring the top of the wall back to level if done right. I had made a giant pair of calipers when I worked at the machine shop anticipating having to check each log as we went—they served me well.

∞

We'd moved to eastern Washington partly because I thought it was always warm and dry during the summer. Maybe June doesn't count as summer. I was irked on a particularly cold and drizzly day.

"This is June!" I griped, my breath visible. "This aint right!"

I mulled the last few days with a mix of satisfaction and worry. We had three layers of logs in place and the footing poured for the chimney, yet there was so much more to be done. I was preoccupied, not thinking about danger. Cold. I wanted warmth.

I fired up the stove to heat some water. We had discovered the joys of International Coffee. I popped the plastic cap off the little metal tin, and spooned a big scoop of Vienna into my cup. Caffeine and sugar and flavor—I was working my tail off—I needed the energy. As I waited for the water to boil, I decided to start the camper's propane furnace. I would get warm and I would go back to work.

Thea was in the shed changing Luke's diaper and Jacob was in the camper with me on the top bunk. I had closed the door of the camper, lying on the floor on my right side. I removed the grill from the furnace so I could see the pilot light. I opened the valve to the furnace, and lit a match. I held it to the pilot light.

Nothing.

The match went out.

I could hear the hissing of the gas.

I kept the button pushed and lit another match.

Whump! I clamped my eyes shut, but then blinked them open to find I was inside a ball of blue flame. The fire rolled through the interior of the camper toward Jacob in the upper bunk. The explosion blasted open the door of the camper.

{ 14 }

THEA DASHED FROM THE SHED. I dragged myself from the floor, and looked in the bathroom door mirror. Thick strings of melted flesh hung from the left side of my face. Tight little curls of crispy charred hair clung to my chin where my beard had been. It smelled funny. *Pretty weird.* I had been wearing a hat, which kept the flames from burning my head hair, but my left eyebrow was gone.

The world had slowed down. I looked to the left at Jacob and absorbed the horror on his five year-old face. I turned to the right and saw Thea standing in the door. Holding my arm, she gathered me up and helped me walk to the Land Cruiser.

"Let's get you downtown to the clinic," she said. "Come on, Jacob, climb in the back."

She returned to the shed to collect Luke and buckled him into his car seat. Jacob climbed in the back in silence. Thea drove. She could see Jacob's face in the rear view mirror. His eyes were still wide. His lips were drawn tight.

"Dad will be okay," she said. Jacob burst into tears.

"I'll be fine, bud," I turned to say. "We just need to get me to a doctor to take care of this burn." He nodded, but kept crying.

Thea helped me into the waiting room at the clinic. When the receptionist saw me, things happened fast. A nurse came running and escorted me back to an exam room.

"Ooh, what happened to you?" the doctor asked. "This is pretty severe!"

He prescribed Silvadene cream to help the burn heal. I looked like an alien with my face plastered in silver goo. My face hurt as the shock wore off, but the doctor had prescribed some powerful pain killers, so I sat in la-la land for a week while the burn healed.

Before I burned my face off, we had arranged to have a "peeling party" at our place to get as many logs peeled as possible. That way, I could spend the next week hoisting them into place. I sort of remember it, but I mostly just sat there, slumped over in a lawn chair, watching all my neighbors peeling my logs for me. They were all building log homes too, so they brought their own drawknives. Thea stayed busy keeping the children out of the way and making sure everyone had enough to eat and drink. I think they peeled twelve logs in one day. I felt blessed.

I looked at the furnace more closely after my burns healed. The pipe supplying propane from the tank to the furnace had rusted through, just before the pilot light. Gas had poured straight out into the camper. I didn't bother trying to fix it. Winter was coming, but I figured we had enough time to get into the house before the first snow fell.

I must have been healthy because I was working again in a couple of days. The walls rose rapidly with all the logs the neighbors had peeled. Following Skip's method of building, I wouldn't cut any doors or windows until the walls were complete. Skip had been adamant. He had shown us pictures of the results of some who ignored his advice. The walls were uneven at the top of the openings, a problem impossible to remedy. I crawled into and out of the house under the bottom logs. They were about eighteen inches above the ground, so it was easy to do. I had planned the placement of doors and windows and was careful not to put any rebar where they would eventually be cut.

I designed the downstairs doors to line up from front to back so during the hot summers, the afternoon breeze would pass through and ventilate the house. I lined up the upstairs windows in the front and back bedrooms for the same effect.

While it was nice to have neighbors help with peeling parties, most times the parties were limited to two people—Thea and me. Then, too, on occasion, we returned the favor to our neighbors when we had peeling parties at their places. Spending so much time pulling on drawknives and come-a-longs, we found our hands permanently curled to the shape of the handles. It hurt to straighten our fingers.

During one of the peeling parties, a fine older gentleman named Wayne Leatherman had come to help. Wayne would give you the shirt off his back if he thought you needed it. He lived snug and comfortable in a little one-room house he'd built into the side of a hill.

Wayne used an axe to peel his log so it wasn't finished smooth like the rest of the logs. He made multiple chop marks where he'd swung the axe to remove the bark. It wasn't bad—it just looked different. We chose Wayne's log as one of the second floor support logs that crossed the building from side to side. We put it right above the fireplace to showcase its unique appearance.

I had to place the four cross logs with precision. I would lay the second story floor joists across the cross logs, so they needed to be level with each other for the second floor to be level. I notched the wall logs, and shimmed a little here and there to get them just right.

◌୫ঈ◌

July brought the sun and heat I had expected and hoped for in an eastern Washington summer. Thea's garden began to produce a few vegetables. Dan Matthews, our nearest neighbor, had come by to visit and stayed till dinner time.

"Well, I better go," he said.

"Stay and have dinner with us," Thea said.

"Oh, I don't know..." He looked around warily.

"There's plenty of food. I picked some zucchini fresh today, and baked them with tomato sauce and onions and garlic."

"Well, all right." He sat down at the table reluctantly. Thea sprinkled some cheese over the hot baked zucchini, and served our plates with rice.

We lived in the shed and camper while building the house.

Dan took his first bite and looked at Thea, surprised. "You're a good cook," he said.

"Thank you," she said.

"She sure is!" I said, beaming. "Every meal is as good as this. Good job, dear."

In addition to growing her little garden, cooking and caring for the boys, Thea also tried to keep up with our dirty laundry. We'd purchased a 1940s Maytag wringer washer in Wenatchee—it was in mint condition and worked like a charm. But the charm was lost in the work.

Thea loaded the clothes in the washer and added the soap and water. She let the machine agitate the clothes, then lifted the heavy soaking wet clothes to pass through the wringer. The still wet and heavy clothes emerged from the wringer to drop into the rinse tray. Thea used her hands to swish and move the clothes through the clean water to remove the soap and remaining dirt. Then she hefted the sopping wet clothes into the wringer again. The wringer squished the clothes one more time, and pushed them into the final laundry tray, this one dry. Thea then hung the wet, mostly clean clothes on the line to dry. She had to drain the dirty water in the washer and the rinse tray and fill them back up for each load. She did this for us all summer and into the fall.

∞

It was now already August—time to finish the walls. It had taken three months to get this far. I wondered when the snow would start falling. I had planned to have at least four feet above the second floor for better head room near the outside walls. The roof would come down at a forty-five degree angle, so height would be limited where the roof met the walls.

I struggled hardest to place the last logs. I could not get one of the logs to fit. I had already spiked it into place, but I realized the problem before I had gone much further. It had a funky bend and a gnarly burl, but I thought I could make it work. I thought wrong. I figured wrong, too, that I could just pry the log up and off the top of the wall. No, it took me most of two full days to remove it without ruining the log below.

A few guys from Greenwood Christian Church came to help for the weekend, and I was glad when they arrived. I worked the northwest and southwest corners of the house, and my help worked the northeast and southeast corners.

I had explained, "The outside can stagger in and out according to size. Roll the logs up against the vertical 2 x 4 to keep the inside plumb." We worked all day and finished three layers. We had placed twelve logs—I was pleased.

The next Monday, while admiring the work we had been able to complete, I was horrified to see my help had plumbed all three logs on the *outside* of the wall.

I swore and yelled, "Nooo!"

The wall at that corner was leaning out away from the building. The inside dimension was almost a foot wider. The rafters would lie on the top log, and the roof would end up skewed, not square. Metal roofing is less forgiving with such a discrepancy. The problem started three layers down. Two days to remove each log times twelve logs equaled twenty-four days, just to be back where I had started. I could not tear it out. I put my head in my hands. *Now what?*

I stared at the wall and thought. I considered different alternatives, but the pressure of winter's arrival ultimately guided my decision. I had to place the final log where it was supposed to be. The wall would make a very obvious step at the top in that corner.

I hoisted the log into place and measured the diagonal. I adjusted the log. I measured the width and adjusted the log again. I measured the height of that final corner, and, satisfied, I spiked it into place.

The temperatures were still high, but every day the sun rose later and set earlier. Soon the temperatures would decrease like the daylight. I always felt rushed. Winter was coming. We had eight more logs peeled for two more layers, but the upstairs walls were tall enough—there just wasn't time.

The following week, my wife and I managed to raise the ridge pole support logs. These logs needed to be stood up on end and bolted to the front and back walls. The ridge pole would sit on top of them and support the rafters. At that stage, the building would look like a log basket with a handle.

Getting those vertical logs in place was an engineering feat. They were twenty-four feet long, twelve inches through at the big end, nine inches on the small end. I calculated their weight at more than a thousand pounds each. We would hoist the logs using the two industrial strength cast steel come-a-longs I had bought to lift the wall logs into place. They were rated for two tons.

We started with the pole at the back of the house, the north side. Thea and I dragged and twisted and rolled the log into position on the ground, perpendicular to the house. We used a come-a-long to lift the butt end onto the center pier block. We had positioned the pier block to leave a shelf to support the ridge-pole support log. Once the end was in place, I chained it from side to side so it wouldn't fall off the pier as we raised it to its final upright position.

I attached a come-a-long to each upper corner of the house, and the other end to a strap tied to the log about ten feet down from the tip.

Thea and I climbed to the top of the wall, holding the lifting poles to steady ourselves. First I cranked my handle. Click, click, click. The log rose an inch and angled west. Then Thea cranked her handle. Click, click, click. The log rose an inch and came back to center. I cranked my handle and counted the clicks. Thea cranked her handle and counted the same number of clicks. The log crept higher.

Since the tip was up it cranked into position with some effort, but we finished that afternoon. Once I was satisfied it was plumb and in the right spot, I drilled through the pole and through the center of each wall log. Then I secured it to each horizontal log with a two foot length of three-quarter inch threaded rod with a nut and washer on both ends. It wasn't going anywhere.

The front log was much harder. The ridge pole tapered about four inches over its length of forty-two feet. We had decided the thickest end would point south. The vertical support log would therefore need to stand big end up to match the size of the ridge pole. We lifted the small end onto the pier and I chained it in place as I had with the other log. I rigged up the straps and come-a-longs to hoist the log, and we started cranking.

First I cranked my handle. Click, click, click. The log rose an inch and angled east. Then Thea cranked her handle. Click. She pulled again. Click. She took a breath and tried once more. No clicks. I scampered over to her side and helped her get the last click. Then we pulled for three more. The log was angled west.

{ 137 }

Dancing on the top wall log, I returned to my side. I cranked to center then east, walked back to Thea's side and cranked to center, then west. Back and forth, back and forth, click, click, click, click. That giant log swayed first one way and then the other, steadily climbing. It stuck out like the prow of an old sailing ship. I had to jump down more than once to re-tighten the chains holding it on the pier, but eventually, we stood it up against the front wall.

I was glad nothing slipped or jumped or broke or fell—it could have been fatal. Once the log was in position, I secured it the same way as the back one. We were relieved to have that part done. The next step was to raise the forty-two foot ridge pole and balance it on top of those vertical poles. I was going to need some extra help.

{ 15 }

MEANTIME, I DECIDED TO GATHER my rafters. I wanted to use logs between six and eight inches in diameter on four-foot centers. I'd need eleven for each side, so twenty-two all together. The top of the ridge pole would be twelve feet above the top of the walls and the house was twenty-four feet wide. That would make the roof a twelve-twelve pitch, or forty-five degrees. I wanted a steep roof for space upstairs and to convince the snow to slide off before it piled up too deep during the winter. Wet snow can crush roofs and I didn't want my roof crushed. I was going to use R-30 insulation on the roof also, so there was no concern about losing heat through the roof.

"I'm looking for some tall skinny trees to use as rafters. Do you know someone who might sell me what I need?" I asked among our friends in Union Valley.

"Dan is the man you want," I was told. Dan lived near Church Camp and had hundreds of small trees growing thick on his property.

"You can have them for free," he said. "I wanted to thin them anyway. Just come and get 'em."

I showed up the next day with my chainsaw and buzzed down my choice of trees. Then I tried to move them. Ugh! They were heavy! Still green and full of sap.

I cut the trees to twenty-three feet, zipped off the limbs, and stacked the branches. I piled five or six logs into the bed of the pickup, tied them in and hauled them to our place. It took most of a day to make the repeat trips. The late August sun was hot and the work was hard, but I couldn't beat the price.

Thea and I peeled those twenty-two rafters in the next day and a half. Being green made them easy to peel. The bark fell off compared to the wall logs. We set them aside to dry and wait until after we'd lifted the ridge pole.

❧

Thea drove back to the Coast with the boys to help a friend with the annual ski sale called Ski Bonkers, put on by Olympic Sporting Goods in Seattle. She wouldn't be there for the ridge pole project.

Thea called from Seattle when she arrived. "I'm sitting here with my dad," she said. "His shoulder and right arm are swollen like balloons."

"Oh, no. From what?" I asked.

"It's an infection. I keep telling him he needs to go to the hospital, but he won't listen. He's protesting because it's the weekend. I've told him it doesn't make any difference whether it's a weekday, a weekend, or what. He needs to go to the hospital. He says he'll just go to bed and sleep it off."

"He knows it's Labor Day Weekend, right? The weekend will go into Monday."

"Yes, I've told him. He says, 'Then I'll go on Tuesday.' I hope he makes it that long. I'll be worrying about him all day while I'm working Ski Bonkers."

"I'm sorry, dear. I wish there was something I could do."

"There's nothing anyone can do. If he won't go, he won't go."

☙❧

Several good friends from Greenwood Church, including our Pastor Jim Shields, had offered to come over on Labor Day Weekend and help. They brought a camp trailer and Donna, Jim's wife, kept an eye on us and kept us well fed.

Before we lifted the ridge pole, there were many other tasks we did. The walls were up, the pad for the fireplace was in, and now it was time to cut the door. We would be installing the floor next, and wouldn't be able to crawl under to get in the house. I marked the center of both front and back walls. I measured the width of the back door, thirty-six inches, and added three inches for the jamb. I would be making the doors myself, so there was some room for adjustment. I measured and marked the level of the floor inside, and fired up my chainsaw. I notched the second log halfway through and cut the door opening. It was the first time we could walk into the building without crawling over or under the wall.

Steve, a friend from church, cut three short sets of logs and stood them on end. He tacked some scrap 2 x 12 boards across the tops to use as temporary stairs to reach the bottom log.

"Promise me you'll replace these as soon as you can," he said.

"I promise."

Somehow I just never got around to it. They worked so well, we're still using them thirty years later. Good job, Steve.

I'd planned to use 2 x 12 boards for first floor joists for two reasons: insulation factor and strength. I had purchased enough R-30 insulation to fill a moving van for both the floor and the roof. R-30 insulation is twelve inches thick. I knew winter temperatures would drop below zero degrees Fahrenheit, and I didn't want a cold floor.

The joists would be twelve feet long. They would lie east-west across the building and meet in the middle. I had placed with great care a log down the center of the house from north to south. We nailed 2 x 12 rim joists to the center log and each side of the house. I wanted to lay my joists on twenty-four inch centers, so I divided the length of the house, twenty-eight feet, by two. Fourteen boards, plus one to start.

I planned for the back twelve feet of the floor to be tile in the bathroom, vinyl in the kitchen, using particle board for the sub flooring. The stairwell and the living room in the front sixteen feet of the house would be 2 x 6 car-decking.

The guys began bringing in the joists to nail in place. There was a problem. I had only bought enough for one side—typical. I'd only calculated for one run of joists, but there were two sides to the house. Dang it! Well, I had to buy fifteen more boards.

"I'm going to town to buy the boards for the other side," I said. "While I'm gone, set the first joist sixteen feet back from the front wall. Starting from there, set the joists on two-foot centers going away to the front and back wall. If the last joists are slightly less than two feet, it'll be fine."

I thought they understood. I thought they would do what I asked. They had finished the first side by the time I returned, and it appeared to be done well. I was happy with their progress. I didn't learn until later they had done it wrong. And it mattered. Ignorant of this, we installed the second half. We calculated where the chimney would come through the floor and nailed it all into place.

I wanted to use the extra hands while I had them, so we started hefting the second floor joists into place. As a temporary measure, we laid out some plywood on the first floor to be able to walk around. I had purchased some semi-green, rough cut 4 x 8 beams from a guy who had built his house near the road on the way up from town. Thea and I had stacked them in the shade under a tarp so they could dry slowly.

We pulled back the cover to a mess. Several of the beams had warped and twisted, making them unusable. The rest were covered with black mold. We set the straight moldy beams on saw horses and scrubbed off the mold with bleach. I knew another guy with a saw mill and he had some nice timbers of dry fir. I bought enough from him to finish the job.

I was so glad for the help with the big beams. The original beams were over twelve feet long and nearly a hundred pounds apiece. The new beams were over sixteen feet long and nearly a hundred twenty-five pounds. I notched the beams to overlap and staggered the joints on the cross logs. The original beams were whitened by the bleach and had been cut with a band saw. The new beams were slightly darker and had been cut on a huge circular saw, so the texture was different as well. We just alternated the beams as we worked. It looked like we'd planned it that way.

One beam did get away from us. It dropped right onto a main floor joist, breaking it. We had to install another joist to replace it, but at least it hadn't landed on any of us. We also cut shorter vertical logs to temporarily support the center of the cross logs.

Between jobs, our friend Sendi had discovered Thea's garden and her peppers. They weren't bell peppers at all—they were jalapenos.

"Oooh, may I try one?" he asked.

"Of course," I said. "They're too hot for us."

He tugged one off the plant and bit into with a crunch.

"Oh, these are so good! You don't like them? Can I have them?"

"Take 'em," I said. "All of 'em!" He grinned and chomped a second pepper.

Next, we prepared to lift the ridge pole. It was forty-two feet long, and I calculated a weight of nearly 1,800 pounds!

First, we needed to secure the lifting poles in place. We tacked down a couple of sheets of plywood on the second floor, and set a ladder on the plywood, leaning it against the ridge pole support log. I tied ropes to the top of the pole that would serve as guy lines before we lifted the pole into place. Perched at the limits of the ladder, I lashed one small pole to the side of each vertical ridge pole support log, lashing them as tight as possible because the entire weight of the ridge pole would be hanging on them as it was raised into position. It wouldn't do to have them come loose or spin around with the ridge pole halfway up. I climbed back down the ladder and attached the guy lines from the top of the pole to the corners of the building.

Next, I climbed up to hang a heavy-duty pulley from each pole as high as I could reach, and ran a cable through each pulley that would attach to the ridge pole on one end and a come-a-long on the other. I chained the come-a-longs at the bottom so we could crank while standing on a solid floor and not have to lift this massive log while balancing at the top of a ladder.

Then, we nailed stout planks to the butts of the wall logs so the ridge pole could slide up the side of the house. We hoisted the ridge pole onto the top of the walls and rolled it to the center of the building until it rested against the vertical support logs.

Raising the ridge pole

We attached the come-a-alongs to each end of the ridge pole, and cranked on the handles. Click, click, click. Upward it climbed. Two of us were pulling on the handles and the rest of the crew craned their necks to watch the progress. Minutes passed as the log rose. Click, click, click. Just before it reached the top, the crowd drew a collective breath. When it thunked into place, they shouted and danced and high-fived.

I had cut the top of the poles so the top of the tapered ridge pole log would end up parallel and level with the top of the walls. I climbed up to straddle the ridge pole so I could drill and spike it permanently into place. I looked around I realized I was sitting more than twenty-five feet in the air. Quite a view.

This was a major milestone. It was so good to have it done and I was deeply grateful for the help from the Greenwood guys.

୯୫୬

Thea drove back to Chelan on Tuesday. Her dad had promised to check himself in to the hospital. Thea called her mom from the phone on the tree for a status update. Her mom was beside herself, scared, alone, couldn't drive, didn't understand. Thea called the hospital—the very one she'd been working in when we first met.

"How's your dad?" I asked after the call.

"I was able to confirm dad is there, and he's not on his deathbed, so I don't need to rush back."

"Good."

"I told him dad was going to sign out AMA once he was feeling better—maybe three or four days—but to do everything they could until then. The nurse confirmed dad was on IV antibiotics. I told him my mom wasn't going to be any help, she knows nothing medical, doesn't know how to ask questions, doesn't need to know. I asked him to call me if it got bad and he said he would make a note."

"That's as good as we can hope for, I guess," I said.

Three days later Thea's dad signed himself out "Against Medical Advice." The infection was staph. The antibiotics were stopped too soon. The bacteria slowly ate away the ball and socket of his shoulder.

{ 16 }

MORE AND MORE, I FELT THE PRESSURE of the coming winter. It turns cold early at 3,000 feet and time was wasting. I wanted to hang the rafters as soon as possible, but I couldn't just nail them in place as they were. The rafters varied in size more than I thought and the ridge pole did, too. We needed to cut them flat on one side to reduce the size variation and also to be able to nail the car-decking to an even, level surface.

We were attending the Little Stone Church in town, and on Sunday after Labor Day I was talking with a friend Phil Hale about our progress on the build.

"I have a saw mill at Twenty-Five Mile Creek," he said. "I'd be glad to cut your rafters for you. I can load them onto my truck get started right away, if you like."

"Fantastic!" I said. "Can you come up to our place tomorrow?" I felt a tickle in my throat, but I didn't let on. I didn't have time to be sick.

Phil showed up early and we started loading the rafters onto his truck. It was a rainy, icky day. I felt sicker by the minute, but I tried to push through. By the time we got to his place, I could barely hold up my head. I felt like I'd been run over. "Why now?" I moaned. It was a bad, achy flu that came on quick. I felt horrible.

"Sorry, Phil," I said.

Phil had wanted my help, but he'd worked by himself before. It took longer without me, but he cut and loaded all the rafters by himself. He had some nice rough-cut 1 x 12 lumber for sale and I bought enough of it to use as fascia and the board and batten for the upper end walls. Three of the boards were over twenty-four feet long, so the fascia would be one piece. I liked that.

I felt much better the next day. Back to work! The next task was to get those rafters up onto the ridge pole. I climbed the extension ladder from the second floor to the ridge pole and sat on it. I threw one end of a rope down to Thea on the west side of the house, and she tied a clove hitch on the butt end of the first rafter. The other end of the rope was connected to the winch on the Land Cruiser parked on the east side of the house.

Thea ran the winch on the Toyota and hauled on the first rafter. It was lying parallel to the house so it wouldn't catch on the logs as it was lifted up the wall. When it cleared the side of the house, the weight made it hang below the rope. She kept hauling on the winch, and the rafter tip would have gone under the ridge pole, so I used a peavey to roll it onto the rope. I kept it balanced there until it slid up and over the ridge pole into place. One down, twenty-one to go.

Some of the rafters still needed to be adjusted for thickness so they'd line up with each other where they sat on the ridge pole. I had the chain saw up there with me to get the fit just right. I'd also fabricated some steel straps that I lagged to each pair of rafters for added assurance they wouldn't move. It took us a few days, but finally we had all twenty-two rafters up and spiked into place. Thea and I worked pretty well together. I was glad for that—I couldn't have done it without her.

The rafters in place, it was time for the car decking to go up. Our neighbor Ken had some building experience and came over with Ron and Chuck to help me nail on all that lumber. Ron and Chuck had moved to Union Valley with their wives, Cathy and Sue, a few months before us. Chuck and Ron were old Navy buddies. All four together had taken Skip's class, so we were all on the same page for building our houses and helping one another.

I'd bought over 5,000 linear feet of car decking and more than half was for the roof. Car decking is tongue-and-groove 2 x 6 with one side sanded and beveled for appearance. The other side is left rough because it usually doesn't show. We would see the underside of the roof from inside, so we put the nice side down. Ken had us check for square before we started. We measured diagonally and bumped the end rafters to make the numbers match. We nailed on the first row of boards.

Most of the lumber came in four-foot increments—twelve-footers, sixteens, and twenties—so we did little cutting. We let the boards hang over the edge as we went and trimmed the ends evenly after it was all nailed on. Two guys on the ground would feed the lumber up and the other two would nail. We traded positions every so often. Nailing was easier than handing those long boards up onto the roof. The bottom edge of the roof is probably eleven feet from the ground. It really looked like a house with the roof nailed on.

The mid-September days were still warm, but rarely hot, and the nights were crisp. Winter was nearer every day, and it didn't care whether we were ready. I felt the urgency of nailing down the floor on the main level and moving in. First, I nailed up the plywood from underneath, starting in the southwest corner. I laid on my back and pulled the first sheet of plywood over the top of myself. I pushed up the plywood, held it against the bottom of the joists with my knees, then nailed it in place. One down, twenty to go.

Once the plywood was in place, I dropped in the two-foot by four-foot bats of R-30 insulation. I had scored a big sale on that, too. Now I was ready to bring in the car decking that would serve as our floor.

I had saved a bunch of 2 x 6 car-decking boards eighteen feet long and was able to span the whole front of the house without any seams. That made me happy. I nailed them all in place, leaving the ends to hang beyond the length I desired. Once they were in, I measured sixteen feet from the front wall and snapped a chalk line across the ends. I adjusted the skill saw to the depth of the boards and started cutting.

The ends of the boards were hanging over empty space.

"What the heck!" I shouted.

They should have ended right on top of the joist below.

I measured again. Sixteen feet. I was right. So what was wrong?

"Ah!" I had it. My 'help' with the joists had started at the north end of the house. They had ignored my instructions to start the first joist at sixteen feet and go away each direction on two-foot centers.

Now what? The front room floor needed to end at sixteen feet so there would be twelve feet for the bathroom and kitchen. The bathroom and kitchen sub floor would be particle board: three sheets wide, three sheets long, and two sheets thick. I had only one option. I had to hang another joist where it belonged. I growled under my breath.

I pulled out the insulation and threw it aside. I crawled under the house and took down the plywood where the new joist needed to go. I nailed the joist in where it was supposed to have been all along. I pushed the plywood back up into place. I cut the insulation to fit the new spacing and plunked it back in.

Winter was two hours closer, but I wasn't two hours more ready.

I brought in the first piece of particle board and nailed it into place. One down, seventeen to go. We would later install ceramic tile for the bathroom and linoleum with a large terra cotta brick pattern for the kitchen. I left a hole in the floor above the footing where the chimney would be.

I'd designed the chimney to be centered front to back, and one quarter of the way from the east wall of the house. That way the wood cookstove in the kitchen and the fireplace in the living room would be back to back and share the same chimney.

I called around to hire a mason—a job like this needed to be done right, by an experienced person. I didn't want to learn by myself on such a critical project and create a monument to my ignorance. The first guy I called drove up to see what we had in mind.

"I'll do it," he said. "We'll get started on it next week."

Two days later he called me back. "I'm sorry, Jim. I can't do your job, after all. I have a bigger job that will require my attention for at least a month, maybe more."

"Well, thanks for not leaving us hanging," I said. He wasn't the only mason in the area.

I made another phone call to a guy named Tim and explained the project. "I can build your chimney for you," he said, "but I'm going to need your help. I don't have a hod carrier."

"Well, it's my chimney, and I want to learn, so of course I'll be your helper," I said.

"Okay. I'll see you tomorrow then."

We measured and located the corners of the chimney with a plumb bob, and marked them on the footing. The chimney needed to come up right between the two cross logs that supported the upstairs floor. We mixed the mortar with the cement mixer and set the first row. We used 100% concrete blocks for durability, because the chimney was going to get heavy. We plopped mortar on the first row of blocks and set the second. Row by row, we built the chimney higher until it was above the level of the first floor.

The fireplace within the chimney would hold the Quaker stove insert, so we built a form for the fire box that was just a few inches bigger than the stove and built around it. Tim advised me to use separate flues, so we installed an 8 x 10 terra cotta liner for the fireplace and an 8 x 8 liner for the cookstove. Once started, we worked fast. We could only go so far each day because the weight of the blocks would be too much for the mortar until it dried.

I built a ladder out of 2 x 4's to access the second floor. We laid more sheets of plywood, then worked from there. About a third of the way up, we switched to lighter blocks with a lower percentage of cement because there would be much less weight on them the closer they were to the top. When we were within a foot or so of the roof, Tim used a straightedge to locate where the hole would be cut for us to pass through to the outside.

Earlier in the summer, while I was exploring the area around us, I had found an old '46 Chevy one and a half ton flatbed truck abandoned in a field not far from our place. I found out who owned it and asked whether it was for sale. The owner was glad to sell—he needed the money. I paid him two hundred, towed it home, and got it running in no time. I was sure it would come in handy. I had parked the truck next to the house so we could use it as a platform to stage the blocks and other supplies for the rest of the chimney.

We used a step ladder to get to the bed of the truck, and then put up an extension ladder to access the roof. From there we nailed 2 x 4 cleats on the roof so we could climb up to the hole where the chimney would emerge. We built a platform from a pallet right by the hole and braced it well. We stacked blocks on the platform and worked from it. We built the chimney to stand two feet taller than the peak of the roof to get good draw.

Fortunately for me, we had started using the lightest blocks available. As hod carrier, I had the job of getting them from the ground to the platform we had built. I'd carry one in each hand—up the step ladder, up the extension ladder, then up the cleats on the roof and finally to the platform.

From the beginning, we had poked rods of half-inch rebar into the openings of the blocks as we worked upward. We also inserted thin metal tabs here and there anticipating covering the blocks with river rock in the future. These would add support to the fascia and give the mortar something to stick to. Every three layers, we'd fill the voids with mortar to tie it all together and make a solid, stout chimney to last us many years. We continued inserting the rebar and filling the blocks all the way to the top.

Guess who hefted all that mortar... I hurried to mix batches of mortar, fill two five-gallon buckets about two-thirds full, and carry one in each hand up to the top of the roof. Muscles straining, lungs heaving, I'd hand the buckets to Tim and he'd pour them into the blocks. He'd hand them back to me and call out with a grin, "More!"

I lost count of my trips, but I was totaled by the time we were finished. We then built a form around the top of the chimney and poured it full of mortar to finish it off. In all, it took three days, start to finish, and it looked terrific. It was twenty-seven feet tall.

The chimney done, it was time to put on the metal roof. First, I covered the entire roof with heavy tar paper. I then nailed 2 x 12 boards on edge, end to end, running parallel to the ridge and two feet apart on both sides of the roof. I created a checkerboard pattern of two-foot by four-foot boxes, staggering twenty-two-and-a-half inch long 2 x 12 boards on four foot centers between the main runs. I would fill the grid with bats of R-30 insulation the next day.

The next morning I went to the shed for an arm load of insulation. I had left the ladder up against the eave overnight.

"Where's Jacob?" I asked Thea.

"I haven't seen him. I thought he was with you."

"Well, he was, but now I don't know."

"Maybe he's at the house. It's dangerous over there."

I walked from the shed with the insulation and looked up to see Jacob sitting inside one of the grid boxes on the roof.

"Hi, Dad," he said with a big grin.

My heart jumped, but I saw he was fine, so I called out Thea, "Thea, come see where your son has gotten himself!"

Jacob on the roof

"*My* son?" she asked, when she saw him up on the roof. "I would never climb up that high."

"Come on down, Jacob." I said, "And be careful!"

Once he was back on the ground, I said, "Jacob, please only climb ladders when I am around, okay? It's too dangerous otherwise."

"Okay, Dad," he said.

He had turned five in June. Boys!

❧

I'd placed all the insulation by myself, but I would need some help with the metal roofing. Phil's dad, David Hale, volunteered, along with Gordon Hyde, pastor of Little Stone Church. The metal was long and unwieldy. It needed to start square. I didn't want a "saw edge" along the bottom when we'd finished.

We hefted the first piece up onto the roof, measuring the distance at the top and at the bottom. We wiggled the sheet sideways a bit. We measured the upper diagonal and measured the lower diagonal, wiggling the sheet back a little and tacking it into place. We hoisted the second sheet into place, aligned it carefully with the first, and drove the nails. Each sheet covered two feet of the roof, top to bottom, so we made quick progress. We had to cut the sheets to fit around the chimney, which slowed us a little, but we finished the first side by early afternoon. I had purchased a "cricket" from the local sheet metal man which fit on the roof above the chimney. A cricket diverts the snow and prevents it from building up above the chimney. It would keep leaks to a minimum.

We hadn't started the first sheet perfectly—we ended up with a minor saw edge. We figured out the trick when we installed the second side—we measured ahead of ourselves every other sheet so we could make slight adjustments as we went. The second side came out better and went quicker. We didn't have to work around a chimney, and finished in less than three more hours.

The equinox was approaching. The days were getting shorter and the nights longer. Daily high temperatures were in the upper fifties to low sixties. Frost glinted from blades of grass when I awoke each morning. We were sleeping in the camper and had to add two layers of blankets to stay warm through the night. Three days after my birthday in mid-September, I awoke to see the needle of the thermometer pointing at seventeen degrees. The sky was leaden and dropping. At nine o'clock in the morning, the first flurries of snow floated down through the cold, still air. At noon, the flakes began to stick.

The house wouldn't be ready for us for a month or more. We wouldn't make it through a winter in the camper.

{ 17 }

I HAVE TO GO GET MORE FIREWOOD," I said to Thea. Most of the snow had melted, but there was a tiny berm under the edge of the roof. We'd nailed that metal on just in time.

"Are you going out to the Burn?" Thea asked.

Wildfires in the late sixties and early seventies had burned through the forests a few miles beyond our property. The trees had died and fallen like pick-up-sticks. Thousands of acres of dry fire wood lay out there for the taking. Plenty was accessible right off the roads.

"Yes, and I think I can be more efficient than I have been. I don't need to cut it to length out there. The wood is light enough I can put whole trees in the truck and let the tips stick out the back."

"Okay, I'll stay here in the camper and try to keep the babies warm with the stove."

I returned from the Burn with my first long load in less time than it had taken before, and with four times the wood. I unloaded it under the phone tree and went back out for more. The tips of the trees sticking out the back of the truck had scratched long furrows in the dirt all the way from The Burn to the house. I made three trips that same day, but I still had work to do on the house.

I needed to frame in the upper end walls, insulate them, and nail up the board and batten outside. As in the first floor, I used 2 x 12 boards for my framing so the walls would be thick enough to keep out the cold. The ridge pole support logs were outside the log wall so the framing would lay right on the top log. I started on the back wall, measuring the distance along the roof from the peak to where it met the wall: seventeen feet.

It made me happy to be able to use one eighteen foot length of wood cut to fit—except for the weight—it was too heavy for me to hold up the board and start the nails alone. I set the board on the floor and started all the nails. I cut a brace to hold the board in place and leaned it against the ridge pole support log, lifting the board back up into place and tapping in the brace. I climbed a ladder to reach the nails up high and pounded them in, repeating the process for the other side. Then I cut 2 x 12 studs and nailed them into place. They were cut at forty-five degrees on the top to fit the angle of the roof.

The second floor above the kitchen and bathroom would be the boys' bedrooms. They were mirror images of each other. I had framed in a three-foot by four-foot window box in each room, but I didn't have time to build the window frames and install the glass at that point. I cut two pieces of plywood to size and put them into the window boxes, filling the boxes with insulation until I could build the window frames.

I moved to the front of the house and installed studs and framing. The front room would be the master bedroom and measure twelve by twenty feet. The remaining four feet of width would be used for the stairwell when the time came. Between the front and back bedrooms was a four-foot hall that ended at the chimney. The windows in the master bedroom were quite a bit bigger to take advantage of the winter sun. The room faced due south. During the winter the sun is lower in the sky, so the solar gain would be maximized during those colder months.

I had bought three-quarter inch thick thermo-pane glass designed for sliding glass doors, so the two panels were tempered safety glass. Each one was three feet wide, six feet-six inches tall and ridiculously heavy. I built the window frames upstairs on a pair of sawhorses. I cut the center out of two sheets of three-quarter inch thick plywood to fit the glass and prevent the frames from racking, sandwiching the glass and plywood between 1 x 6 trim, gluing and bolting through in several spots around the perimeter. I used barn door hinges to open them during the summer.

The real trick was standing them up into the window opening. By the time they were ready to install, they weighed over a hundred pounds apiece. I set the bottom edge on the sill and with a mighty shove, stood them up. The sill was twenty-four inches up, so I had to climb a stepladder while supporting all that weight and holding them in place.

Those windows were the only source of outside light for the whole house. I had only cut the back door and no other windows had been cut in yet. Without the upstairs windows, the house would be pitch black inside when the door was closed, even during the day. We planned to use kerosene lamps for light at night.

After getting the windows in place, I climbed up on the outside to finish the walls with the rough-cut 1 x 12 boards I'd bought from Phil. I covered the cracks with 1 x 2 battens. It looked real nice. I stuffed the end walls with insulation, and sealed the inside with clear plastic house wrap.

Then I set about building the back door, using three rough-cut 1 x 12 boards for the outside, and seven lengths of 2 x 6 tongue-and-groove car decking for the inside. I sandwiched the two layers of wood together between metal straps three inches wide that formed a Z on both sides. I drilled holes through the straps every few inches and bolted them together with carriage bolts. The door was two and a half inches thick—beefy, to say the least. As with the upstairs windows, I used barn door hinges to support its weight. I had painted the straps and hinges black to prevent rust.

☙❧

One Sunday at church a friend told us about a job opening. "Did you hear North Country Fruit is looking for a swamper?"

"What's a swamper?" I asked.

"Swampers clean up the packing shed at the end of the day. They sweep up the apple leaves, clean the machines and get everything ready for the next day. It's harvest, and they're super busy."

We jumped at the chance. Thea went to the North Country Fruit packing shed and found the foreman. She asked whether she and I could share the job—four hours each. He agreed, so we started the next day. We swept out giant heaps of apple leaves, ran the machines to be sure everything worked, and cleaned them out for the next day. We brought the boys with us, and they helped us fetch apples that had rolled back against the wall in places we couldn't reach.

I asked the foreman whether I could take home the bins of apple leaves we were gathering, and he said sure, but wondered why. I explained we'd use the leaves as mulch for our garden. He nodded.

I was happy about the leaves, but Thea was happy about the sinks. She had running water to wash her pretty, long hair. This became a perk she would look for in future jobs until we had the well.

"Hey, Thea, come look at this!" I said one night. "I'm always finding sawdust here on the floor, and I never knew where it was coming from until now."

I poked the ceiling with my broom handle, and a puff of sawdust rained down.

"I think this whole place is insulated with sawdust. I don't think this is good."

One Friday, I was at a point on the house where I just couldn't stop, so I asked Thea to call the foreman about coming in on Saturday instead. He wanted to be sure we weren't skipping out for the weekend, but Thea assured him it would be clean for Monday morning, so he agreed.

"Do you hear that?" Thea asked me a few hours later. I was engrossed in my work.

I stopped to listen. "It sounds like a siren," I said.

The sound grew louder and persisted. "Are we seeing a glow from town?" I asked.

Thea switched on our battery-powered radio to hear the local station describing the fire:

The North Country Fruit packing shed is fully engulfed in flames. Fire fighters are doing all they can just to keep the fire from spreading to other nearby structures.

"We were supposed to be there tonight," I said.

"Thank God we're not," Thea said.

The investigation determined the cause of fire to be arson. There was enough evidence to convict a local young man, the son of the woman who owned the laundromat where we washed our clothes.

※

One Sunday morning in late September, on the way to church, we had our first taste of another aspect of winter. It had rained overnight—the first snow after my birthday had been only a warning and not the immediate start of winter. We piled in the van, drove down Sawmill, turned onto the Loop, and drove up and around the corner past Buzz Hunter's.

"Zzzzzipppp!" The rear tires of the van spun out on the slick film of mud.

"We've just started this little climb," I said to Thea. "We sure won't make it up the steeper part, and I'm not going down Switchback, not with this wetness."

"I guess we just go back home," she said.

"Yep. This van is useless here. We'll be able to drive it for five months a year."

We started looking for other vehicles in the local paper, and a couple of weeks later, we found an ad for a four wheel drive Suburban in Spokane. We called, and it was still available. We sold our van to Del, a friend of ours in town, and used the money to buy the Suburban. It was a much better rig for dirt and mud and snow.

{ 18 }

BACK IN JULY, OUR FRIEND HANS came over with his dog Grout. Hans was a bricklayer and tilesetter. Grout was a beautiful male golden retriever. Our dog Danny hadn't come home one summer evening, though we called and called, so we picked up a female golden retriever from Wenatchee in August as a companion for Clowd. We called her Goldie. We all thought it would be a great idea for Grout and Goldie to get together.

They made a fine couple. It became obvious Goldie had become pregnant and we looked forward to a litter of golden retriever puppies. Many people we told were very interested in buying a pup when they were ready.

On the day of the blessed event, Goldie had disappeared and we were concerned she had gone away to have her babies. We were still cooking in the camper then, and Thea thought she heard a puppy squeak. Goldie had crawled under the shed to have her babies in a safe place. I had to dig a bit to get under there and started to hand out the babies one by one. My gosh, there was a bunch of babies! 10...11...12...

Thirteen perfect little golden retriever puppies! She only had twelve nipples. We let her get them started and she would just trade off, so all got their share. I built a chicken wire pen about 6 by 12 feet—low, so Goldie could get out for a while to catch a break. It was so fun to see so many puppies running to greet mom when she would return from being away.

Many people were anxious to get their puppies, but we had to make sure they were ready. We started feeding them oatmeal and would mix up a large pan to be sure all got their fill. When we'd place it in the pen, the whole group would turn and gallop to the other end to be first at the dish. We called them the "thundering herd" because they raised so much dust.

After those who had chosen a puppy took them home, we still had five or six left. We gave one to Wayne Leatherman, the older gentleman who had peeled the log with his axe, and he was tickled. We ran an ad in the paper and got a few more calls.

It was autumn, and hunting season had begun. We had posted signs, but still had occasional trespassers whom we would admonish. We didn't want any shooting because we had children and dogs that could be in danger. They understood, but Thea was still nervous.

One day a fellow in a red plaid jacket, wearing blaze orange, came walking down the driveway carrying a rifle. Thea ducked into the shed and retrieved a 12-gauge shotgun. She held it angled across her chest and asked if he'd seen the no trespassing signs.

He stammered that he'd heard we had some Golden Retriever puppies for sale. She relaxed a little and instructed him to lean his rifle against the nearest tree. She confirmed we did have a couple dogs left.

We had dropped the price to $40 and he was glad to pay it. She continued to hold the shotgun until he was out of sight. We did keep two of the puppies.

The boy we called Banjo and the girl Ginger. Sadly, Banjo got into something and didn't survive. He might have swallowed a chicken bone—we didn't have any poison on the property. Ginger was a good dog for the boys and they enjoyed watching her grow.

⊗⊗⊙

We drove over to Chuck and Sue's to help them get ready for winter. Chuck and Sue and Ron and Cathy had set up large army tents as temporary shelters while building their houses. Ron built a nice floor for his tent, but Chuck threw chunks of old carpet directly onto the dirt. Their floor rolled like the sea. The tents were twenty by forty feet—plenty roomy, but I didn't figure a thin canvas wall would offer much protection from the cold.

"The army made it through the winter in tents. We'll be fine."

I stayed quiet. Chuck was a few years older than me. He'd been a fire chief and he knew his stuff. He had advice for me on various topics which I accepted in the helpful spirit he intended, even though I often disagreed.

"You're going to regret those fat tires on that Land Cruiser," he told me. "You need skinny tires like I have on my truck. You want to get down through the snow or mud to solid ground where you can get a grip. You'll just stay up on top with those fat tires and spin out."

"I think I'll be okay," I said. "My experience has been with the Seattle Jeep Club, and we rolled through some mud so deep that staying on top was an advantage. I never had any trouble, and I've driven through some serious situations. Anyway, weren't we going to be doing some work on your house today? Didn't you need some help?"

"Yeah, I was going to put insulation in the floor, but there's a football game I want to watch. I'll fire up the generator and we can have a beer and watch the game. There'll be plenty of time to put in the insulation afterwards."

"Okay, well, I'm going to go then. I still have work to do. Winter's coming."

"You sure you don't want to watch the game with us?"

"Yeah, I'm sure. Thanks, anyway. See you guys later."

I drove back home shaking my head. I just didn't get it. The first snow had already fallen, and even though it had melted, more would be coming soon. I figured it would start piling up. Why they thought they had time to watch a football game with so much work still to do on their houses I had no idea.

Our next project was to seal the gaps between the logs, called chinking. Skip had told us to chink the logs temporarily with paper maché made by soaking newspaper in a mixture of flour and water.

Thea and I were in the midst of applying our first batch of chinking when Dan and Vicki came to visit with guests from Norway. They had stopped by to see our progress and show their friends what we were up to.

"Do you mind if we help?" Dan asked.

"Heck, no!" I said. "Please do."

We mixed up two more batches of flour and water and threw in the torn strips of newspaper. Each couple had a bucket and a section of the walls. We talked and laughed for hours and almost finished chinking the whole house that same day. The four of them came back the next day and helped us finish. No more cold air blew in between the logs. It was almost warm in the cabin.

Halloween morning greeted us with two inches of fresh snow. It was beautiful. We were almost ready to move into the house, so it wasn't as scary as it would have been otherwise. Dan came by to see how we were doing with the snow, and we asked him to take a picture of our family at the back door of the cabin.

I had been on unemployment since April, and registered with the office in town when we moved. The phone rang on the tree with a call I didn't want to take.

"I found you a job." It was Carol from the unemployment office.

"Ooh, I'm not really interested."

"Well, if you don't take it, you lose your unemployment."

"Fine. What do I need to do?"

I still had to install all the plumbing and fixtures inside the house, but what could I do?

I showed up for work the next day. The manager explained the job was building maintenance for several local stores. It was the night shift and we'd wash and wax the floors in grocery stores from Chelan to Pateros—about an hour, round trip. I had done that work in the past and I thought I knew what it would entail.

I was wrong. This outfit didn't have floor machines for washing, just waxing. They expected me to scrub the floors by hand and scrape off all the gum and shoe marks on my hands and knees like a bearded Cinderella. I lasted only a couple of nights and threw in the towel. No way was I going to ruin my knees crawling around on linoleum, night after night. So I lost my unemployment. I had been getting about $300 a month. Our land payment was $192, and the remaining $108 covered everything else. Though we still had a few dollars saved, we wouldn't last long without some income.

{ 19 }

AT LEAST I COULD INSTALL the toilet. We were using an outhouse a football field away beyond the shed. That wouldn't work once the snow piled up. I had a marine toilet that required very little water to flush, and wanted to use it. I wasn't sure about plumbing, so I asked around for a plumber who could come up and help.

Ken introduced me to Art, a young fellow who said, "I know how to do that. I can help you get it done."

"You rode up here in the snow on your motorcycle?" I asked when he arrived.

"Well, I don't own a car," he said.

"Okay, well, let's get to work."

He only had a few tools, but I had the pipe and fittings and glue. We cut four drain holes into the floor—toilet, tub, bathroom sink, and on the other side of the house, the kitchen sink. The kid crawled under the house to hang the drain pipes. The main pipe was four-inch black plastic ABS that crossed from the bathroom drains to the kitchen sink, and then turned and exited the house before dumping into the septic tank.

He climbed back out from under the house.

"Now we have to add a vent," he said. "It has to rise at least three feet above the P-trap before it can have any elbows."

{ 175 }

"Fine," I said. "I just don't want the pipe to show behind the sink on the log wall."

I walked outside to collect the two-inch black pipe that would be the vent, and I heard him begin drilling into one of the logs with his big hole saw. Half a minute later I heard a horrible grinding, squealing sound. The drill stopped. A pause. Then it started up again.

When I came back in with the vent pipe and saw what he was doing I hollered, "Stop! You're wrecking the place! That looks horrible!"

"Yeah, well, it's to code," he tried to explain.

"I don't care about codes," I yelled. "This is my log house and that looks like heck! Nothing else is to code!"

I looked closer at his holes. He'd hit rebar with his first attempt. That explained the horrible squealing sound. But then he'd just moved his hole saw a couple of inches sideways and started drilling again. They were well above the sink, in plain sight. He was trying to stuff his first hole with sawdust and woodchips, as if that would look the same as the side of a log.

I bent over to peer into his second hole. He had already cut through to the outside.

"Get out of here, you idiot!" I shouted.

He stood there stunned.

"I said get out of here!"

He packed up his four tools, put them in his bag, and fled down the snowy driveway on his motorcycle.

I considered cutting plugs to fill the holes, but never got around to it. I ended up running the vent pipe through the hole he'd drilled.

"At least the toilet works," I said to Thea. "Just like downtown." It was a phrase that came to be a sort of inside joke. She smiled.

☙❧

We moved into the house the day before Thanksgiving. Seven months earlier we had barely scratched the dirt, and now we were moving into the home we'd built. We had four walls, a floor, a roof, and two windows, but that was all. It was enough. We were deeply grateful to God for the blessing of this home.

We hustled to move our beds and dressers from the shed into our new house. We set our bed in the living room against the front wall across from the fireplace on the main floor. There was no second floor yet, just the heavy beam floor joists, so it was open to the peak inside. We set Luke's crib at the foot of our bed and Jacob's bed went next to my side. We were huddled in front of the only heat source that would keep fire overnight. Even at that, we stayed completely dressed and kept our coats on when we went to bed. Temperatures in the early morning when I awoke were often in the teens or low twenties.

A couple of weeks later, the toilet backed up and wouldn't flush. It hadn't been as warm as thirty-five degrees since we installed the plumbing.

Moving in with the snow falling. No door, no windows. Grateful!

"Now what?" I wondered out loud.

I crawled under the house to look. Art had only put support straps near the ends of the twenty foot-long four-inch diameter drain pipe. The middle was sagging down with a big belly, and it was frozen solid. I climbed back out from under the house, cursing and growling. I returned with my propane torch and waved the flame back and forth over the surface of the black plastic. ABS pipe doesn't conduct heat very well, so nothing happened. I crawled back out from under the house again, cussing and grunting.

I heated some water to boiling and poured it down the sink and toilet drains to melt the ice at the elbows. I crawled back under the house and sawed off the pipe at both ends. Oh, it stunk! It was heavy, too—a twenty foot-long, four inch-through pipe of frozen poo. I waited for the air to clear a little before I returned to install the new length of drain pipe. I supported it with straps every few feet and made sure it angled enough to drain. So much for hiring qualified help, I should have just done it myself.

We had installed our claw-footed tub and pedestal sink with drains, but there was still no supply of running water. With snow on the ground, we weren't using the solar shower anymore. Our Saturday evening bathing routine had to be modified in the cold. Thea and I took sponge baths during the week, but the water bath on Saturday evening was pure luxury.

We placed a metal eighteen-gallon round wash tub on the cookstove and warmed up the water. We set the tub on the floor and gave Luke a bath. Jacob went in the tub next, and we rinsed him off with clean water. Then it was Thea's turn. The house was cold inside, so we kept open the oven door of the cookstove. Once, Thea backed into the oven's open door and sizzled a little line on her calf. I bathed last, and by the time I had rinsed, the tub was full.

I carried the dirty bath water outside and pitched it beyond the bank. I now understood what was meant by the saying *Don't throw the baby out with the bathwater.* The water was so dirty we might not have been able to see the baby in it.

We had been getting our water from Dan Wright's hose in the ground, but that froze solid as the temperatures dove and stayed under. Fortunately, just two hundred yards farther down the valley was a square cement cattle trough fed by a hose of running water that never froze. It was our half-inch diameter creek and it never wavered. It was faithful, but it wasn't friendly.

The new water source meant we couldn't fill our fifty-five gallon drums anymore, so we switched to gallon milk jugs. I loaded six empty gallon milk jugs into my hiking backpack. I hand-carried four jugs, Thea carried two, and, Jacob carried one. We walked the half mile down to the trough and filled up our thirteen jugs from the hose. We hiked back up the hill to the house with our hundred pounds of water. Jacob, at five years old, always wanted the jug with the skinny handle—he figured it weighed less.

Giardia in the water beat me down. Maybe the little parasites hit me harder because of my intestinal issues and surgeries. My guts cramped like balled fists, roiling and burbling in fits and spasms, a sulfury taste in my mouth. For two weeks I spent hours using the shoddy work of the plumber kid with the motorcycle. I was dizzy with nausea and my vision was blurry at times.

We made three trips a week to the trough—we had no other source of water. Jacob didn't always come with us, and sometimes even Thea stayed at the house. For all our drinking, cooking, washing and bathing needs, we could get by on thirty-two gallons of water a week for our family of four. It helped when more snow fell, because we were able to bathe with melted snow. The snow was so cold and dry, though, that a heaping mountain of snow filling the metal tub would melt down to less than two inches of water. It took a lot of snow to take a bath.

Having recovered from my fight with giardia, I searched the property for a Christmas tree. I cut the best one I could find—too spindly and funny looking even for Charlie Brown. We did have our decorations, so at least it wasn't a bare tree. I didn't know whether we'd be able to put anything under it for Christmas morning. Since I'd lost unemployment, we didn't have an extra penny for any gifts. Thea had to stand in line at the food bank for commodities.

"You need to bring an electric bill," the man said at the entrance.

"We don't have an electric bill," Thea said. "We don't have electricity. We have propane."

"You have to prove you're living in a house."

"We are living in a house. Can I bring our phone bill? My husband is not working, and I'm not working—that's why we're here. We sold our house, but we only get so much for it each month, and it pays our house payments. It's good we don't have electricity, we couldn't pay it anyway."

"This first time is okay," he said. "But next time you have to bring your phone bill."

"Shame!" yelled the plain white labels and generic black text. Thea hustled the bags of government supplements into the Suburban and drove back up the hill. She came home with a five-pound block of cheddar cheese, a pound of butter, a big box of powdered milk, four packets of powdered eggs, a five-pound bag of rice, and six cans of beans.

On December 16th, the temperatures plunged from the twenties to the single digits. They dropped again to zero and held steady a few days. Then they dropped again— minus ten, minus twenty, minus thirty on Christmas Eve. Jacob wanted to go outside to play in the snow, so we bundled him up with every layer of snow clothes that fit, and sent him tottering out. In less than two minutes he came back in the house. "It's cold, Mom, it's cold. It's too cold."

The Sunday before Christmas, the pastor greeted us as we entered and said, "We need to talk to you after church."

Curious, we found the pastor after the service and he ushered us into his office. "We have this for you," he said.

It was a great big box of food.

I was stunned silent. Then I remembered to say "Thank you." It came out in a whisper. It wasn't supposed to be like this. We were supposed to be the ones to help others.

"Also, the Blessins would like to have you over for lunch today," said the pastor. "They're waiting outside."

"Okay," I said. I was numb. I picked up the box of food in a daze and walked out of the office.

"What's that for, Dad?" Jacob asked.

"It's food for us, bud," I said. "I guess we're poor."

The Blessins gave us more than lunch. Hanna said, "I have a bunch of toys here I want you to take home for your boys. They have to have something."

She had a stuffed embroidered puppy for Jacob and a kitten for Luke. She gave us mittens and a brand new fire truck. She gave us two pillows Thea embroidered with *Jacob* and *Luke*.

The boys had gifts under the tree.

Thea said, "To have a happy wife, you need to bring the refrigerator over from the shed."

So, on Christmas Eve day, in record breaking cold temperatures, I brought the refrigerator into the house. I drilled two holes in a piece of plywood, and poked a rope through the holes for a handle. I put the fridge on the plywood, and dragged it through the snow from the shed to the house.

We had been keeping our milk in the northeast corner of the kitchen with the Jell-O and other perishables. It was as cold as a fridge in that corner—the chinking wasn't the best. In the deep cold, however, the milk and other items had been freezing. We needed the fridge in the house to keep them from freezing.

"BANG!" It sounded like a gun had gone off inside the house.

"What the heck was that?" I looked at Thea. Her eyes were big with surprise.

I looked around the house and spied a giant crack in one of the logs. Our logs were not green when we spiked them into place, but they hadn't cured either. Wrapped in bark and peeled only just before we used them to build the house, they were still damp. The low humidity air outside and the heat of the fire inside were drying the logs quickly. Big checks formed with loud cracks.

The logs shrank to their own centers, a positive feature of Skip's design for preventing settling, but not so good for the paper maché chinking. One morning, after a blizzardy night, we awoke to find small berms of snow piled up on the plywood floor. The paper maché had pulled away from the logs, and fine snow whistled in through the gaps. We did some patch work.

Around year's end, the temperatures climbed briefly to the thirties, but they fell again to the twenties and teens. Winter had come and only just begun. It was getting to be too much for Thea.

"I burned Jacob's Ernie doll last night," she told me one morning.

"What? How?"

"Well, I get up in the middle of the night to stoke the fire because it's so freezing cold even inside the house, but the fire was still warm, and I couldn't find a glove, so I used the Ernie doll to close the door of the fireplace. Then I realized I had burnt off the back of Ernie's shirt."

"The gloves should be right by the fireplace all the time."

"I know, but I couldn't find them last night. I can't let Jacob see his Ernie all melted. I'll make him a vest out of felt. I'll tell Jacob Ernie has been getting cold, too." A couple days later she had stitched Jacob's Ernie doll an orange felt vest, and Jacob never suspected a thing.

Days later, the metal of both the fireplace and the wood cookstove were popping and pinging from the intensity of the heat, but the floor was still cold.

"All of the heat is up in the rafters," Thea said.

"I know," I said with a sigh.

"We can't keep sleeping down here on the first floor. We need to sleep up higher where the heat is."

Then she delivered her ultimatum.

"I'm taking our babies downtown to a hotel until you put up the second floor."

{ 20 }

YOU DON'T NEED TO GO DOWNTOWN," I said. "I'll bring in the boards."

I had covered the pile of second floor decking with a lumber wrap, but the pile was buried under two feet of snow. I swept the pile clear, pulled back the tarp, and brought the boards in the house four at a time. Snow often came along for the ride.

The second floor level was above freezing—more than could be said for the first floor. The snow melted off the boards I'd retrieved, and the drips fell to the kitchen floor. Much to our surprise, the drops would freeze when they hit the linoleum. Squat stalagmites of ice built up on the floor as we watched.

It was then I decided we could wait no longer to skirt and insulate the crawl space around the house to help keep the cold out. Even with the twelve inches of insulation, the floor was freezing. For skirting, I used the plywood that had served as pier block forms. It was already cut to match the angles of the piers, so it worked very nicely. The floors were noticeably warmer.

Once the boards of the second floor dried out, I covered them with an old oriental pattern rug we'd been given. It was thick wool with long fringe along two sides. One spot was worn thin, but I placed the bed over that.

I leaned the 2 x 4 ladder I'd made next to the chimney to get up to the second floor. I brought in only enough lumber to cover the kitchen. There was room for our bed, Jacob's bed, Luke's crib, and our dresser, but there were no walls—it was essentially a loft, but it was warm.

"I can't be crawling down that ladder in the middle of the night when I have to go potty," Thea said after our third night on the second floor.

"All right, I'll see what I can come up with," I said.

I found a five-gallon bucket at the shed and made some measurements. I built a little box out of plywood that fit over the bucket and created a seat. I rounded and smoothed the edges of the hole, added a peg on the side for a roll of toilet paper, and attached a lid with a length of piano hinge. I painted it all brown and presented it to Thea with a flourish.

"Ta-da!" I opened and closed the lid with a goofy smile.

"It's very nice," she said.

The proof was in the pudding. I set up the bucket and box near the chimney, at the foot of Luke's crib. Thea didn't have to use the ladder that night—she was very happy. That sucker got brim-full several times. I had to carry it down the ladder and through the house downstairs to take it outside, and I never spilled a drop!

We had not been able to use the wringer washer since before we moved into the house. Thea's hands would turn bright red in the cold fall air, and we didn't want to risk having the water freeze in the washer and break something. Thea had been taking the clothes downtown to the laundromat to wash, and she brought the wet clothes home to hang dry on the line outside. This worked even in the cold. The clothing would freeze stiff on the line outside, and when it warmed up inside, it would be dry.

After I brought in the boards for the second floor, I strung a clothesline inside the house. I used some extra boards to make a walkway, and Thea was able to dry our clothes in the relative warmth of the second floor.

The snow began piling up in January. There was rarely enough snow on Washington's west side to build a snowman, and even then bits of grass often added color to the ugly shapes we could form. We had plenty of snow at the log house, but now it was a different challenge—the snow wouldn't pack! Cold and dry, the ice crystals spilled like sugar from our gloved hands.

Big sheets of snow broke loose with a roar from the steep roof, and landed with a thump to form massive berms under the eaves. The Land Cruiser charged through nearly two feet of snow unhindered, but after that I had to use chains. Even those only worked up to about three feet of snow, and then we needed help. Deep, fresh snow wasn't the problem. The ruts and packed snow are what made it difficult. No one was plowing, so we tried to drive in our own tracks, but it occasionally snowed up to a foot overnight. It started to get difficult even with chains.

In late January, a big storm brought a generous gift of deep snow and more cold temperatures. Three days after the storm, Lee Howe knocked on our door. He lived about two miles beyond us in a ramshackle little cabin he and Earnest had built on a foundation of firewood rounds.

Two by fours spanned the stumps and supported an apple bin plywood floor. The walls were built the same way—when he moved around inside the whole place wiggled and sagged and gaped. They kept it all upright by tying a wall to a nearby tree—the shack moved when the wind blew. The shed roof at least had some rolled roofing to keep out the water. It was about eight by twelve feet inside and had one single pane window and an old interior door. There was an old steel framed single bed and a round tin stove. The first time I visited I wondered aloud how he thought he'd make it through a winter. He assured me he'd be fine.

He was riding his skeletal horse. Lee usually appeared with his Jeep, or since the snow started to get deep, on his snowmobile.

"Hey, Jim, can you help me out?"

"Hi, Lee, how have you been?"

"I'm good, but my Jeep is kind of stuck."

"And you rode your horse? What about your snowmobile?"

"Snow's too deep and fluffy. I can't get up on top of it."

"All right," I said. "I'll be out in about an hour."

I fired up my Land Cruiser with its big fat tires, and its chains made for a semi. The road was not plowed to Lee's place—just a horse track through the snow. The snow was belly deep to the horse. *Well, I'm not going that way!* Lee had turned north on Sawmill, a steep dirt road with three feet of snow that might have stopped even my Land Cruiser.

I turned west on Open Road instead until I reached the head of the draw, at which point I turned north into the trees. I followed a path through gaps in the woods and popped out onto a hundred-acre field. Sixty years earlier the hopeful had cleared it and planted wheat. By the mid-eighties, it was only a summer range area for cattle.

The snow was as deep as my front fenders. I chugged across that field pushing a growing wall of snow. The snow piled up before me, fell back onto the hood, and slid up against the windshield. It grew to half the height of the windshield before it fell off down the sides.

I made it to Lee's place to find his Cadillac and his Ford pickup buried to their windows in the white stuff. There was a track in the snow down the hill from his place to the creek. At the end of the track was Lee's little blue mail truck Jeep—it looked like it was actually *in* the creek.

I drove down the track to his Jeep, and sure enough, it was frozen solid into the creek.

How do you even do that?

"I drove down near the creek to get water," Lee explained as if he had read my mind. "I loaded my jugs of water into the Jeep, and when I went to leave, I slid down into the creek. Instead of going up the hill, it slid back in. I couldn't figure out how to get it out, so I said 'Screw it,' and took my jugs of water and walked back up the hill to my house."

I was taking in the whole situation, trying to form a plan.

"I think the rear end might be broken," he said, "because I'm only getting my front wheels to spin."

"Did you try to drive it after it was frozen into the creek?"

"Well, yeah. I came back the next day to get it, but then I heard a bang, and that's when I came to get you."

Are you kidding me? Oh, man!

So I turned around and backed down to him. Since he'd been maneuvering around, the snow wasn't as deep there. I hooked his rig up to my bumper hitch, and started to pull. It wouldn't come, wouldn't even budge.

I gave it a little bump and broke it loose. I checked the mirror, and a big ugly chunk of ice was attached to the back of his rig. His back wheels were not even moving. It's like I was dragging a giant rock, or an anchor.

I better not stop—at least I'm moving.

I pushed on the gas to get some momentum.

Lee ran after, calling out, "Hey, wait for me!"

"Sorry, pal. If I stop now I don't know if I'll get moving again."

His shack was about five hundred feet from the creek. I dragged his Jeep with its giant ice block anchor all the way up. I had carved a huge trough in the snow all the way up the hill like a high speed glacier in reverse.

I had unhooked his Jeep by the time he made it up the hill, breathing hard in the cold air.

"I don't know, man," I said. "But if the rear end is blown, you have to get that ice off before you can fix anything, so good luck with that." I could imagine him building a bonfire under his Jeep to melt the ice.

Jake Beaty

{ 21 }

THEA APPLIED FOR A JOB with Dr. Bruce Hurst, the local chiropractor, when we lost my unemployment. She was hired as the receptionist, a great match for her office and people skills. She enjoyed working for Bruce and learned a lot about the practice.

I swung by the office one day, and Bruce was gearing up for a group snowmobile trip.

"Sounds like a great time," I said, "I'd love to be able to join you guys."

"Well, you need to have all the right equipment. It's super cold at high speed."

"Oh, I have all the equipment."

"Are you sure?"

"Oh, yeah. I've always had all the equipment. Anything you want to do, I've got all the equipment. Well, except fishing, I don't fish."

He didn't invite me on that trip, but a couple weeks later he called the house. I packed my gear in ten minutes. It was to be a weekend trip a few weeks before Thea's birthday. Friends on snow machines would drop us off at the South Navarre, and five of us were going to snowshoe from there to the North Navarre for some camping in the snow. It's a ten or twelve-mile hike on a high ridgeline with steep drops—too hairy for snowmobiles, but worth it for views of the lake and mountains.

We drove up the Methow Valley, which is separated from Lake Chelan by the ridge we planned to climb. We unloaded the snowmobiles at a snow park near Lake Alta, in the bottom of the valley, and headed up into the hills. We followed snow covered roads that diminished to trails, and then trails that faded to suggestions. We were flying through the snow, creating a billowing cloud of pulverized ice crystals that settled slowly in our wake.

The snowmobilers dropped us off and sped away. The silence of the snowy woods engulfed us. Bliss. We strapped on our snowshoes and strode out for the top of North Navarre. We could see it clearly the whole time and felt like we were making reasonable time, working our way up the slope. The sun went behind the ridge, casting long shadows, and then behind some clouds. We were a long way from our goal, but the darkening sky compelled us to set up camp. There were no stars to be seen.

We found a little hollow spot, set up our tents and cooked some dinner. I shared my tent with Chris, a friend of Bruce's from Manson. We were all exhausted, so we crawled into bed and went to sleep. Scattered snowflakes drifted down.

Next morning, I opened my eyes to very faint light. The roof of the tent was pressing down on my chest, barely inches away from my face. I pushed up, hard. It barely moved. I struggled to turn around, unzipped the door, and a bunch of snow fell into the tent. The top of the snow was high enough we had to crawl up to get out of the tent. The tents of our camp were buried, barely visible under a thick white quilt of snow. More than a foot had fallen overnight.

I learned later the wives on the hill were in a state. Thick snow had fallen there, too. Thea, Maryann, Sue, and Cathy were each home alone with their kids, all the husbands away for different reasons. They all telephoned each other. *How are you doing?... What's going on?... Are you okay?... Does anybody need anything downtown, or are we just safe at home?... Does everybody have firewood?* There had been no plowing for any of the ladies to get out. They each waited for the husbands' return.

If we'd had any doubts about forging ahead versus returning to where we'd started, the difficulty of packing up our gear in the new deep fluff erased them all. It was hard to walk around. We sank deep into the powder, even with snowshoes.

We worked our way back down to where the snowmobiles had let us off the day before, and then waited...and waited. We didn't want to leave our spot and not get found if they returned. But we had no communication to know whether they were even coming. So we waited some more.

"Shh! Did you hear that?"

We all strained to listen. Distant. Faint and muffled— we heard the barest whine of a snow machine.

"It's them! It *has* to be them."

The sound grew louder, and it was more than one machine. We saw them coming across the slope.

"We're so glad you guys found us. It snowed so heavy."

"Glad you guys are all right. It snowed real heavy down below, too, and we were just worried sick about you. If we hadn't come in yesterday, and made tracks, we never would have found you. Yesterday's track was hardly even a dent."

One of the other snowmobilers had been standing up the walls on his snowmobile trailer while we talked. It was a plywood box shaped like a tall dog sled we could stack the packs in. There was room for a guy to stand on the tails of the skis, and there were two handles.

"You ride the trailer to stabilize it," the driver said to me. I looked around. *Are you talking to me?*

"The snow is so deep, the packs will tip it over. Ride with it to keep it upright."

"Ah, okay." I stepped onto the skis and grabbed the handles. I expected the driver to slowly gain speed, but he nailed it and we blasted off.

We came to a steep hillside, and the guy leaned into it, still flying. He made a track, but the trailer felt like it wanted to fall down the hill. I leaned and pulled hard, putting most of my weight on the uphill ski. If the trailer had tipped there, our gear would have fallen a long, long way down. My arms and hands ached from the strain and the vibration, but there was no stopping, so I held on and held on.

I was the last in line, behind the last snowmobile of the five, perpetually swathed in a cloud of snow dust. It became harder and harder to see. I could just see my driver through a narrow slit. I was not wearing goggles, only my balaclava. It had to have been an hour and a half before we made it back to the parking lot.

I stepped off the trailer. My hands and arms and back and shoulders were all tingling—electric. Reaching to remove my hat, instead I grappled with a thick layer of snow. I scratched through the crust and pulled—my eyelashes and beard were frozen to the hat. I needed to break up the ice before I could extract my head. Then I saw the thick snow shellacking my chest and arms, a shield which had protected me from the wind. I wasn't cold at all.

සැ

Ray called one morning after another big storm increased the snow depth to nearly four feet. "You guys stuck up there with all this snow? Hang tight, and I'll be right up with my bulldozer."

Four hours later we heard his bulldozer rumble down Open Road. He crawled down our driveway, hidden behind the gigantic roll of snow he was pushing. He took it right down to the dirt, unfazed by the packed snow and ice. He turned around by the house and came in to get warm.

We chatted over lunch for about an hour. He said, "I best get back home before dark," and walked out to his little dozer.

He pulled the handle on the pony motor, a small gasoline motor that was used to start the main diesel engine. Nothing happened. He pulled again, and again. And again. The pony motor refused to start. Ray never complained

{ 199 }

and never gave up. He must have pulled the starter rope a hundred times. Half an hour later it sputtered to life. He started the dozer, and waved goodbye, smiling as he headed back up the driveway.

We followed his path down to town, his work appearing most dramatic through Roller Coaster. Five-foot discs of snow had broken off at regular intervals, flanking the road like big white boulders. I would need my own plow for next winter.

I measured the snow depth often throughout the winter—it was deeper than my yardstick before the end of January. I used a tape measure after that. The deepest snow I recorded was fifty-four inches, or four feet, six inches. The snow that slid off the roof almost reached the eaves—I think it helped cut the wind against the house. There had been more snow than I expected, and colder temperatures, but February suggested spring.

"I think we made it, dear." I said one warm, sunny day.

"Just barely," Thea said. "We need to make some improvements before next winter, because I won't make it through another one like that."

⋘⋙

"She's down again, Dad!" Jacob yelled one morning before church.

I walked gingerly around the corner to see Thea lying on her back in a shallow melt water lake. She was holding her elbow and laughing.

"It's true!" she said. "I always fall when I come out in the snow."

I looked for a place with traction, and braced myself to help Thea stand.

"That's cold water," she said, shivering. "I was getting into the car, and next I knew, I was on my back. I think I hit my elbow."

"I saw the whole thing, Dad," Jacob said. "It was just like last time. Her feet went up really high."

We had compacted the snow by driving on it all winter. The daytime high temperatures were above freezing, so the snow would melt. It would re-freeze overnight as a big flat sheet of ice. The ice would melt again the next day, and the thin layer of water on top made it even more slippery.

One such morning in late February, Thea drove the Suburban to town with Jacob. The next time I saw her, she was telling me about the accident.

{ 22 }

WHAT ARE YOU DOING HERE?" I asked. She and Jacob had appeared at the house about an hour after driving away. "Where's the Suburban? What happened?"

"The car went off the road."

"What?"

"Sawmill was slippery, and that angled bump was scary, of course. But it was like a normal day. I don't think I was driving that fast. I came around the corner past Buzz Hunter's, and you know the road doesn't slant the right way, like they should way up in the mountains?"

"Angled down toward the inside of the corner?"

"Right. It's flat there. Well, I drove into the shade and turned right to follow the road, but the car kept going straight."

"Toward the outside of the curve." I said.

"And all of a sudden, we're off the road, and we're hanging on by the passenger front tire."

"You drove off the road?"

"It's like a skating rink."

"But you didn't roll? The car went over the edge and stopped? It's a long way to the bottom!"

"The one tire is on the road, but the rest of the vehicle is over the bank. Jacob fell into me, and I told Jacob, I said, 'I'm going to open your door and push you out onto the road. But don't be scared. You might get wet and cold, but you'll be okay. I will crawl out of the car after you, and then we'll go get dad.'"

"And, so?"

"I stood up. The car's like this, you know?" She held her hand to show a steep angle. "I stood against the driver's door and got the passenger door open—it was so heavy! I took Jacob by his butt and pushed him out onto the road, and I crawled out on top, and I said, 'Okay, now we have to walk back to the house and tell dad what happened'."

"I'm so glad you're okay!"

"It was like we were skating, dad," Jacob chimed in. "I was pretty scared in the car. The door was too heavy for me to open."

I hugged him tight. I choked up. What would I do without my Jakey?

Our neighbor Lee had come to visit soon after Thea and Jacob drove out the driveway that morning. He was there listening to Thea's story.

Lee said, "Well, I'll go down. I'll take you and Jacob so you can go to work and he can go to school, and Jim can come down and we'll figure out how to pull the car out."

I in my Land Cruiser and Lee following in his car, drove cautiously to where the Suburban had gone off the road. I couldn't believe the car hadn't rolled.

Lee stepped out of his car and walked across the ice to the Suburban. He put his foot on the only tire still on the road, and shoved against it, grunting.

"Stop it!" I yelled. "What are you doing?"

Startled, he turned to look at me. "I was checking to see how stuck it was..."

"We don't want it to go on down the hill, man! Let's just leave it hang right where it's at and we'll see if we can pull it from there. If it goes all the way down into the valley, it'll probably tumble and the car will be destroyed."

"Oh. Yeah. Okay."

I took a deep breath. Then I said, "Thea, when you get downtown, please call Mike Talley and ask him to come up with his tow truck."

Mike Talley brought his wrecker and hooked up to the front of the Suburban. He hauled in on the hook, but the Suburban didn't budge. His truck did. He pulled his parked tow truck across the ice toward the Suburban.

"I'm going to call my friend with a bulldozer," I said to Mike.

"Oh, I think I can get it," Mike said.

"Well, just in case, I'm still going to call." I drove back home and called Ray Hill.

"I'll be right up, Jim," he said.

Ray came up with his little bulldozer, and we chained his rig to a stump on the side of the hill, up above the road.

Ray said, "Mike, if you keep your line taut, I'll pull from the back end, and hopefully the car will come up back end first."

Ray chained up to the Suburban and backed away. His bulldozer slid sideways on the ice. He adjusted his angle so his tracks were perpendicular to the pull and the Suburban jumped back up on the road.

"Thanks, Ray, you're a life saver," I said.

I drove downtown to pick up Jacob and Thea. "Mike is charging us $180," I said to Thea.

"We don't have that kind of money!" she said.

"He didn't even do anything. He wasted his time slipping and sliding on the ice, but he didn't get us out of the hole. Ray did. I think that guy is an angel disguised as a mechanic."

"How are we going to pay Mike?"

"I got a job today at the Chevron station, pumping gas. They made me take out my earring."

"That's great! The extra cash sure will help."

"We get paid by the gallon. We have to keep track of how much gas we sell, but that shouldn't be too tough."

Thea's birthday was in early March, and I wanted to give her a special treat—a kitchen window—but it was still too cold. I promised to make it happen when the weather warmed.

March was one of the ickier months up on the hill. The snow melted away to reveal fields of dried autumn grass and dead arrowleaf balsam root leaves crushed flat and grey. The run-off turned the dirt roads to slop and carved them with channels. Our tires chewed and spat gobs of mud all over our cars. Puddles gathered in dips to earn names—Lake Chelan, Puget Sound. Our parking area became such a mud hole I set out pieces of plywood on either side of the car to serve as docks.

Watson Grade was one particularly difficult stretch of road to navigate. The ruts were mid-calf to almost knee deep. A driver couldn't head straight down the road, but had to tack like a sailboat, crossing the ruts at an angle to avoid high-centering. Chuck and his skinny tires apparently missed the memo. He had all four spinning in air. He called me from Ken's house.

"Hey, Jim, it's Chuck. Can you come help? I'm stuck on Watson Grade just below Ken's house."

"Yeah, I'll be right there. I still have my chains on the Land Cruiser."

I drove up and around behind Ken's place and down to Chuck. His truck was high centered, tires spinning in air. I latched onto his truck and drug it back up the hill, my chains merrily flicking mud twenty feet into the air. Ken watched the whole thing. "The County needs to see this," he said. He made some phone calls and arranged to drive two County Commissioners, Jim Wall and John Connelly, up the hill to see the condition of the roads.

As they approached the place where Chuck high-centered, they put their hands against the dash and stood against the floor boards.

"No, No!"

"Don't go down there!"

"People live down there," Ken said. "They drive this hill every day. They have to take their kids to school."

"Well, that's okay, don't go down there!"

"Oh, my gosh, how do they do it?"

"Well, it's not easy," Ken said.

A week later, the County sent up a grader to fix the roads. Most of the snow had melted, so the roads were never again as rutted or muddy as they had been. My Land Cruiser and I, however, had secured a reputation as the combo to call for rescue.

{ 23 }

DID YOU HEAR THAT?" Thea said one night shortly after we blew out the kerosene lamp.

It was the pitter patter of rodent feet. "Yeah. It's just a mouse, or something. There's not much we can do to keep them out until we finish the chinking."

We didn't hear them every night, but that was probably because we fell asleep so quickly.

One night, it wasn't skittering feet we heard, but chomping. It was close. Stealthily, I reached for my flashlight and aimed it at the floor beyond the foot of our bed. I switched it on to catch a pack rat, red-handed, munching on a tassel at the edge of our carpet. He was the size of a grey squirrel, but had a pointy nose and an ugly, hairless tail. He froze for half a second, then dropped his loot and ran.

I hoped the light would be enough to scare him off, but seconds after I switched it off, he was back. This time he was munching on the fringe at the head of our bed. I shone my flashlight on him again, and he jumped up onto the log wall behind the head of our bed.

"I got you now, you bugger!"

I pulled a hunting arrow from my quiver and held it in my right hand near the fletching. Aiming the flashlight with my left hand, I closed in on the dirty rodent.

Dlump, dlump, dlump—he came running toward me.

{ 209 }

My heart skipped a beat before I regrouped and clutched the arrow tighter. I stepped aside to let him come by and as he emerged into the open, I lunged at him with the arrow. I hit him right behind his rib cage and pressed him against the wall. He kept right on going. He moved beyond the reach of my arrow and my flashlight beam tracked him across a second floor beam to the south wall. He took a short hop and disappeared between two logs. I didn't know there was a hole there.

I grabbed my .22 revolver, scrambled down the ladder, slipped on my boots and out the back door. I crept around the west side of the house, holding my flashlight over my pistol the way the police do in the movies. I popped out from behind the corner and caught him with my light. He was perched on the fourth log down.

Boom!

He dropped like a stone.

I crawled back into bed and switched off my light. I listened carefully. No more chomping—for now.

The next day, I plugged the hole between the logs and went around the house filling any gaps that had formed as the logs dried. I jammed rocks and chunks of wood in every critter entrance I could find.

∽∾

Thea called her dad on Palm Sunday. During the conversation, he said he and Thea's mom would be coming over for Easter. They'd stay with Pat and Larry, but visit us at the cabin.

{ 210 }

After she hung up, Thea said to me, "You know, my parents are convinced you dragged me over here against my will."

"We could tease them," I said. "We could have you chained to the tree with a collar when they come down the driveway,"

"And you could pretend to be unhooking me!" she said.

We had a laugh picturing that scene and their reaction, until we realized they probably wouldn't see the humor in it. Maybe we'd better not.

We did our best to prepare the house for their visit, but there was only so much we could do. We squared away the kitchen table and the stacks of firewood by the fireplace and cookstove. Thea swept the linoleum in the kitchen. We looked around one last time as they drove in the driveway. We shrugged our shoulders.

Thea's dad parked the car. Thea's mom wouldn't get out. "I'm not going in there," she said.

"Don't you want to see what we've done, Mom?"

"No," she spat. "Just look at you. You're a mess. You're wearing plaid? You shouldn't wear plaid. You've got runs in your nylons, ..." Still drunk, and still mean after months apart, she maintained the barrage of insults even as Thea stepped away, obviously hurt.

Thea's dad poked his head inside the house and ranted, "God, you have so much to do. No electricity? Running water? You still use the outhouse? It's just ridiculous. You have so much to do here."

Thea interrupted, "Can you say something positive?"

"What in the hell are you talking about?"

"Can you say something positive, please?"

"Like what?"

"Like we've done a lot?"

"That goes without saying."

"No, it doesn't. We've done a lot here."

"Okay, I guess so." He shook his head. "Well, we should probably go."

He got back in the car and they drove away.

They hadn't been there five minutes. Thea was visibly upset. She had endured years of ill treatment from her mother, but it was never any easier. I needed to lighten the mood.

I fetched the chainsaw and brought it into the kitchen.

"What are you doing?" Thea asked, curious.

"Happy belated birthday, dear," I said. "I'm going to cut you a window."

"I'll get the broom," she said.

I measured the logs and marked them with a permanent marker, having planned the window location before building, making sure there was no rebar. I fired up the chainsaw and revved the engine, placed the bar for the first cut, and pulled the trigger. Big chips burst forth. The sweet smell of alpine fir sawdust and two-stroke exhaust blossomed into the kitchen. I switched to the other side and pushed out each log as it was cut through.

I sliced the bottom half of the top log and the top half of the bottom log like a loaf of bread, whacking out the individual slices with a hammer and chiseling flat to the line. I nailed in a 2 x 10 frame, sandwiching a strip of insulation against the logs. Two rings of 1 x 2 boards clamped the thermo-pane window in place. Thea had her birthday present on Easter Sunday.

She had the faintest smile as she swept up the sawdust and chisel chips. "Thank you, dear."

છ૪ા

Tiny white woodland stars were the first flowers to spring to life after the snow melted. Then the itty bity purple, yellow and black bonneville shooting stars bloomed. Arrowleaf balsam root sunflowers shone bright as the stars faded, spotting the green fields with clumps of happy yellow. They were joined at the margins by shy purple lupines, comfortable to stay in the shadows. Lomatium flowers, unpretentious, like miniature heads of cauliflower in yellow and brown, also bloomed in late spring, adding to the variety of wildflowers growing on the hill. They all made us happy.

As much as Thea and I loved to watch the wildflowers sprout and grow, they weren't going to feed us. By mid-May, the morning lows were rarely below thirty degrees, so I felt it was safe to start working on the garden. Last fall we had tilled the apple leaves into an area thirty by forty feet in front of the house. In the spring, I added and rototilled four pickup loads of horse manure we collected from the stables.

Across the deep, soft soil enriched with mulch and manure we laid a paper tube irrigation system. Two columns of eight parallel rows sprouted from a central supply line. I heaped soil on the tubes, creating both the mounds in which we would plant our vegetables, and the aisles between them where we would walk.

The paper tubes would allow the water to seep into the soil without being lost to evaporation. I supplied the system with water each day by filling a 55-gallon drum with water from the hose at Dan Wright's spring. The barrel drained into the soil each night.

We planted potatoes, tomatoes, carrots, green beans, peas, three kinds of squash, radishes, onions, asparagus, lettuce, rhubarb, chamomile, broccoli, cauliflower, and catnip. I built a fence around the garden to keep out the deer.

It remained to be seen whether our efforts would pay off.

C3ED

As spring turned into summer, I was still working at the gas station, which might have meant more money, but the owner kept hiring more people. We had to be cut-throat, running and shoving to get to the cars that came in. Our individual wages, low as they already were, dropped because we weren't actually pumping much more gas. Then the owner hired a guy with thirteen earrings up one of his ears—he didn't have to take them out. So I quit.

I drove up the road to Mike Talley's. After the Suburban rescue, I felt like I knew him. I also still owed him, so if he gave me a job, he could be sure he'd get his money. He didn't take much convincing. The busy season was coming so he hired me to help with the auto repair and muffler work part of his business. I hated even the infrequent trips Thea had to make for commodities, so now that I had a decent job, I was glad to leave those trips behind for good.

{ 215 }

My Land Cruiser, with a Chevy 350 V8, burned a lot of gas and a lot of my paycheck. I did some searching and found a Yamaha Enduro motorcycle for a hundred dollars. I saved that much in gas in under two months, but my Land Cruiser never made me bleed as much as that motorcycle.

I was riding home from work, having taken the steep, gnarly Switchback. Starting up, I saw a fire growing fast in the back of the draw. Cabins above were in danger. I cranked the throttle and raced up the hill to warn the neighbors and get help. I crested the hill going fast and took the corner wide. My front tire dropped into a rut. The motorcycle twisted and slammed me down. I wasn't wearing a helmet.

Boggled, I found myself prone in the dirt next to a motorcycle lying on its side, motor running. I thought maybe I should pick it up and ride it somewhere. The handles were twisted off-center. As I rode, I watched someone's blood dripping, dripping, dripping onto the speedometer. I heard a noise in the distance—*ka-chook, ka-chook, ka-chook*—so I rode toward it.

I rolled into Ron and Cathy's driveway. They were having their well drilled. Chuck and Sue were there also, and they all waved hi. I had no idea who any of them were. I stopped the bike and fell over.

"Oh, my God!" They came running.

"He's covered in blood!"

"His ear is dangling from his head."

"We need to get him downtown."

"There's a fire at the bottom of switchback," I managed.

Thea was downtown at the lake with the Union Valley kids, and Sue came to find her.

"Thea, there's been an accident. You have to come!"

"Is Chuck hurt?" Thea asked.

"No, *your* husband's hurt."

{ 24 }

SUE AND THEA PULLED THE KIDS from the water and raced to the clinic where Ron and Chuck had taken me. Thea rushed in and knelt in front of me. I was leaning forward, my elbows on my knees, but still wobbling. I recognized her.

Dr. Pleyte said, "He's going to the hospital."

Thea repeated. "Jim you're going to the hospital. Is that okay?"

"It doesn't make any difference if he's okay with it or not," the doc said, "he's going to the hospital."

I was admitted to the hospital and spent two nights. They sewed my ear back on—my necklace had jumped up around my ear and sliced it down to the lobe. They confirmed a concussion and said I had crushed the labyrinth in my ear—I would need to see a specialist in Wenatchee.

I went back to work for Talley a week later and laid down on a creeper to roll under a car for a muffler job. I got so dizzy—everything was spinning and spinning. I could see only a whirling blur. I lay still and the spinning persisted for a long time, maybe two minutes. Finally, my vision cleared and I could work, but it was the same every time I lay down. At least it wasn't as bad when I stood up. I gradually healed over the next two months and started riding the motorcycle again.

All the guys on the hill had served in fire service at one time, so we had formed our own Union Valley Fire Department. We were attached to the Chelan Fire Department and their insurance covered my hospital expenses. Someone had reported the fire and they'd put it out before it burned any homes.

⊗

The first day of summer arrived with a cloudburst. Two inches of rain fell in less than two hours. The total amount of rain that falls in an entire year is commonly less than twelve inches. The sky opened as it must have in the days of Noah, and rivers of water carved canyons into the dirt roads. We piled into the Suburban as the firmament broke and we drove downtown via Switchback. As we drove through the narrow exit of the valley bottom, enough water was flowing to hoist the Suburban and carry it along until the valley opened again. The town was flooded with muddy water deeper than the curbs that washed into the businesses along Main Street. What kind of place was this?

The Suburban started to give us fits. It wouldn't always start with the key anymore, so we had to pop the hood and short the starter with a screwdriver. The hinges were stiff, and the hood didn't close easily. I pulled hard once, and the hood folded just past the end of the hinge. I managed to straighten the hood well enough and get it to close again. I don't know why I didn't think to grease the hinges.

Thea didn't have the strength or finesse to get the hood closed as it got stiffer, and one day she was in a hurry to get downtown.

I noticed the damage that night.

"I couldn't get it closed," Thea said.

"So what did you do?"

"Used the sledgehammer."

"That we used to pound in the rebar spikes?"

"I was in a hurry."

I had no reply.

CS80

On the Fourth of July, we had another Union Valley party, this time at Chuck and Ginger Langer's. Chuck was a retired Navy chief. His solar system was the envy of the entire hill. The panels, which charged a big bank of batteries in his basement, were motorized to follow the sun's path through the sky. Upstairs, if we hadn't known about the solar panels and battery bank, we would have sworn he was connected to city power. He had light switches—just like downtown.

The chill of winter still hadn't given way at night. Even around the fire, we needed to wear our jackets, but it seemed like summer arrived the very next day. We caught up with our neighbors around the fire. Ken and Maryann were there, with their son Payson, a newborn.

CS80

{ 221 }

One day, a thin, small man who looked to be in his late fifties, grey hair and white, scraggly beard, wandered up to our house. He wore a gray tweed jacket.

"Are you guys hippies?" he asked.

"My name is Jim Beaty," I said. "Who are you?"

"I'm Earnest. What happened to the Stiles?"

"They sold us this property. We're the owners now."

"The Stiles were hippies," Earnest said. He chuckled. "They were going to live off the land."

"Where do you live?" I asked. "I haven't seen you around before."

"I just live over there, past the brow of that hill." He pointed to the west.

"By Dan Wright's spring?" I asked.

"Yup, in a corner of the old barn down there in the valley."

It was a hovel.

"We go down there all the time for our water. I've never seen anyone there."

"Well, I just got back from Medical Lake. I got family there. So you guys aint hippies, huh? You know they call this Hippie Hill, right?"

"Yes, we've heard, but never knew why."

"'Cause there was hippies up here! Naked hippies!" He smiled big and his eyes glinted.

"Is that so?"

"Other side of Dan and Vicki's place. You know them?"

"Yes, they live that way," I said, pointing north east.

"Well, there was a bunch of hippies would run around naked across the road from them. Free love, and all that. They made tents by covering tree branches with clear plastic. They looked like wigwams. It was a whole village of 'em! They were gonna make it through the winter in them tents. None of 'em did." He laughed till he coughed.

"Well, I can see why. This last winter was a bear, and winter's comin' again."

"Yup, I'll be ready. I figure I'll stay pretty warm. I got a good stove and my little dog, Levi. We'll keep each other warm. Almost had some hippies come visit. You could sometime, if you wanted."

"Thanks for the offer."

"Well, bye," he said, and walked away as abruptly as he had appeared.

⊂ℬℱ⊃

Some friends of ours from the log house class, Stephanie and Carl had found property and decided to build in Colville, about three hours north and east. They drove up to our place to see how we were doing and swap stories. Thea and I drooled all over their brand new 1984 Isuzu Trooper. "Ohhhh, maaan! What a beautiful little rig!" I loved the big windows and 360 degree visibility.

As they drove away, Thea said, "That's the car I want. That's what you're going to buy me. We have to have that car."

I fetched my chainsaw before the dust had settled. "I'm going to cut the front windows in," I said.

{ 223 }

"Oh, that will be great," Thea said. "It's still so dark inside."

I marked and cut the openings on both the front wall and the east wall toward the driveway. They were larger than the kitchen window and it really added daylight.

We were going to use an old bank door with a wood frame for the front door. Ron wanted it for his upstairs deck and wondered if we'd trade for a set of hospital French doors. They were nice—much heavier than those available at the time—so we made the trade. The doors were taller than the cross log holding up the second floor, so they had to open out. The doors were four feet wide and all glass—the front room was flooded with light. Thea was pleased. I was on a roll, so the next day I installed the kitchen window at the back of the house, and finally, the small bathroom window, framed and hinged.

CB&O

We could hear them coming before we saw them, clatter, clatter, clatter, flying through the air. They were light brown, as big as my index finger, long and skinny, their antennae almost as long as their bodies. They were pine sawyer beetles. It was no fun to step on them—crunchy and slippery.

It was especially bad at night. They were attracted to our reading lights, Coleman lanterns mounted on a three-foot pipe above a five-gallon bottle of propane. I'd be engrossed in a Louis L'Amour novel and yanked from my concentration by the sound of an aerial attack. Where,

where, where! Then, BAM, I'd be hit—thumped in the forehead or struck in the chest.

Pine sawyer beetles eat downed timber, but they weren't eating our log house logs. They were more of a nuisance than anything. I figured any beetle willing to kamikaze me should also be willing to feed the dog. I'd throw them to Ginger after they crashed into me, and she would gobble them down like tortilla chips—crunch, munch, crunch. I never did get used to the sound or the idea, but at least I would have a few more minutes of peaceful reading until the next air raid.

{ 25 }

Written from Thea's perspective

JIM AND I HAD HOPED FOR SIX KIDS. We had six boys' names picked out, but could only agree on one girl's name. We already had Jacob Randolph and Lucas Paul. Next would be Kale James, then Christopher Charles, Patrick Edward, and Nolan Thatcher.

In August, I figured I might be pregnant. I was so excited. We had tried for three years to get pregnant with Jacob, then three more years for Luke. We hadn't tried at all for this baby—it felt like a gift from God. I was having a bit of a time with the two, but three babies would be okay.

We'd met friends at Campbell's Resort, and there was a hot tub. I whispered to my friend, "I think I might be pregnant."

She said, "Don't go into the hot tub—it's not good for pregnant women."

September came and still no period. So, with little money and no insurance, I went to the community clinic, held at the hospital every other Thursday. Only our Mexican migrant worker population usually used it, but where else was I to go?

I checked in at the front desk, and filled out the paperwork. The receptionist almost jumped over the desk to look at my tummy. I wasn't showing.

"How far along are you?" she asked.

"Three months, I think."

"Oh, good."

The nurse practitioner checked me out, confirming I was about three months along. She set me up for a new patient exam the following week.

I drove up the hill and stopped by the West house to tell Maryann I was pregnant. Then I told Cathy Forrest. I couldn't wait until Jim got home. I met him at the door and told him the news. Then I told Jacob and Lucas, "You're going to have a baby sister or brother come spring!"

I still had my maternity clothes and all the boys' baby clothes and all those wonderful old cloth diapers. Luke wasn't out of diapers yet, but he would be almost three when the baby came. *Maybe the baby will be born on my birthday,* I thought to myself.

I had a cold coming on, so I started taking Vitamin C. I thought it was strange I'd felt so good for so long—I had no nausea, which was so different from Jacob and Lucas. But now a cold. Why now?

I went back for my next appointment. "Is something wrong?" I asked the nurse as she moved her probe all over my belly.

"I should be able to hear a heartbeat," she said. "And I can't. Let's do a pregnancy test."

The test came back. Not pregnant.

I wasn't bleeding. I had a faint stomach ache. "What do you mean I'm not pregnant?"

"The baby has died. Come back to the hospital at nine tomorrow for a D&C. You'll be out Saturday morning—that's all there is to it."

Numb, angry, disbelieving, confused, hurt. *Why, God? So freely given, so quickly taken!* I couldn't cry. I went to Safeway to get some food for dinner, then drove home.

Jacob was in school until three. Luke was at Sue's. Cathy Forrest brought Jacob home from school. When Jim came home, I told him the baby was dead. He hugged me, said he was sorry. I cooked dinner.

Friday morning, I woke up, got Jacob ready for school. Jim took Luke to Sue's and I went to the hospital. I filled out the papers, turned them in.

The receptionist said, "Since you're married, the state will not help pay for this procedure. How are you going to pay today?"

"Even though I'm married, we still don't have any money."

"Can you make payments?"

"I guess. Can we pay ten dollars a week?"

They took me to a room on the maternity ward, which at first I did not realize. They took me from my room and wheeled me to the operating room. Then I was back in my room. The nurse kept coming into my room, checking on me, asking questions.

I kept my eyes closed and turned my head away in silence. *Why should I talk to her? Why answer any questions? Why even open my eyes? Why bother? Go away. Leave me alone, you have no idea how I feel—go AWAY!*

The next morning came. I opened my eyes.

Again the nurse, "How do you feel?"

"When can I leave?"

"Soon as the doctor checks you out."

I heard the doctor talking to one of the new moms, heard babies crying. *I'm on the maternity ward! How unjust. How unfair. How rude.*

I waited and waited—no doctor, no Jim.

I'd had it. I rang the nurse's bell. She came in all smiles. Now I was really mad.

"Take this IV out of my arm so I can leave."

"Oh, but the doctor hasn't talked with you. Your ride isn't here."

"Fine. I'll take the IV out myself."

"No! Wait just one moment, okay?" She yelled out the door, "Doctor!"

The doctor came in, and the nurse removed the IV.

"The surgery went well," said the doctor. "Sorry you lost your baby, but you can always have another one." He kept talking but all I heard was blather.

I stood up and dressed while the doctor yammered.

"Do you have any questions?" he asked.

"Can I go now?"

"Your ride's not here."

"I can walk home."

Jim appeared at the door and we drove home.

We had company that weekend. Ted and Marylynn came over from the coast. I wasn't much of a hostess.

The neighbor ladies came over to offer condolences and asked to take Luke.

"No, thank you. I'll keep my child. One's already been taken."

Many months before, a friend of mine had miscarried, and I'd written her a note:

I'm so sorry you lost your baby. I had to write you this note because I don't know how to talk to you on the phone. If you want to call me, I'll listen and cry with you, but I don't know how losing a baby feels. I'm so sorry.

Well, now I did know how it felt. We lived in a tiny town, so word traveled. My friend called me when she heard the news. We cried together. She was the only one who understood.

Everyone at church was so kind. But they didn't get it. They had lots of hugs, but I had empty arms. There were far too many well-meaning people who said, "Oh, so you lost your baby. It'll be okay—you can have another one." When Hanna at Little Stone said that, we quit going to church.

I don't want another baby—I wanted this one!

For the next nine months I read three books a month: one self-help, one romance, and one non-fiction. We had library service by mail, and every month a zipper bag would arrive in our big mailbox, near where the pavement ended, with the books I'd chosen the month before. I'd return the books I'd read, and mark three more books in the check-out pamphlet to be delivered the next month.

I wasn't getting answers from God, so I told Him to go to hell, told Him He wasn't in my life anymore. For three years, no church, no prayers, my heart turned to stone.

As for my husband, he wasn't there for me. He didn't know what to do when I cried, or when I was angry. He was quite happy another child hadn't come to live with us. He didn't like how I treated the children we already had. Years later we straightened out that mess, but in the worst times I felt alone, lonely, lost, and sad.

For years, September was always a sad month because that was the month I'd lost the baby. March was sad too, because that's when the baby would have been born. Time has softened the memory, but at times I still wonder: What if...

{ 26 }

LATE SUMMER AND EARLY FALL saw our garden producing in abundance. It paid off, all our work of hauling and tilling the leaves and manure, placing the irrigation tubes, and gravity-feeding fifty-five gallons of water every night. We had a bumper crop.

We harvested over a hundred pounds of green beans alone—six paper grocery bags brim full, not to mention the potatoes, carrots, and peas. The squash had cross-pollinated and we harvested two hundred fifty pounds of hybrids. We gave squash to everyone, even if they resisted. We insisted, so it wouldn't go to waste. We had a full row of plump red cherry tomatoes, and a few big boy tomato plants near the house that lived up to their name.

The fence I built around the garden did keep out the deer, but it didn't keep out Jacob. I caught him several times gobbling handfuls of peas and stuffing his face with cherry tomatoes.

Vicki actually seemed a little upset by our success. "How did you get your tomatoes to grow so well?" she asked accusingly. "Mine don't look half as good as yours."

"Maybe it's the sun and the heat on our southern slope," I offered.

Thea canned all those big, red, juicy tomatoes. She used to can stewed tomatoes before she and I married—she thought it was something a wife needed to know how to do. She figured as a wife she needed to know how to sew, how to cook, how to make repairs, and how to make do.

She'd read all these recipes for stewing tomatoes, and said, "I'm going to put the onions, the green peppers and the celery right in with the tomatoes. Then I can take my quart of stewed tomatoes and I can make chili, I can make spaghetti sauce, I can make tomato soup, I can do anything with it. It'll already be made. I don't have to do the onions and celery and green pepper separately, or add them to the tomatoes later."

First, she cooked the stewed tomato mix so it was ready to go into the jars. Then she sterilized the jars by immersing them in boiling water. She'd grab the jars with special tongs, dump the water, and pour in the stewed tomato mix. The rings and lids were kept in hot water so the rubber on the lid would be soft to make a good seal. She placed the lid on top of the jar, and screwed down the ring. Then she would put the filled, sealed jars in a hot water bath for half an hour.

We always checked the lids for a good seal after letting them cool. The lids would suck down with a pop or a ping, and we'd know we'd done it right. We'd tap each one with a finger, and if it was concave and didn't flex, we could store it away for months.

Thea canned our green beans, and canned pears and peaches we'd picked from Uncle Larry's trees. She liked to can the pears and peaches dead ripe. She may have overdone it: The peaches just disintegrated in the juice and became peach syrup. Tasty stuff!

We came to know a family downtown, the Adamses— they grew grapes. They shared a bunch with us and told us how to make grape juice. They said to strain it through gauze, but we didn't have the money to go buy gauze, so we used pantyhose. It worked great—our juice tasted just like Welch's, so purple and so good.

We weren't going to need any government supplements this winter. We had grown our own garden, kept it watered and safe from the deer, and harvested a bountiful crop. We had stored much away for the winter. We were ready. It's hard to describe the feelings of satisfaction and gratefulness that came with raising our own food. I like to think we rather understood the feelings of the Pilgrims after they came through their first starving winter and prepared to enter the second with abundance. Thank You, Lord.

I called my mom one day to share with her the success of our gardening and canning efforts. "Do you have a cellar to store what you've canned?" she asked.

"No, but we can keep the jars under the house for the next few months until the temperatures are too low."

"Now tell me about your kitchen," she said.

I chuckled. "Well, our counter is a piece of plywood resting on two sawhorses."

"Does Thea have cupboards?"

"No, we just stack our dishes."

"How does she do it? I'll buy you cupboards."

"You know, Ma, we don't need the cupboards as much as we need a snow plow. It snows so much up here we can't get in and out without one."

"Really? How much does a snow plow cost?"

"I've been looking into it—about fifteen hundred dollars."

"Okay, I'll send you a check. You really should try to install some cupboards though, Jimmy."

"Yes, Mom. And, thanks!"

So we bought the plow. I was working at Talley's and, at his shop, I welded a custom frame to mount the plow to the Land Cruiser. I had taken a welding class years before, and could weld pretty much anything I wanted. I did a good job on that frame, and with the plow, we were in like Flynn.

Winter was comin', and this time we'd be ready!

◌⑂∽

Our neighbor, Earnest, wasn't. He came to visit a few more times after his first appearance and, in November, he invited us to dinner. We accepted his offer with some hesitation, and on the appointed day our whole family trooped down to his shack.

His place was even smaller than it looked from the outside. He had walled off a room in the part of the barn that was collapsing the least, making his total living space about seventy-five square feet. He'd set a lumpy old mattress on a wire frame bed at one end, made presentable with a tan wool blanket spread smooth. He had a small tin barrel cookstove at the other end and one chair.

Earnest served us with paper plates and plastic utensils. He sat on his chair, we sat on his bed with Luke, and Jacob sat on the floor.

"So, what are we having for dinner?" I asked.

"We're having goat stew."

{ 237 }

I'd eaten goat meat before—ghastly. The milk from Leif was no better. My reaction was involuntary, and though it was brief, Earnest saw me shudder.

"You're going to love it," he said. "Do you hunt deer?"

"Yeah...?"

"Well, you know a deer is a goat."

I had to think about that for a while. "Hmm. Well, I suppose they're related."

Even though it smelled good, I braced myself for my first bite, expecting to gag. I stabbed the first piece of meat and lifted it to my mouth. Earnest watched. I paused and smiled, maybe too big.

I took the bite and my eyes widened. Earnest chuckled from his chair by the stove.

It was great! Delicate, delicious, tender, and tasty. He had cooked it in a tomato and onion sauce with thinly sliced potatoes. All the flavors came together perfectly. Thea and the boys enjoyed it, too.

"Is this where you're going to spend the winter?" I asked as we finished dinner.

"Yup. Cozy, isn't it?"

Not what I was thinking.

Thea blurted, "You can't stay here! You'll freeze. " She looked at me.

"Come live with us," I said.

"Nah, I'll be fine, me and my little dog. Isn't that right, Levi? We'll be fine."

"No, Earnest," I said. "How will you get in and out? The snow gets deep, you know, and you're down here in this valley living in a—well, it's not a proper house."

"I'll be snug as a bug down here."

Thea chimed in, "Earnest, we have a bed at the house. You can come and stay and be warm. Bring your dog."

"You don't want to get run off the hill by winter like those hippies, do you?" I asked.

He looked at me hard. "I'll come live with you as long as you let me cook. But you have to cook one meal a week." He looked at Thea.

"I would love that," she said.

"And you have to do the dishes," he said.

"I can do the dishes."

"Well, okay," he said.

We should have asked other neighbors first about Earnest's reputation, but we were more kind than wise, a dangerous position.

{ 27 }

EARNEST SPENT A FEW MORE CHILLY NIGHTS in his cabin before he came to live with us. Our logs were done shrinking and checking, and we had done a better job of chinking, so no more snow would be blowing in. We set his bed up on the first floor against the west wall. His dog slept curled up on the foot of his bed.

Earnest jumped right in and took over the cooking. He was a big help, often having dinner ready when we came home from work. He helped us cook our Thanksgiving turkey in the wood cookstove, which required hours of constant stoking with scraps of small wood. When he pulled the turkey out of the oven, however, he set the pan directly on our card table. A card table with a vinyl top.

"No!" Thea shouted.

"What?" he said as he yanked the pan back.

The pan had already burnt a perfect oval ring into the vinyl.

"Well, I thought it was wood," he said, upset.

"It's just vinyl printed with a wood grain pattern. Here, set it on these," Thea said as she laid out two scraps of decking that would have been fire wood for the stove. "I guess I should have had these out already."

The turkey turned out wonderfully well, and it was a lovely Thanksgiving with a friend at our table.

Earnest cooked dinner for us six nights a week. He cooked potatoes with every meal. Potatoes with pork chops. Potatoes with chicken. Potatoes with eggs. Potatoes with soup. Potatoes with potatoes.

After a few of Thea's weekly meals he said to her, "I don't like how you cook."

She said, "What do you mean? You don't like my food?"

"You have never once made potatoes. When you cook, you either cook noodles or rice or squash or something else, but you never cook potatoes."

"Well, we're eating potatoes six nights a week. I thought maybe we could have rice or noodles."

"I want *you* to cook *me* potatoes."

The next week, she cooked some potatoes for Earnest.

"You're a pretty good cook," he said at last.

ॐ

I wanted to bake my own bread for the family, so I asked a friend for a recipe and set to work. I imagined big, fluffy golden brown loaves that puffed up in a dome over the edges of the pan. They'd be just like store-bought, only better, and they'd be *mine*.

I mixed the ingredients and followed the directions to a T. I let the bread rise next to the chimney for the set period of time, and placed them in the wood cookstove oven when it was just the right temperature. I stoked the firebox carefully to maintain a constant temperature and only checked when I knew the bread was almost done.

I rubbed my hands together in anticipation. The smell! *Oh, this is going to be great...*I opened the oven door and looked in to see my homemade bread.

It was flat. Barely a curve. No puffing up at all. *What the heck!*

The color was decent. The toothpick came out clean. It smelled great. *Why didn't it rise?*

We had it with dinner that night, and it tasted all right, but it was a lot thicker and denser than I had expected or wanted. Maybe I'd added too much flour or done something else wrong. I would try again and see whether I could get it to rise next time.

⊂⋛⋚⊃

The wind blew hard many days during November, and I wanted to catch some with my windmill and turn it into electricity. The windmill's instructions suggested mounting the tower on the roof. I did not want it rattling the house day and night, so I built a ten-foot log pole platform and set the tower on that. I struggled to lift the heavy, awkward power unit to the top of the tower.

I set the brake and connected all the wires below— wires from the windmill to the control panel, wires from the control panel to a 12-volt car battery. The battery would be able to power a few lights, like we had in the camper. Once the wires were connected, I climbed back up and attached the propeller.

The wind was blowing hard and steady. I released the brake and stepped back. The blade started to spin—faster and faster—it sounded like a helicopter. I heard a click, and the blade slowed down, accompanied by a change in the sound. The needle on the voltmeter jumped—we were making power!

Another click. The needle on the voltmeter dropped. The blade spun back up, whirling and chopping, but accomplishing nothing. I heard a click again, the blade slowed, and the needle jumped. And off again.

Grrr! After all that? The wind wasn't fast enough, or the tower wasn't tall enough, or both. The windmill was an alternator, which uses energy to make energy, and after that first bit of energy was used up, there wasn't any left to charge the battery. This was harder than I expected.

I set the brake and planned to return to the project later. Maybe I could build a taller platform? Maybe I could find a taller tower somewhere that had already been made? Maybe I ...

СВso

We were still going to and from the second floor with the ladder near the chimney. Hans Carlson, who owned Grout the golden retriever, during one of his visits taught Luke to climb the short step ladder. Luke was hesitant, but soon scrambled up without help. He'd never tried climbing the tall ladder.

Thump! We heard it from the kitchen.

Jacob called out, "Luke just fell off the ladder!"

We found Luke on the floor, his forehead sporting a big goose egg. He wasn't crying. The next day, he wasn't using his arm. Guarding it. Thea touched it gently—he winced.

Thea said, "I'll take him to the office, see if Bruce will take an x-ray for us." The x-ray showed a green stick fracture of his little forearm.

The chiropractor said we should get him casted at the hospital. When Thea worried about paying, he reminded her the x-ray had been free, and the casting wouldn't cost much. Luke came home wearing the tiniest cast I'd ever seen. He healed quickly, and learned to use it persuasively on Jacob.

{ 28 }

WORK SLOWED AT THE AUTO REPAIR SHOP after harvest ended. Once or twice a week Mike Talley would tell me, "Well, there's nothing going on today, you can go ahead and go home for the day."

I needed the job. I couldn't take days with no pay, and I told him so.

After being sent home a third day in a row, I left him a note:

Mike, I have a family with two kids I need to feed. I have to have a full paycheck. I need to keep working every day, or I need to be laid off so I can get back on unemployment. I can't take days without pay. So either I work all the time, or you need to lay me off.

Mike glowered and growled at me the next day when I came in. "I got your note," he said, waving it at me. "So, I guess you're laid off. If anybody asks, you're laid off."

I went to the unemployment office and filed my claim. Two weeks later it came back: "Denied." I hadn't worked with Talley long enough. *Now what are we going to do?*

Thea was listening to the radio one morning and there was a talent contest on the *Second Cup of Coffee* program. We listened to a few people call in to play piano, or violin, or sing. Thea called in.

Welcome to Second Cup of Coffee. What's your talent this morning?

{ 247 }

Thea said, "I was going to dance, but I slipped on the ice and hurt my hip, so I can't dance for you, but my husband sometimes sings. So I'm going to hold the phone for him, and he's going to sing."

It was the dead of winter, so I started singing "Summertime."

Summertime,
And the livin' is easy
Fish are jumpin'
And the cotton is high...

I was being accompanied by a live piano in the studio, and we kept time pretty well together. In the studio was Leah Sluis, an organizer of the fledgling Chelan Valley Players, and part owner of the Ruby Theater. When I finished, Leah said, "Well, you win! You win! Where are you? Who are you? You have to come down! I have a kazoo for you and a *Second Cup* cup for you. Come down to the theater, I'll be in the ticket booth."

I drove down to the Ruby Theater, and when I introduced myself, Leah asked, "Are you the guy? Oh my gosh, you're the guy! Sing for me again!"

I started singing "Summertime" again and she smiled and clasped her hands.

"I want you to be Mottle. We're going to do *Fiddler on the Roof.*"

I had only sung one other time before an audience, in the Easter Cantata at Greenwood Church in Seattle. I broke into a cold sweat just thinking about it. I barely moved my mouth when I sang, like a ventriloquist, and hid even that movement behind my big beard and mustache. I could see the crowd jostling and shifting to try to discover who was singing, which was fine with me. Now this lady wanted me to sing a solo on stage in front of a bunch of people?

My face betrayed my thoughts.

"Have you done any community theater or musicals?" she asked.

"I sang one time in church for Easter, but I was very nervous, almost physically ill."

"So maybe you'd like a non-singing role first?"

"That might help."

"We're going to put on *A Christmas Carol* first. I'd like you to please come try out."

She'd given me a kazoo and a coffee mug—how could I say no? It also felt good to hear she liked my singing so much. Maybe there was something to it? I went to the theater and tried out. I was to be Fred, Scrooge's nephew. My lines included no singing, to help ease me past my stage fright.

We prepared the old Ruby Theater for the show. Built in 1913, it was the oldest functioning movie theater in Washington State. We removed the first two rows of seats and extended the stage about twelve feet beyond the proscenium arch. So, when the curtain closed, we still had twelve feet of stage out front. Originally it had been a vaudeville theater, so the fly space had all kinds of room for sets and for scene and costume changes.

In the play, my character Fred was married to Beth. The lady who played Beth was also named Beth in real life. We had many lines together, so we often rehearsed at her house. Beth was married to Joe Collins, the Sheriff of Chelan County. Beth's best friend was Judy Wall, and Judy's husband Jim was the Chelan County Commissioner, who had come to see the bad roads in Union Valley. Joe and Jim were buddies, and through the plays, I found myself at the fringes of their influential circle.

We had sledding parties together up on the hill. Sawmill was a mile-long road of nearly continuous descent. We'd sled down the road top to bottom, lying on our chests and pumping our legs to get over the short rise in the middle, and Joe would tow us back up the hill behind his truck to do it all over again.

One afternoon Jim Wall said to me, "You know what—I have an orchard out on Howard Flats, and I need a guy to do the winter pruning."

"I've never done that before," I said.

"You can learn. I'll show you."

Just like that, I was hired. It was my job to climb up in the trees with a little one-hand top-loader chainsaw, and take out the big leaders—vertical, fast-growing branches as big around as an arm that steal energy from fruit production. Jim told me we needed to keep the trees open, so when we sprayed, we could get the spray inside.

There were five of us pruning the orchard, me with the chainsaw, and four other guys with long-handled loppers. The other four guys were high all the time—they reeked of pot. I outpaced them hour after hour, day after day—and there were *four* of them! All they had to do was the lopping, the small branches. Every time I'd look back, they were huddled around a tree, "Yeah man, gotta get some of this."

I'd been a hippie, I knew what it was about. But even then my nickname was "Red Neck Jim." I'd never gone as far as a lot of my friends in the wild things they did. Maybe God was protecting me. In any case, when at work it was time to work—no messing around smoking joints under apple trees. Jim was impressed with the work I did.

One advantage of orchard work was that I could start my day a little later. I'd work until it was time to rehearse for the play, stay downtown for rehearsal, then get home some nights as late as eleven o'clock.

The snow crystals reflected our headlights driving home at night, sparkling like fields of diamonds, flashing like paparazzi cameras. The stars shone bright in the clear cold of altitude, twinkling and shimmering by the thousands. We could see the stars' colors, blues and reds, and easily discern the Big Dipper's double stars—in fact, all the principal stars of Ursa Major.

Clouds filled the lake valley in December, though Union Valley remained above them for many weeks. Weekday mornings we dropped into town from sunny blue skies, looking over white puffy cloud tops, through a foggy soup, to overcast dreariness. Cold, dense air filled in below the clouds, pressing them up like foam on a latte, the fog layer reaching the cabin by January. The fog persisted for weeks, and froze to everything. Frost radiated full circle in growing spikes around fence wires, pine needles, and bitterbrush branches. It became a cold, ghostly landscape of black and white, blurred by mist, silent and motionless.

Snow fell throughout the winter, the smallest flakes falling when it was coldest. Even the finest flakes could accumulate several inches to a foot or more overnight. It didn't snow every night, but when it did, I needed to be out there plowing. I'd plow until three in the morning sometimes, completely losing track of time. I'd make my first pass down Sawmill at the outside edge of the road, putting my passenger side tires on the crumbling lip of the dirt road. I'd come back up on the inside, pushing the snow away from the high side so I could come back down again and push it the rest of the way off the downhill side.

Of course I was never satisfied with just three passes. In a few spots, the road was wider than two blades, so I'd need to come through again. In other spots, snow bounced off the tree trunks at the edge of the road and rolled back into the middle. I'd make another whole trip down the road to remove a snowball. I'd plow Schoolhouse as wide as possible, then come down the driveway and open it all up near the house.

Dan and Vicki had been cross country skiing in and out for years, and asked if I would extend my plow route to include their place. I saved them about a mile each way and they paid me twenty dollars a month for gas. I tried to refuse, and I did love the work, but they insisted.

When I was done, the roads were flat-smooth—free of ruts, ridges and chunks. I'd roll back home, spent and satisfied, for a few hours' sleep. Once, hours past midnight, I was making my final pass when a person appeared in the road coming toward me. *Who is this?*

It was Thea, charging down the road in her bathrobe and rubber boots. She opened the door, panting, "You never came home. I was worried something had happened."

"I'm fine, just making the final pass."

"It's so late! Let's go home."

౪౸

Through that second winter, we were still getting water from the spring in the valley bottom. One of the times we were getting water, the snow had fallen the night before and added another several inches to the snow pack. Our boots made fresh tracks in our path on the way down. The water only flowed about a gallon a minute, so it took about ten minutes to fill the jugs. We started back up the hill to the house, retracing our path.

We came to the corner of the trail, starting the steep part of the climb. There was a large animal track on top of ours. A cougar. The print was the size of Thea's hand.

Thea and I looked at one another, wide-eyed, our faces drained of color. The hair on the back of my neck stood up. Time slowed. We froze in place and searched every inch of the woods and slopes around us. We listened for any sound, but all was silent. Cats are quiet hunters and a blanket of muffling snow would be to their advantage. *I wish I had a gun right now!* I kept scanning the trees and the bushes all around us.

I looked for more tracks. The tracks disappeared. *Which way did he go?*

Thea moved slowly up the path in front. Jacob walked in the middle, and I walked backwards, looking behind. Step by step we inched closer to the safety of the cabin. We didn't see any more tracks or the big cat himself. Once inside the cabin, I shut the big door with a thump and leaned against it with a sigh. *Next time we go for water, I'm taking a gun!*

{ 29 }

WE REHEARSED FOR *A Christmas Carol* throughout November. We performed each evening the first week of December, giving matinees on Wednesday and Saturday and the finale on Sunday.

Section Two   December 5, 1984   Page 17

Chelan Valley **MIRROR**

'Chelan County's Progressive Community Newspaper'

Some of the cast of Charles Dickens' play 'A Christmas Carol' during curtain call on opening night Monday at the Ruby Theatre.

'A Christmas Carol' at the Ruby Theatre

The community responded enthusiastically to the play, packing the Ruby Theatre every night. I was amazed how much I enjoyed the whole process. I forgot my nerves, and the shows went off without a hitch—well, most of them.

I, as nephew Fred, opened a scene by throwing a snowball at Scrooge's back. Scrooge was upset, but Fred just laughed it off. In the following scene, Beth and Fred are walking arm in arm, and Beth said, "So, you really hit your uncle with a screw ball?" The audience laughed, and my face registered confusion. Beth then realized what she'd said, but I regained my composure and replied, "Well, actually, it was a snowball, my dear. He didn't think it was funny." The audience laughed again and seemed to miss that we'd messed up. I became comfortable in front of a crowd. I also made some good friends and our relationships continued even after the final curtain.

⊂୫ℰ⊃

Earnest was spending nights with us, days at his place. He would come back in the afternoon to cook dinner. We appreciated his help, but he crossed some lines, and I should have stopped him sooner.

Thea told me about it on our drive down town one day.

"I caught Earnest watching me this morning."

"What do you mean?"

"Before you got up, I was washing in the living room standing next to the fire, trying to stay warm while I took my clothes off and washed. Of course the house was pitch black, but I saw his eyes watching me in the light of the kerosene lamp. And when I realized he was watching, I blew the lantern out."

"Did he do anything?" My heart raced.

"No. I don't know how long he was watching. Or how many times it's been. He probably saw all of me. Not good."

"No, it's not. Maybe you can bathe upstairs in our bedroom?"

"And climb the ladder with a bowl of hot water?"

"Well, no, in the kettle, and pour it out into the bowl once you get up. It's warmer upstairs anyway."

"I guess."

"It'll be spring soon, and we can send him back to his little hovel."

Thea stayed quiet.

"And he didn't really do anything," I continued.

"Put yourself in my place, and tell me he didn't really *do anything*."

"Yes, dear, I'm sorry. We were just trying to be good neighbors and help an old guy out."

"Maybe there's a reason he's old and alone, living up here in the middle of nowhere in a barn. He might be a pervert."

In my naivety, I let Earnest's leering slide and I never said a word to him.

⊰⊱

One day I asked Jim Wall what was going to happen with all the leaders and other branches we were pruning from his apple trees and heaping into a pile.

"We dump them in the ravine over there."

"May I take some home?"

"Sure, take as much as you want."

They'd been dumping for years—the pile was endless. I loaded the pickup that same day after work with as much apple wood as I could fit in the bed, and unloaded it at the house. I did it again the next day, and the next, and the next. There was something about that large and growing pile of wood that made me feel secure and prepared. *A guy can never have too much wood*, I thought to myself each day as I nabbed one more load.

After winter pruning ended at Jim Wall's orchard, I started working on Stan Mettler's orchards. He had five acres on Howard Flats and ten near town called the school orchard. The school district had bought the land planning to build a new high school, but then chose a different site across town. Mettler's dad and brother, a Seattle architect, had bought the land from the school district, and just let it go. It needed a ton of work to produce a good crop. Mettler asked me to prune aggressively, insert spreaders, and tie the branches of one tree to another to open them up. They had grown up—we needed them to grow out.

Fifteen acres meant the work would be full time. Stan explained I would move the sprinklers in the spring, spray in the summer, and thin and prop and harvest in the fall. I'd be a one-man show, which was right up my alley.

❧

Beth Collins invited us to dinner with a few other couples. After dinner, I stepped outside to smoke a cigarette. I returned to a conversation about grandparents who smoked, remarks about what an awful a habit it is, and details of their horrible, drawn-out deaths. Beth said she couldn't understand why someone who breathed the Chelan valley's amazingly clean air would ever want to inhale smoke. Several ladies agreed.

They were talking to me, and I knew it. A while later, I went back out, letting them think I hadn't heeded their warning. Passing through the kitchen, I pulled out my remaining cigarettes, crumpled them into a wad, and threw them in the trash. I didn't tell anyone. But I was determined to quit.

I craved the nicotine, and felt anxious, but I endured. Weeks passed and I overreacted to something small. Thea wondered why I made such a big deal.

I said, "Did you notice I quit smoking a couple weeks ago?"

"No, but I did notice you were chewing a lot of gum and were really grumpy."

"I didn't want to say so until I was sure I could do it."

I did quit. And felt better. It was easier over time—only a strong urge now and then.

❧

Winter gave way to spring and Earnest and his dog spent more and more time at their shack. We drove him downtown or back up the hill occasionally. One day he went too far. When Thea told me, I wanted to kill him.

"Earnest grabbed me today."

"He did what!"

"We were coming up the hill and I stopped to let him out. I leaned over to give him a hug goodbye, and he leaned in, and he grabbed me, here. I said, 'Get out of the car, Earnest. You're done.' He said, 'Well, I didn't do anything wrong.' I said, 'You're done. You stepped over the line'."

I paced and clenched my fists while Thea talked. "I'm going to kill him."

I stalked down to his place and banged hard on his door.

I said, "We gave you a place to stay! We were friendly, and you do *this* to us?"

"I didn't do nothin'."

"Yes, you did. It may seem innocent to you, but that's off limits. You're done. You don't live with us anymore."

A couple of days later he brought back my dad's heavy wool military coat and one or two other things we had loaned him.

Thea was talking with Vicki a few days later and warned her about Earnest.

"I'm so sorry!" Vicki said. "He attacked me, too."

"What? He did? When?"

"Remember that night I was at your house for dinner when Dan was away? And you wanted to send Earnest home with me?"

"Yes. It was dark, and there are animals. But you didn't want him to come with you."

"I felt weird about it. I just had a feeling."

"But he didn't go with you. So how did he attack you?"

"He came later and caught up with me. And he grabbed me. But I fought him off."

"Why didn't you tell us? He was living with us! He could have done that to me. He *did* do that to me!"

"Well, I don't know. I just thought you guys were friends, and, well...I felt ashamed and thought it was maybe just me."

"No, Vicki, we were being nice to a poor, lonely old man. We didn't know he was a pervert. You have to talk. We have to communicate"

"You're right, I'm sorry."

"I'm sorry, too. I'm sorry I tried to send him off with you. I didn't know."

Vicki wasn't the only one who knew Earnest's reputation. We never saw him again after he brought back my dad's coat, but he stayed up on the hill. Clowd followed him and lived with him because she liked Levi, his little dog.

I felt so betrayed by that dang dog. She was the best I'd ever had. We were friends, I thought. I'd had her from just a tiny puppy. She started going deaf, so she couldn't hear me when I'd call. She just liked Levi. Fine. Earnest went back and forth to Medical Lake for malaria treatments at the Asylum, and he took Levi with him. Clowd would come back when Levi was gone, but it was different. I knew who and what was more important to her.

08&20

Thea's dad came over for Easter again, and we braced ourselves for a repeat of last year's criticism. He came alone and sober, however, and it was much better.

"We're going to go to church," Thea said.

Paul said, "I'm going to stay here, then. I'm going to keep the stove going so that when you get home, we can have dinner."

He wanted a turkey, and stayed to stoke the cookstove.

Jake, Thea's dad Paul, and Luke

We came home after leaving Paul in the silence for several hours. He greeted us from his chair by the stove.

"This is hard work," he said about cooking the turkey. "I thought I was just going to sit and watch it, but I had to keep adding wood. But not too much, 'cause then it would get too hot. My grandmother used to cook with a stove like this—they all did back then, in the thirties. I was just a kid. I always had to get the wood for the fire-box, but I never cooked, I never had to maintain the fire, or stoke the stove. I had no idea how much work it is!"

"It sure smells great," I said. "I do love the smell of cooking turkey."

Paul wore a faraway look on his face.

"I get it now," he said. "If I was twenty, no, thirty years younger, I'd be right here with you doing this. I totally understand what you're doing now. It's quiet. It's peace-ful."

"It's nice, isn't it, Dad?" Thea said.

"Yes, it's great. And you've done a lot, Jim. You're building yourself a log house." he said, looking at me.

"Thanks, Paul. It's not perfect. The walls aren't all square, and they're not all plumb..."

"You're not building the Taj Mahal," he said, inter-rupting.

I nodded. "You're right. I'm not building the Taj Ma-hal. I'm just building a log house." Somehow it helped me to hear that.

The turkey was moist and delicious. I told Paul as much and thanked him. He smiled big—he was proud of his contribution.

This is how it's supposed to be, I thought to myself as I looked around the table. *Thank You, Lord.*

∞

A Christmas Carol had gone so well, packing out the Ruby Theater night after night for a full week, that we started rehearsing for *Fiddler on the Roof* right away. I was to play Mottle. My song was *Miracle of Miracles*, a love song to Tzeitel after we got permission to be engaged.

Wonder of wonders, miracle of miracles
God took the tailor by the hand
Turned him around and
miracle of miracles
Led him to the promised land!

Leah Sluis had acted professionally as Golde in one production, and Yente the matchmaker in another. She played Yente again this time. Edd Lamar, owner of the Lake Chelan Building Supply, a lumberyard between Chelan and Manson, played Lazar Wolf. A few weeks into rehearsals, Edd offered me a job at the lumberyard.

"Thanks, Edd, I really want to accept your offer, but I also want to finish what I've started at the school orchard. They haven't harvested yet, and I want to do the harvest with them, run the tractor, finish the whole process."

Edd said, "Okay, well, whenever you're done with harvest, just come on down. Jim Wall put in a good word for you."

※

Several weeks after Paul's visit for Easter, Thea had trouble with her dad's truck. I was downtown rehearsing for *Fiddler*. Ron Forrest called me at the theater. "Thea won't be able to come get you. She burnt her hand real bad and the truck won't start."

{ 30 }

IS SHE OKAY? WHAT HAPPENED?"

"She's okay. You'll see when you come get her. It was an electrical fire. The truck's okay, too."

"Thanks Ron, I'll be up soon."

She explained what happened when I came to pick her up. "I was taking the kids to Ron and Cathy's when sparks and smoke started coming out from under the dash. I stopped the truck and said, 'All you kids get in the back. I'm going to drive very slowly, and if the truck catches on fire, I'll stop, and you leap out, run into the field, and get away from the truck.' Everybody was like, 'Okay, okay,' so we started up the hill. The sparking and smoke got real bad, so I slammed on the brakes, and yelled at everybody to jump out of the truck. I reached up underneath, and with my hand, pulled out all the wires."

"Bare handed. Wow."

"I burnt it bad, real deep. I was scared at first it was burnt to the bone, as I could see white, but I think now it was tendons I saw. I kept looking at my hand, and I thought, *Wow, it doesn't hurt. But the truck's not going to move.*"

"You just ripped the wiring out?"

"I knew you'd be mad. I kept thinking, *I need to get downtown. I'm going to get in so much trouble. Jim's going to be so mad because I ripped the wires out.* So we all

{ 267 }

got out of the truck and we all walked up to Ron and Cathy's, and I was just shaking my head. Ron said, 'Let me see your hand.'"

"I'm not mad, dear. I'm sorry you were hurt. We can fix the truck." I turned to Ron. "You were a Marine medic in Viet Nam?" I asked him.

"A Navy corpsman," he said.

Thea continued, "He looked at my hand, and he said, 'Thea, your hand is so severely burned. Get in here. I've got to fix it.' And I said, 'It doesn't hurt. I'm just upset.'

He said, 'This is really bad! You could lose the feeling in your hand.' I said I had to get downtown to get you, but I didn't know what I was going to drive. He said, 'We'll get a hold of Jim, we'll work it all out. It'll be okay.'"

"And here I am," I said.

"Ron put all this goo on my hand, and wrapped it all up."

"I need her to come over and see me every day. I have to debride the burns, keep them clean and make sure there's no infection, all of that."

"Yeah, we can do that. Thanks, Ron."

Thea went back every day for a dressing change and Ron took great care of her. There was never an infection and Thea continually marveled that her hand never hurt.

∞

Leah called on some acquaintances from her earlier *Fiddler* productions to improve our performance. The Russian dancer joined us from Seattle, and Tevye came from Wenatchee. We had a live orchestra—musicians from the Seattle Symphony, Spokane Symphony, and other professionals. We accommodated the orchestra by removing a couple more rows of seats. We built all the sets ourselves.

Chelan Valley Mirror   May 8, 1985   Page 20

Much hard work, including hours and hours of rehearsals like this one on Monday of last week, goes into a production like 'Fiddler on the Roof', set to go into performance for six days beginning next Tuesday. Collins Loupe is the conductor and musical director of the production. Marcia Ericksen is the choral director. Valerie Weimar will play piano; Sandy Rydy, the clarinet; Steve Walter, the accordion; and Joe Curry, the violin.

'Fiddler' opens Tuesday, May 14

I felt privileged to be part of such a fantastic production—the sound quality of the singers and orchestra rivaled the movie. The "Chelan Valley Mirror," the local paper, wrote, "The Chelan Valley Players sang their hearts out to capacity crowds, and succeeded with a great deal of verve and growing polish. Bravo!" The *Fiddler on the Roof* was an ambitious project for a small community theater group, and we nailed it—Chelan had never seen such a successful live theater performance. I enjoyed every minute, and never felt nervous.

{ 269 }

Cora Hartley attended the Wednesday night *Fiddler* performance and asked Leah to introduce us. Cora had retired to Manson from California's Occidental College where she had been head of the music department. She was the teacher's teacher, supervising and instructing instrumentalists and vocalists.

Cora loved Johann Sebastian Bach. She originated the annual Lake Chelan Bach Fest held every summer. It had grown from a simple weekend to ten days of performances around the valley in July. She had started to include music from other composers: Handel, Mozart, Vivaldi—and wanted to add opera singing, too. The Bach Fest earned acclaim in music circles nationwide.

She asked me, "Where did you receive your training?"

"For singing? Oh, I have no training. I can't even read music. I sang in church a few times, and here in Chelan twice."

"No. I don't believe it. I've never heard a tenor like you," she said.

"Really?" Leah had explained Cora's credentials in our introduction, her praises boggled my mind.

"You don't even know. I'd like you to sing in the Bach Fest this summer. I want to train you myself. Come to my house."

"I don't have any money. I can't afford lessons."

"I don't want you to pay me—I will teach you for free!"

"Really? Okay. Wow. I work with Edd and Sharon. I could come after work?"

She was pleased. We went over the basics, she taught me to read the notes, and we practiced over and over. It was fairly easy to sing after I'd heard it once. Then she'd play the accompaniment, and I'd sing the words.

಄ઠ෩

Thea and I readied our garden for another season. We were anticipating another bumper crop. I removed the paper watering tubes, tilled, placed the paper tubing, and mounded planting rows. We planted seeds, and I filled the watering barrels. The following morning, I checked the first barrel, expecting it to be empty—nearly full. I disconnected the hose at the garden, and water gushed out. *So the siphon is working, but the paper tubes aren't letting it seep.* I looked closer—a fine white powder clogged the entire system.

The water was loaded with minerals, and they precipitated out, clogging the tubes. We periodically descaled the hard white crust in our tea kettle with vinegar, but there was no way to descale the tubes. The system wasn't cheap and we couldn't afford to replace it. We'd have to spend all day hand watering our garden if we wanted to keep it. Thea and I were both disappointed. Only the asparagus grew.

಄ઠ෩

Any homesteader I ever read about worth their salt had chickens, and it was time for us to join their ranks. Joe St. Louise, an old timer with a long family history in the valley, had a big hutch full of chickens. We asked if he'd sell us some chicks, and he snagged them off their roosts and stuffed them in boxes: "There you go."

We came home with a dozen Araucana and Barred Rock hens, and a Rhode Island Red rooster—we called him George. I built a coop from apple bins with three nesting boxes and a raised roost. We fed the chickens in the morning and let them range free the rest of the day. We collected eight or nine eggs a day.

The hens started pecking on this one chicken for some reason, and yanking out the feathers on her back. I'd yell at the others, "Why are you guys picking on her?" I'd kick at them. "Leave her alone!" Every time I'd turn my back, they were on her again—the whole gang running and squawking, like they were saying "Get her, get her!" She tried to get away, wings flapping and legs pumping, but they never let up.

Well, I do have a solution for this. She's going to die at their hands anyway, so let's just end this. I came out with my shotgun, found the poor hen, and made the shot. It was sad, but there are 800 trillion chickens on the planet. I didn't remember stories like that in any of the homesteading books I'd read, but that's how it happened for us.

℘

I shot another bird, too, but it was a bigger challenge. I was getting home late from rehearsal and needed all the sleep I could get before leaving for work. It would start singing at five o'clock in the morning, as soon as the sun came up. It sat on the peak of the roof, whistling a Chinese water torture song with two notes repeated: tu-tu, toot-toot. Then it whistled again about a minute later: tu-tu, toot-toot. *Oh, shutup! I'm trying to sleep!* Tu-tu, toot-toot.

The first morning, I just lay in bed frustrated, hoping it would go away. Tu-tu, toot-toot.

The second and third mornings, I went outside to chase it away. Tu-tu, toot-toot.

The fourth morning I went out with my 12 gauge shotgun. Tu-tu, toot-toot.

He flew from the peak of the roof to a tree branch nearby. I aimed and fired. Boom! Tu-tu, toot-toot. I missed! He flew to another tree about a hundred yards away. I aimed and fired again—Boom!—and missed again! *I bet I scared him good, though!* I thought, consoling myself. *He won't be back again.*

The fifth morning: tu-tu, toot-toot. *Oh, for crying out loud!*

I jumped out of bed in my skivvies, threw on my bathrobe, stepped into a pair of rubber boots, and grabbed my shotgun and a handful of shells on the way out the door. Tu-tu, toot-toot.

Boom! Miss. Run a hundred yards north. Tu-tu, toot-toot.

Boom! Miss. Run a hundred yards west. Tu-tu, toot-toot.

Boom! Miss. Run two hundred yards north. Tu-tu, toot-toot.

Boom! Miss. This time he circled around and came back to the house. *You little...!*

I watched him land on the tallest fence post that formed the gate to the garden. I snuck along the west side of the house like a cowboy in a movie, holding my shotgun vertical. I peeked through the logs ends at the corner, doing my best not to be seen. *He's right there!*

I popped out from behind the corner, raising the gun to my shoulder. "Boom!"

He jumped in fright.

And burst into a silent cloud of yellow feathers.

I got him!

The sixth morning? Sweet, peaceful sleep.

I didn't shoot all the birds on our property—there were some I really liked.

♋♋

In early May, Thea shouted to me from the kitchen, "Come look at this! Come look at these pretty birds!"

"Wow, they're so blue!"

"Like the sky. Have you ever seen such pretty birds? Do you know what they're called?"

"I've never seen them before, but they look like a pair."

The female flew up to the window, and I started talking in a falsetto. "Look Fred, look at this house, let's move here!"

Fred was sitting on the snowplow marker antenna. I dropped my voice to speak as Fred, "Somebody already lives there, Martha. We can't move in there."

She flitted up and down at the window. Falsetto again: "No, no, it's really nice! Oh look at that! We could be very comfortable!"

"I'm telling you, somebody already lives there. We can't do this. You're going to drop your eggs right there. We have to make our own nest."

Martha kept flitting at the window, and Fred kept sitting on the antenna of the plow, looking at the house and Martha. I felt like I could see him shaking his head and thinking *oy, oy, oy.*

"Fred, you have to come look."

Fred came and flitted up and down at the window a few times, and flew back to the plow.

"I'm tellin ya, we can't get in there."

Eventually they flew away, but we kept seeing them around the house. They were a pair of Mountain Bluebirds, and the male was the most vibrant shade of blue, like a highlighter. Even their song was pleasant, rather like a muted toy train whistle.

I continued to make up a dialogue for them whenever we saw them. It was neat to imagine them conversing with each other the way husbands and wives do. They started to feel like familiar friends.

{ 31 }

THEA HAD HAD A ROUGH NINE MONTHS since the death of our baby. She was inconsolable. I tried to help, but it felt hopeless. My efforts made no difference for her, or for the baby we lost. I didn't know what to do, so I didn't do anything.

I didn't respond the way she expected or wanted, and so I became a victim of her wrath. I would see her eyes dilate, and I knew that was my cue to leave. She was mad at God and mad at the world and mad at me.

I'm not sure whether it was the financial pressure, or spring, or that time had begun to heal her wounds, but in June she said she was going to be looking for a job downtown.

The clinic had an opening for a receptionist. She applied, and they were stunned at her qualifications, so they called her in for an interview. The interview went very well until the end, right after they offered her the job and she accepted, when it took a turn for the hills.

"How'd it go?" I asked when she returned.

"I got the job. And I can wash my hair."

"Oh?"

"The interviewer asked me if I had any questions about working there, and I said, 'I have a request for a privilege.' I told him I lived in a house in Union Valley with no electricity and no running water. He just waited to see where I was going. I said, 'It's a lot of work to wash my hair, and I can't use my hair dryer, so it stays wet for a long time. May I have permission to come in an hour early to wash and dry my hair?' 'Well, that's an unusual request, but, yes, that would be okay.' I told him I had all my own stuff, I just needed a source of water and electricity. No one would ever know, never a hair in the sink or even on the floor.' He said it would be fine."

Thea's hair had been very long. Even with the convenience of running water to wash her hair, she was still doing it in a sink. So she cut it short. I liked her hair long, but it was helpful to have the extra income.

⋐⋑

In July, more than two years since I had first witched for water and tried to drill my own well, we decided it was time to have water at the house. We chose to hire the professionals this time. We called MVM Quality Drilling and they brought up their massive drill rig.

I grabbed another set of branches and took another pass at witching. The branches seemed to dive at the same points as two years ago, the best I could remember. There were actually a few options along the length of what appeared from above to be an underground stream, so I chose a spot different from the one I had drilled.

"Dig here," I told the pros, feeling a little like Mr. Kester. *I sure hope there's water down there!*

The boss also did some witching, but used thin bent steel rods. He found the same spot I did. They stood up

{ 278 }

their rig, almost as tall as the peak of the house, and pushed their big six-inch bit into the dirt. Within the first twenty foot length of pipe it was obvious they had hit rock—not the crumbling orange decomposing granite we could see at the surface, but rather the white-grey-black solid granite people love for countertops.

Down their machine chewed, grinding through the hard rock and ejecting a growing plume of grey dust. Fifteen minutes later the fire siren downtown began wailing. The fire lookout on the Butte had seen the plume and reported a fire in Union Valley. We didn't know the siren was wailing for us until the fire crew arrived.

"It's just rock dust. Sorry to be a bother. But thanks for checking."

We hit a little water at a hundred and sixty feet, but the driller said we'd find more deeper. He was right. We drilled to a hundred eighty, and pure, fresh water climbed the stone pipe we'd created to within a hundred feet of the surface. They only cased the top twenty feet because the rest was solid rock.

We lowered my water pump down the well to one hundred sixty feet and connected it to the generator. I was curious how much water we'd have. We were pretty high on the hill, and it'd be a shame to have a limited supply, or seasonal variation.

I started the generator, and switched on the pump. The hose burbled and spat for a few seconds before a solid stream of cold clear water burst from the end of the pipe. We had set up our milk jugs, and aimed the gush of water into the first one, starting the timer. The water filled the jug so fast I scarcely had time to look at my watch. I moved it to the second. We hit the one minute mark just as the eighth gallon jug finished filling. *Wow, eight gallons a minute!*

The generator ran for hours, requiring a refill of gas. The water stream leaving the hose never slowed or sputtered. A sounding line dropped to the water a hundred feet below showed the level hadn't dropped an inch. I installed a faucet at the top of the well, where we could fill our jugs. *No more walking to the spring!*

ଓଃ৪১

A short time later, Mom had taken Luke up stairs for a nap. Still the only second floor boards were over the kitchen, and they weren't nailed down. Luke tripped on a loose board and did a header. He gashed his eyebrow on the edge of the bedroom bench—blood flowed.

Thea called the hospital, alerting them we were coming. "Should I take him to the clinic, or the hospital? He only needs a few stitches."

"Bring him right to the E.R."

A doctor, fire department medic, and nurse met Thea at the door. Brad, the medic, agitated: "Is this the little guy who's critical?"

"Critical?" She looked at Luke, whom she was carrying, to see if she'd missed something.

"We thought you said the child was critical."

"Well, he's hurt, but he's awake and responsive. He has a cut above his eye—just need some stitches." Their tension drained away. They laid him gently on the gurney, wheeling him down the hall, Thea close behind. Three stitches.

Thea came home and urged me to hurry up with the stairs: "Climbing the ladder is getting old." I needed to complete the second floor first, though. After work and on weekends I made gradual progress, leaving open what would become the stairwell. Once the car decking was nailed down, I installed the upstairs north wall windows. The extra light was great. Upstairs access came only through the stairwell, so I moved the ladder.

One afternoon, the boys were climbing up, getting some toys. Luke went first, Jacob waiting below. Luke lost his grip and fell. Jacob attempted to break Luke's fall, and may have softened Luke's landing, but it was a hard impact.

Thea ran to them. Luke seemed stunned—another big goose egg. She rushed to the clinic.

Dr. Pleyte said, "He has a concussion. Watch him closely. Wake him from any sleep every two or three hours for the next twelve. If he should throw up, get him back in here right away."

On cue, Luke threw up. They treated him for his concussion and sent them home.

Thea walked through the door, saying firmly, "It's time you built those stairs." She was right—we couldn't have any more injuries!

⊰⊱

I'd never built stairs before. There are many ways to mess 'em up, but I was sure I could figure it out. Stairs rise about seven and a half inches per step, and treads are about eleven inches deep. I made the treads and stringers from 2 x 12's, the risers from 1 x 8 pine.

I measured between the first and second floor surfaces, and divided by seven and a half to get the number of steps. The plan was to parallel the west wall to a landing, turn east to run up between the center support logs, and terminate on the second floor. The resulting second floor hall would be eight feet long, plenty for three bedroom doors.

So, I laid out the stringers, framed the landing and nailed down the 2 x 12's. The treads and risers all went in without a hitch. Then, the run to the second floor—the last step was super short. *Now what?*

I assumed my troubleshooting position: I sat down and stared at the problem, thinking... *Ah! The final tread thickness!* I measured each rise—all were seven and a half inches, but the top was six—suspicion confirmed. I divided the difference by the number of steps—a quarter inch. I cut the first step one quarter inch shorter, the second step two quarters, the third three, and so on. By the top riser, I'd gained exactly the right amount to make every step the same height.

Wayne Leatherman's log was chest high at the landing, so I installed a support pole at the landing corner, and cut the log so we could pass. A second heavy post next to the bottom step supported the second floor stairwell corner. I installed a bannister between the two vertical supports. The stairs made life in the cabin easier and safer—a milestone project, and deeply satisfying.

{ 32 }

LEE HOWE CAME WALKING IN with his girlfriend one afternoon.

"I popped a tire on my truck," he said.

"So why didn't you change it?" I asked.

"Well, I actually popped all four."

"How did you pop all four tires?"

"Will you come help me?"

What's this dumb guy done this time? My curiosity got the better of me.

"Yeah, Lee, let's go. C'mon."

We drove out to his place, and there was his truck, sitting a hundred feet past a big messy pile of boards. His tracks showed he had driven over the pile of boards, the tires going flat right away, but that he'd kept driving. He tried to make a turn and drove two tires completely off the rims.

"Did you drive over the pile?"

He looked sheepish. "Yeah."

"Is that the house you built with Earnest?"

Still subdued: "Yeah, it was falling over..."

He'd left soon after the first snow the year before and had come back to find his shack collapsed in on itself. So he disassembled the place, leaving the nails in, and stacked the scrap in the middle of his two-track road. He

{ 285 }

drove over the pile to get out. "What were you thinking, man? I just don't get you."

"Well, can you help me or not? Can you take me downtown so I can get some tires?"

We took the rims off his truck, and I drove him to town to buy new tires. I dropped him off at his place with his four tires and drove away. I'm willing to help a guy who makes an honest mistake, but I have to draw the line at future Darwin Award winners.

A few evenings later, in the dead of summer, the fields dry as tinder, the fire ban long since established, we were driving down Open Road. We saw in the darkness the orange glow of a fire at Lee's place. *Is he trying to burn down the whole hill?*

I drove straight home and called the fire department. We drove back out to Open Road for a view of the fire, and fifteen minutes later we saw the lights of three rigs racing out toward Lee's place. Two minutes after that, the fire went out.

I don't know if he got a ticket, or if they told him I'd turned him in—which would've been fine. I'd have told him to his face if he asked. But we never saw Lee Howe again.

∞

Joe Collins had been the Scoutmaster of the local Boy Scout troop. His boys were older than ours, so when I asked about signing them up, he told me he was moving on, so the troop would need a new Scoutmaster, too. Jacob was really just old enough to be a Cub Scout, so I became the Cubmaster. Thea was the Den Mother.

At first there were only three kids, and two of them were ours. Luke was actually too young to be an official Cub Scout, so we pretended he was our Tiger mascot. We spread the word through coworkers, friends on the hill, and *Second Cup of Coffee*. A few kids showed up, then, week after week, still more. Pretty soon we had an average of a dozen kids coming to our Cub Scout meetings. We had such a ball.

We had a great time with knot tying. We bought long red licorice ropes and long black licorice ropes, so the boys could see how the knots came together, then eat the fruits of their labors. After we'd done this whole series on knot tying, Thea said, "Okay, what we're going to do tonight is Mr. Beaty is going to sit in the chair, and you guys get to tie him up with real rope. We want to tie him up so good he can't get out of the knots."

The boys were beside themselves, laughing and hooting and hollering and running around in circles. They wound the rope around me, and wound it around, and wound it around, and tried to tie a knot. Their smiles turned serious as they finished their job, and they stood back in anticipation.

I took about three seconds to get out.

The boys let out a collective sigh of disappointment, and I said, "You didn't do your knots."

Lance, a chubby little guy with a sufficiently high opinion of himself, challenged me, "Why do we need to know how to tie a knot?"

Thea asked, "Do you think someday you're going to grow up? Be a man?"

"Well, yeah."

"Probably going to own a truck, right?"

"Well, yeah!"

"Will you ever need to take anything to the garbage dump? Or move furniture?"

"Or get something from the lumberyard?" I added.

"Well. Yeah."

"Then you're going to need to know how to tie a knot."

Lance was quiet. I could see the wheels turning. His attitude changed, and he wanted to know how to tie knots.

It was neat to see some progress, and we were just getting started.

ଔଲ

Jacob needed shoes every two or three months, he was growing so fast. We could hardly afford to keep up, even shopping at Payless. Luke would wear a pair of shoes for an entire year, and he started to get jealous.

"I want new shoes," Luke said.

"You don't need new shoes," Thea said.

"But I really want new shoes."

"All right, you have to eat what mama puts in front of you. You have to have a quarter of a sandwich at lunch and three grapes, and you have to have half a glass of milk."

"I do?"

"Yes, and you have to eat it all."

"Otherwise you won't grow, and you won't need new shoes," I said.

Thea continued, "I'm going to give you a snack. You're going to have breakfast, a snack, lunch, a snack and then dinner, and then maybe another snack. You have to eat it all. And *then* you'll grow and we can get you new shoes."

So Luke worked hard to eat everything Thea put in front of him. He ate his meals and his snacks and he grew. He finally needed new shoes. We bought his new shoes and he stopped eating again. Food was never Luke's thing.

Jacob, however, was Mr. Food. It worked as a tool for discipline for him: "You can't have lunch." "I'll be good, I'll be good."

Jacob chose a pair of patrol boots to start the school year. They were buckskin leather with a raised forefoot and an even taller heel. Within days of starting school, he was trying to destroy his brand new boots. He would drag the toes on the pavement. We noticed the scuff marks after about a week.

"What are you doing to your boots? You're wrecking them!" I was mad.

Jacob stayed quiet and looked at his feet.

Thea said, "You're not getting any new shoes. No matter what you do to these, you're not getting any new ones, so don't do this."

He kept scuffing them, however, and wore the toes all the way through, a rectangular hole. We wrapped them in duct tape and sent him to school. "Fine, this is what you get."

Looking back on it, the kids at school were likely giving him a hard time. He would have been the only one wearing patrol boots, and they did look unusual. He chose them, however, and we were already spending too much money on shoes.

☙❧

One morning Thea was getting Jacob ready for school and Luke for day care. She opened a drawer to get some long johns for Luke, and when she pulled them out, she screamed. She was staring right in the face of a...mouse. Thea reached slowly for a jar, and dumped the buttons it held on the bed, the mouse motionless, watching her the whole time.

Thea crouched. And slammed the jar over the mouse.

"You got it, Mom!" both boys yelled. She pushed the lid under the jar and screwed it on tight.

"What are you going to do with it, Mom?"

"I think I'll give it to the cat."

"No! It's too cute! Don't give it to the cat...please!"

"All right, I'll let it go outside."

She walked toward the outhouse, the boys following close. Halfway there, she bent down, unscrewed the lid, and let the mouse go. Chomp! The cat appeared, the mouse disappeared. One less country mouse.

❧

Jacob was a bright boy academically, but not socially. He had been held back a year to be part of a class called Transition, allowing him another year to mature before moving on. Once back on track in first grade, he was invited to join the gifted class. There he was given a report assignment that turned out to be pretty tough. He wanted to back out, but we said, "If you do this, you can have anything you want. Just ask, and it's yours."

We couldn't explain any further, because we weren't kidding. He had asked for a bicycle for his birthday, but we just didn't have the money.

Thea said, "We need to figure out how to start saving money to get a new bicycle, because that's what he's going to ask for. He's outgrown his old one."

Jacob persevered to finish his assignment, so after school on the day he turned it in, Thea asked him, "What do you want?"

Thea said she could see the wheels turning as Jacob worked up the nerve to make his big request.

"Can I have a donut from the Judy Jane bakery?"

"What!" she blurted.

Thea said Jacob looked sheepish, like he'd said something wrong.

"Really? That's all you want? A donut from the bakery?"

He paused. "Yeah. Just a donut. Is that okay?"

"Of course it's okay, honey! We just expected you to ask for something different."

"Like what?"

"Let's go get that donut. Did you have anything particular in mind?"

He was timid again. "Can I have a Texas donut?"

Thea chuckled. "Their biggest donut? Yes, dear, you can have a Texas donut."

Jacob had asked before, but we'd always said no. He finally had the power to make any request, and he was not to be refused. Images of that great big donut just may have pulled him through the toughest spots in his assignment.

Later that evening, when Thea was explaining the story to me, I said, "We thought you were going to ask for a bike."

"You mean I could ask for that?"

"We did say anything."

"Wow, I never thought to ask for that." He seemed sad, like he'd missed his chance.

"Well," I said, "Maybe it was good you asked for that donut, because we're going to get you a bike anyway."

"Really?" His eyes were saucers.

Thea and I both smiled big. "Yes, Jacob, you earned more than a donut for your hard work."

"Cool! Thank you!"

Jacob rode that bike up and down the driveway for hours and hours at a time. He'd come bombing down the hill toward the house as fast as he could and stomp the brakes. The back tire would lock up, the bike would go sideways, and he'd scratch a twenty foot long skid mark in the dirt, churning up a billowing cloud of dust. Before the dust had cleared, Jacob and his big grin were already charging back up the driveway to do it again.

{ 33 }

EARLY OCTOBER, I HEARD A CAR on the edge of destruction coming down our driveway. The engine clattered like mad.

"Oh, my word, who *is* that?"

I stepped out of the house to see Thea coming down the driveway in our blue and white Suburban. She rolled up next to the house. Her window was down, she was smiling big and pretty, and she said, "Listen to this!"

She revved the engine a couple times. She was going to blow the engine then and there.

"No, don't do that!" I shouted.

Her face turned serious and she shut the car off.

"The crank bearings are failing," I said. "This rig won't last much longer and winter is coming again. We have to sell it and get another car."

"Let's sell it to Del," Thea said. "He'll buy anything."

"Yeah, it's true. He loves collecting junk."

I called Del and told him about the Suburban. He was thrilled, even as he heard it clattering violently under the hood.

"So, now we have to buy something else," I said.

"Not 'something else,'" Thea said. "We're buying an Isuzu Trooper, remember?"

"Yes, dear."

We drove the Land Cruiser over the mountains a few weeks later and stopped at the Skippers in north Seattle on 145th and Aurora. It was pouring down rain—typical Western Washington. As we stepped out of the car to go inside for some fish and chips, Thea and I looked at one another, stunned.

"It's so loud." I said.

"It's so loud!" Thea echoed.

We weren't used to the traffic noise. Our wilderness experience had really taken hold. After fish and chips we continued on to Thea's parents' place. When I parked, I said to Thea, "You know, the steering's acting weird. It feels wobbly."

I looked underneath, and then stepped back to see the car from directly in front. The driver's side front tire leaned in at the top, and angled out at the bottom. What the heck? I pushed and pulled the top of the tire, and it moved back and forth more than an inch.

I marveled to Thea, "Wow, we drove across Stevens Pass like that."

"God was right there with us. He knew what was going on, and He took care of us."

"Yes, He did. I'm taking it to Tenny's Toyota. They do good work, and I don't have the tools for this."

I hopped back in the rig and drove it all the way from Edmonds to 110th and Lake City Way, almost ten miles.

"You drove over here like this?" asked the guy at the dealership.

"Is it that bad?"

"The knuckle bearings are shot on both sides. The wheels could have fallen off and your whole rig could've rolled off the road."

Thea's dad had followed us there, and he took us the rest of the way north to Harris Ford-Isuzu in south Everett to look at the new Troopers.

"Ooh, look at that sweet little rig!" It was bright shiny red with a fat strip of chrome for the rocker panel.

"Wow, they're fancier than I remember," Thea said. It was an '86—among the first arrivals at the end of 1985—brand spanking new!

Somehow we were approved for the payments, and we drove away in the first new car we'd ever bought. It had the new car smell and everything!

Days later we picked up my Land Cruiser from the dealer. It was an inexpensive and simple fix, and we drove back across the mountains to the Quiet Side.

ᆭ

Back in Chelan, we had finished harvest at the school orchard, the one that had been let go. We didn't expect much of a crop, but the few apples we had looked nice.

"I've enjoyed working with you," I said to Steve, Mettler's foreman. "But I'm going to take a job at the lumberyard."

"That's fine, Jim. Now that we got it cleaned up, we're probably going to sell it."

I started work at the lumberyard, and right away I noticed the heaps of scrap lumber they had. Customers often

{ 297 }

cut their lumber at the yard with our radial arm and table saws because they didn't have them at home, so there were end pieces and long thin strips of all shapes and sizes just lying in heaps among the piles of sawdust. *Man, a guy could burn that in his stove!*

I asked the boss one day if he did anything special with the scrap lumber, or if I could have it, and he said, "Take it! Take it all! Just get it out of here, I don't care."

"Thanks, Edd! Winter's comin'."

I brought in an apple bin and asked the customers who were using the saws to pitch their scraps into the bin. When the bin was full, I would load it into the back of Paul's pickup with a forklift and unload it into at the house. I made a huge pile.

I brought home all the twisted and broken lumber— even if it was full size, we couldn't sell it. I brought pallets home, too, load after load after load. We weren't going to have to worry about firewood for a while, but still I brought home more. You can never have too much wood with winters like ours. The fire had already been burning for months, and it wasn't even Christmas yet.

৪৪৯

The well had been drilled five months before, but I still hadn't had time to plumb the house. We had a garden hose attached to a spigot at the top of the well, and we would fill our water jugs right at the back door. It was so much nicer than hiking down to the spring to contend with giardia and cougars.

Sometimes, though, we made rookie mistakes. We didn't always drain the hose, or drain it well, and any water still left in the hose would freeze. I would have to use the little bit of water we still had left, or get some from right at the well, and heat it up in the kettle. I would pour the boiling water on the hose, starting at one end, and walking down the hose's length, to melt the ice. When I could blow through the hose, I knew it was ready to use. I didn't let the hose freeze often, but every now and then, it just slipped my mind.

⊂᙭ᔓ⊃

As the real cold of winter approached, it seemed Earnest's little shack was warmer than our big cabin, and since she was getting older, Clowd would spend more and more of her time down there with her buddy Levi. That bothered me and I went to get her several times. She must have been losing her hearing, as she wouldn't even react when I'd call her.

Clowd was getting old, pushing fifteen years, but one day in December, the day we trooped into the woods to find our Christmas tree, she seemed to have much more energy than usual. She bounded through the snow wagging her tail and wearing the biggest dog smile on her face. It reminded me of that time with Santo, taking turns running through the snow.

We bundled up the kids and towed the sled up the hill to find just the right tree. Clowd had been right with us, but as we rounded the far corner, I noticed she had lagged behind. I didn't think much of it at the time.

We found the perfect tree, cut it down, and put it on the sled to drag back home. We walked toward home, and I spotted her lying in the middle of our snow-covered driveway. She was lying on her side, her feet pointed up-hill. I felt sick. I called out to her. She didn't move. She had died.

I took her down by the shed to bury her, and the ground was so frozen solid I couldn't scratch the dirt, let alone dig a hole. I hid her under a tree hoping it would thaw soon so I could bury my little dog. Snow fell for three more months and we couldn't bury her until the spring. It prolonged the sadness.

I had lost my best friend. She had given me so many fond memories and so many years of loyal companionship.

{ 34 }

THE FELLOW WHO PLAYED SCROOGE in *A Christmas Carol* the year before worked for KOZI, the local radio station. He wanted to do the play again—as a musical. He wanted me to be a caroler, so I sang "Joy to the World" as I strolled the streets of London. It was easy for me because I had no lines to learn and just sang one song, but I still had fun. Again the community thronged and the critics raved.

Cora Hartley had been teaching me for months. After New Year's, full group Bach Fest rehearsals began. There was a lot to learn.

◌჆ᎦᎥᏇ

A neighbor bought a plow and said he would maintain Open Road. But he would only plow one blade wide, right from the beginning.

I had said, "You can't do it like that. You need to start three blades wide—down the middle plus a whole blade width on each side. It'll get to the point where you can't push the snow anywhere. It will slide up the berm on each side, and then right in behind you. You'll end up with a road four feet wide at the bottom of a snowy V. You have to go as wide as possible from the start. Get out into the field."

"Too much time, too much gas," he said. "Too much wear and tear on my rig."

We had driven over for a visit and the road was so narrow the tires kept sucking us into the bank. Just like I warned. He might have been able to salvage it, but he didn't want to hear it.

"What's the point of plowing the road if you're not going to do it right?" I asked. "Open Road is nearly closed, and we're not halfway through the season."

"I'm not going to do it. I just won't plow Open Road."

"Okay, we won't plow Open Road either."

Thea said, "If you want to come see us, you'll have to go all the way out to the Loop road and then down and back up Sawmill."

"Eh," he said, and shrugged his shoulders.

Sure, enough, he used the temporarily convenient one-blade-wide method for his own long driveway, and about half-way through the season, he had to ask for help from Ken with his blower.

ೲೲ

We didn't like to travel with the crowds, so we tried to avoid crossing the mountains on the holidays. We waited until after the New Year to make Christmas and New Year's visits to my mom and to Thea's parents.

"All my canned goods are going to freeze," Thea said with some despair as we drove away from the cabin.

I don't know how much she thought about that while we were on the west side, but when we returned to the house, we found out she was right. The jars were split and cracked and shattered. Only a few survived. The food within them would have to be eaten quickly after it thawed, or it would spoil and be wasted. Thea had spent endless hours canning that food for us.

"I'm sorry, dear," I said, "I'll look for a propane floor furnace. We should be able to set the thermostat at fifty degrees, and keep the house from freezing, even while we're gone."

I found a nice rectangular unit about two feet by four feet and marked the spot on the floor, just about smack dab in the middle of the first floor. *Measure twice, cut once.* I double checked my marks and made the cut. I removed the insulation and cut the plywood beneath. I slid the unit into the hole. Everything was perfect at first, but one of the corners hit a pier block.

I pulled the heater back out of the hole and looked at my obstacle. The hole was already made, and it really was in the right place up top, so I had one option. I fetched my rock hammer and started whacking away at the pier block. Little chips of cement flaked off. I finally carved away enough cement that the furnace dropped neatly into the hole. *That wasn't so bad.*

We used the furnace a lot after that. We kept the thermostat at fifty when we were downtown at work and it was so nice to come home with the house above freezing. We couldn't even see our breath anymore!

"Just like downtown!" I crowed.

Thea was a little less enthusiastic. "We're still camping, just camping in a house, is all."

Thea was always budget-conscious when shopping for food. She made every piece of meat go for two dinners, and she would only buy what was on sale. If it was ground beef, she'd make a meatloaf that would last two nights. She was most happy when chicken was on sale. With one whole chicken we had a great chicken dinner the first night, leftovers the second night, and then soup on the third.

One of Thea's memorable breakfasts came from Golden Florins, also known as Bear Foods, the health food store downtown. She would soak wheat berries in water overnight, and cook them the next morning. She would toast coconut and toast almonds, and sprinkle them on top with a splash of milk. We didn't even need to add any sugar. Thea smiled with every bite—she loved the crunch and the texture.

❧

I was driving my Land Cruiser to the lumber yard daily, and using it to plow. I'd replaced the original engine when the block cracked with a low-mileage four-bolt 350 V8, and it had started to make a faint clattering sound. It needed to come out, but it wasn't as bad as the Suburban. I figured I could replace the engine, save it, and rebuild it when we could afford it.

Talley sold me another 350 to make the swap. I rigged a stout pole to the top log at the back of the house, then lashed a vertical pole at the other end. It would support the weight of the engine. I swept two feet of snow away from the Land Cruiser so I could work. An old chain-fall, tied to the pole over-head, lifted the motor. My hands ached in the cold, but I had no choice and worked into the night, finally extracting the old motor. I installed the new motor the next day, first shoveling the snow that had fallen overnight. By evening, it was in and running. Back in business.

The experience motivated me to build a carport so we could park out of the snow. I cut seven log rafters and bolted them to the back of the house. A friend from the lumberyard helped me place support poles under the rafters. The footings were coffee cans filled with concrete, a short piece of rebar sticking up, anchoring the poles.

I nailed 2 x 4 purlins on edge every twenty-four inches across the rafters. It got dark early, so I worked several nights biting a small flashlight to keep both hands free. Finally, I nailed down some metal roofing that nearly matched the house.

Parking under the roof was great, allowing me a place to work on projects out of the weather. There was even room to stack our firewood. I walled off one end with a pair of eight foot-square cabana windows and blocked the wind and drifting snow.

CS❧SO

In early February, 1986, Halley's Comet was big news. We joined the St. Louises and the Hills for a comet viewing dinner party.

We stared into the clear black sky filled with stars at the bright blue blob that was the comet. Mike St. Louise said to Jacob, "I saw Halley's comet when I was your age." Jacob's eyes widened. Mike was eighty-two years old. Jacob was seven.

"That means I'll be as old as you when it comes around again." Jacob said. He had been studying the comet in school, and he'd come home quoting stats every day.

Mike smiled big in the darkness. "That's right. You and I are the only ones here who get to see the comet twice."

೧೪ഇ౦

Springtime, I upgraded the sawhorse kitchen counter. I screwed a piece of three-quarter plywood to a custom 2 x 4 frame. A contractor I'd met at the lumber yard had showed me how to glue Formica and finish the edge. I installed a salvaged stainless steel sink and connected the drain plumbing with a P-trap to the crawl space main drain.

Thea was happy to have a real counter. She washed dishes in a big stainless bowl on the stove, rinsed them in another, and dumped the water down the sink when she was done. Just like downtown...almost.

Shortly after, I dug a ditch from the well to the house—forty feet. The ditch came across the north, shady

{ 306 }

side of the house. Digging was easy until about two feet, where the dirt got hard—it was still frozen! I broke through after another foot, but dug one more to ensure the pipes wouldn't freeze. The pipe came up under the house near the back door. Several layers of insulation wrapped the pipe in the crawlspace.

I plumbed the house with copper, soldering a T a foot off the floor. One leg supplied the kitchen sink, the other went up and over the back door and into the bathroom, near the ceiling. The camper's propane demand water heater sent hot water to a shower head—it was our only source of flowing hot water. We were tickled to have an easier way to bathe, and even cold water in the kitchen was a step up. Thea could warm it on the stove for dishes and cooking.

☙❧

We both worked downtown, so during summer we needed someone to watch the boys. Fortunately, we could hire responsible girls from families on the hill. One morning, having left the boys at home with Jenny, we spotted a big black critter on the road below our house—a black bear. We'd seen tracks, but never the animal. We drove forward slowly, hoping to push him down the road, away from our boys.

I had taught Jacob how to move slowly and silently through the woods, stepping under small twigs and sticks that could snap and give away his presence. He could sneak within a few feet of chipmunks before they knew he was there. Would he try to sneak up on a bear?

The bear trotted down the road in front of us, then dashed sideways, uphill toward the house. We raced downtown where Thea called Jenny and warned her not to let the boys outside. The boys weren't happy confined to the house, but kept their noses pressed against the windows, hoping to see the bear. The bear never appeared, but the boys would have been safe if it had.

C3ED

I had always wanted horses, and Thea told me Del, from the clinic, had a horse for sale—or trade. I didn't have much for trade, but I did have the camper, though we'd stripped it clean. We'd taken out the water tank, water heater, stove, toilet, lights and refrigerator—it was essentially a shell. Del was thrilled.

Del wanted that camper so badly he traded us two horses for it. I didn't actually want the second horse, because it wasn't even a horse, but a rotund Shetland pony with a sour attitude.

Del said, "If you take Bimbo, you have to take Lance." Bimbo was the real horse. Too bad he didn't come with a real name. He was a long-legged, good looking Arab. He actually belonged to Del's wife, Joy. She wasn't riding anymore and wanted us to have her horse.

"Oh, all right," I said. "We'll take 'em."

Lance must have felt the rejection, because he snorted and stomped and shied away from the beginning, like some sort of diva. He kept to himself in the corral, which was fine by me. Bimbo was more approachable—he was a good trade for that stripped-out camper.

Thea was eager to ride Bimbo. She had ridden once a long time ago, and though it scared her, she wanted to try again. I was working in the carport when she yelled, "Look at me! I'm riding Bimbo!"

Sure enough—she had climbed up on the chicken coop and straddled Bimbo bare-back. She was turning him back and forth across the corral with just the lead rope.

I had been a farrier and had dealt with some rank horses, so I was concerned. She came back around to the chicken house and climbed off. "That was fun!" she exclaimed.

"I'll need to trim his feet if you're going to ride him."

But he didn't want me near. He kept away, and even when I finally grabbed his foot, he would not settle down. Thea saw the struggle. "Just a second," she said. "Let me try something."

She came back with a bottle of Estee Lauder perfume: "Your handkerchief, please." She spritzed it twice, and tucked it into my back pocket. Bimbo settled right down and cooperated from then on.

Thea said, "He was a lady's horse. He likes a lady's smell."

Once I had trimmed Bimbo's feet, Thea wanted to ride again. I wasn't sure what would happen next, and didn't want her to get hurt. I was sure a halter was not the proper way to control a horse. I placed a running martingale head stall with reins on Bimbo's nose. The reins ran through a pair of rings attached to the saddle pad cinch. Bimbo was agitated, pacing and twirling.

Thea climbed on while I held the reins. I turned him loose—he stepped twice and started bucking. Two mighty bucks and Thea came off. She landed hard on her rear—thump! I heard a crack. Bimbo bucked a few more times, then just quit and stood there staring.

I helped Thea stand. She hurt! She had broken her tailbone, and sat on a round donut support for several months. She was done with horses.

∞

Bach Fest 1986, the first year we sang opera, we planned a single, short Leipzig mass at the Methodist Church to check the community's receptivity. There were nightly instrumental performances all week, and we sang Saturday night. I was a principal. We rehearsed in different basement rooms for different performances. Each room had either musicians or singers practicing their music. I was honored to be involved with such a talented group of people. Sharon, my boss at the lumberyard, sang also—she was an excellent classical soprano.

One night, coming home from rehearsing for the Bach Fest, I had a serious fright. My headlights projected horizontally into the trees for a beat before shining down Roller Coaster. As my lights illuminated the road, a massive owl swooped in from above. His wing span exceeded the Land Cruiser's width. He came out of nowhere. He skimmed the top of the hood, and soared down the road in front of me just above my lights. I watched his head turn left and right—scanning for prey? He didn't plunge after anything, but sailed off into the night.

I was looking for him the second night, but I was still startled when he dropped in. I was able to get a better look at him, and based on the bird guide, and the big feather tufts on his head, I figured he was a Great Horned Owl. On the third night I was able to enjoy hunting with him, even though we didn't get anything. I looked forward to that part of my drive home. He flew with me for many nights.

{ 35 }

I MET A LOT OF FINE PEOPLE while I worked at the lumberyard. An old guy used to come in and we'd chat about horses. I mentioned how much I enjoyed horses, but that I didn't have a lot of experience.

He said, "Well, I have a horse for sale. It's an old Quarter Horse. She's excellent. We used her to round up cattle, and she knows how to work her way through the brush. She has a lot of experience. So, for a guy that doesn't, she's the perfect horse."

"I'd like to take a look," I said. So Thea and I went out after work one day.

"Her name is Cricket," he said.

"Nice horse," we said. I'd earned certification as a farrier, but I hadn't ridden a horse since my youth. She seemed docile.

He said, "I've got this old saddle. I was going to give it to the tavern so they could hang it in the rafters. If you want it, I'll throw it in with the horse."

"You've got a deal," I said.

I learned in time that the saddle did not fit the horse—it was too narrow. I don't know if he knew. I'm pretty sure it wasn't the saddle he used. I didn't know a saddle had to fit the horse, so I put it on her and rode anyway. I had to cinch it extra tight or it would slip side to side.

Cricket was a barrel of a horse with a nice round body, and I was using this deep gullet, narrow tree saddle.

Luke sometimes rode with me, sitting behind me on Cricket's rump, gripping my waist. A couple times he fell off, but Luke was like a little cat. Once, we rode straight up the hill out of the valley instead of following the draw, and Cricket balked.

I coaxed her. "C'mon, we're going up the hill." She lunged up the hill. Luke's grip failed. I looked behind as he rolled backward, his head hitting her tail, his legs splayed up in the air. He kept rolling through the air as he fell, and he landed on his feet. He was five years old.

◌჻◌

A young man named Michael Landon ran the lumberyard that Edd owned in Waterville. He came by regularly and once mentioned he was looking for a pony for his kids.

"You know anyone with a pony?" he asked me.

"We have a black and white Shetland, but he's a real stinker. I don't think your kids would like him."

"Oh, he can't be *that* bad."

"If you come get him, he's yours—free."

"Deal!"

Michael fetched Lance the next week and took him home in the back of his pickup. It was over a month before he was back at the Manson lumberyard. The more time went by, the more I relaxed. If Lance had been horrible for them, surely I would've heard about it sooner than later.

He came to find me and was all smiles. He said, "That horse is just the best thing my kids could have ever had. They love him, he loves them. They ride him all the time, all over the place. Thanks so much for giving us that horse!"

"You bet, Michael. That's great news. I'm happy you're happy."

ᏣᏕᏚᏃ

Later that summer, Bimbo started losing weight. We couldn't get enough food in him. His ribs showed clearly, his hips poked up against his hide. He even started to lose hair.

"I don't like this," I said to Thea. "Something is wrong, and we don't have the money for a vet bill. I'm going to see if I can sell him to the meat packer guys."

The guy drove his truck up to our place, and raised his eyebrows when he saw Bimbo. "Whoa, that's a rough-looking horse."

"Yeah, he's been losing weight for a while now," I said. "We haven't changed his diet at all."

He said, "He may have eaten some bailing twine. That'll wreck a horse."

I had always made a point to be careful, but I was even more so after Bimbo. It only takes once.

Bimbo sold for $75 at the auction.

ᏣᏕᏚᏃ

{ 315 }

We were down to one horse now, and the pasture seemed empty. Cricket needed a friend. Again through the lumberyard I heard about a pair of horses up for sale—Ebony and Moon. Ebony was a black Quarter Horse-Morgan, short to the shoulder, and with a short back—she was friendly and gentle and easy—and untrained.

Moon was the great granddaughter of Prince Plaudit, and he was the poster boy best leopard Appaloosa in the world. Ever. Moon had much of his look, minus the spots. But her conformation—all her proportions were fantastic. Her gaskins, the muscles in her back legs, were enormous, giving her racecar acceleration—dig and go! She was the greatest looking horse I'd ever seen up close.

Even in a horse, looks aren't everything. Moon was not well trained—and neither was I. She had such great potential, but I was too green. I rode her only once. We were at the far corner of the pasture, walking down the hill toward the corral—a gentle slope. She accelerated from a walk to a trot to a lope, and my heart raced.

I pulled back on the reins, but she resisted and shook her head, gaining speed.

Oh, oh, oh! I'm gettin' off!

I bailed. I didn't fall, but I got off and ran beside her. I held onto the reins and pulled her back around. *Oh my gosh, that was such a scare. I need to learn more before I can ride Moon.*

Cricket was so much easier to ride. Just climb on and go for hours. Once, we were gone for twelve hours. On the way back home, we came across a field near Lee Howe's place. Cricket stopped. She wouldn't budge.

"C'mon, you dang horse. What are you doing?" She stopped in the middle of the field. I gave her a little kick and surged in my saddle. Nothing.

I looked at the ground. Cricket's legs were tangled in a mess of barbed wire.

I scrambled off in a panic. *She's going to freak out!*

{ 36 }

SHE WAS THE PICTURE OF PATIENCE. She looked at me as if to say, "Would you just undo me?"

I picked up her foot and slipped off the first coil. I went to the other side and pulled out her other foot. She stood still the whole time. She wasn't even nicked. I climbed back on and she picked her way through the remaining two strands of wire. That was that and off we went. I patted the side of her neck and smiled big.

☙❧

One big reason for having horses was to use them for hunting. We could cover more ground and, from the back of a horse, I wouldn't sound, smell or look like a man. As the air began to bite with chill in the fall, I was overcome with the urge to go hunting. I needed to get out into the woods and bring home some meat for my family.

Cricket and I rode out toward an area we called the Bowl. It was above and behind the Church Camp, no-man's land. We weren't even in the area I considered prime when I saw four bucks all at the same time. The first was on the slope right in front of me, about seventy-five yards away. There was another buck on the next ridge over, about two hundred yards away, and then there were two bucks standing together the top of the far ridge above Church Camp, a little over a quarter mile away.

{ 319 }

Look at all these deer!

The first buck saw me and dropped over the back side of the ridge. I lost sight of the other three when I tried to follow the first one. By the time I cleared the ridge and could see again, they were all gone. I don't know where they went—up or down, left or right.

Later in the day we came across a set of huge tracks. The toes were splayed out and in the back were two big old dew claw marks. *Wow, where is that guy?* We saw many more tracks out there, but you can't eat deer tracks.

I went back out the next day, stopping to sit and look from a hillside above the Bowl. It was a good view. I was just sitting there, taking it easy, scanning the brush, enjoying the sights and the smells and the quiet. Down the slope, a coyote was trotting up the hill towards me. He was sniffing around, exploring, looking, hunting. *I could shoot me a coyote!... I'll just watch a little longer...* I imagined him mumbling to himself as he trotted along: *There's some chipmunk tracks, but the wife says we can't eat tracks. Where's them doggone chipmunks?*

He came directly up the hill to within fifty yards, then turned left and disappeared. I had watched him at least five minutes. *This is so cool. I'm seeing wild animals out here, watching this coyote sniff around, check under logs, in the brush, looking for something to eat.* I didn't get a deer that day, but I had fun in the fresh air with the critters.

ᘓᘔᘓ

Joe Collins, the County Sherriff, said the County was hiring deputies. "You'd probably do fine as a deputy. But you can't have a beard." I was okay with work at the lumberyard, but I was also curious about other opportunities, so I shaved my beard on the day of the written test.

Thea said, "The boys might not recognize you without your beard. They should watch when you shave it off."

Jacob stood between the tub and the toilet. Thea and Luke sat together on the toilet. They were looking at my left side as I trimmed my beard close with the clippers. I lathered up with shaving foam and took it down to the hide. I kept my mustache.

I finished and turned to face the family with a big smile. Jacob's eyes widened. Luke burst into tears and started squalling.

"It's okay, honey," Thea tried to reassure him. "That's your daddy. He just shaved his beard off for a job interview."

"That's not my daddy!" he shouted through sobs.

I went in for the interview, and there was a nurse on the board. She stiffened and glared when I said I was a friend of Joe. She tore into me hard with technical questions meant for an experienced deputy.

"You don't know much about this job, do you?" she asked. *Was I imagining her German accent?*

I said, "Well, I'm not a trained deputy, if that's what you're getting at. I'm here to learn. I've been a logger, I've been a machinist, managed an orchard, the lumberyard. I built a log house with my own hands. I learned those jobs, I can learn this one."

"Thanks for your time," she said. "You'll hear from us soon."

I left the interview pretty sure that, if they did bother to contact me, the answer would be "no," but I was okay with that. Even as they asked the questions, I realized that to be a deputy required the kind of aggressiveness I just didn't have.

So I let the beard grow back. First and last time I ever shaved.

One fall day, Luke had a day off school, so I brought him to work with me.

"You know, my dad doesn't like you," Luke said to Hank. Luke was five years old.

Geez, Luke! Do you see how big he is? Hank had been a bouncer and bail skip enforcer. He pursued and retrieved the roughest criminals who'd skipped without paying bail.

"What's he mean?" Hank asked, his brows furrowed.

"Oh, I don't know. Probably I had a bad day."

"Oh, okay." Hank's tone of voice said he believed me, but he frowned and turned away like he knew better.

Luke was right, but I hadn't said it in so many words. Or so few, I suppose. I often complained about him at dinner. Hank was big and strong, but slow and unmotivated. He was disorganized, didn't care, and spent most of his time yacking with customers instead of filling their orders. The actual work was left to me, and I scrambled to make it happen.

I turned Hank in one day. He was a talker, and he grew up in the area, so he knew a lot of the orchardists, and especially the guys our age. They were the sons of the original orchardists. They were taking on more responsibility.

One of them came in, a friend of Hank's, and he was parked in his pickup down by the finished lumber. He and Hank were standing side by side, leaning on the bed of the pickup, just talking. He wasn't loading lumber, he wasn't doing anything. I waited on five customers, and Hank didn't move.

I went in to Edd and said, "Doggone it! I am out there busting my tail, and Hank is leaning on a pickup. Look out your door right now. He's talking with Robert. He's been there for fifteen or twenty minutes. I've helped five customers, and he's been jawing the whole time."

Edd said, "All right, I'll take care of it."

I don't know what he ever said to Hank, Hank did maybe work a little harder, or something—I don't really remember, it wasn't extreme. He just lost interest in the lumberyard.

"Edd gave us a raise today," Hank said a few months later.

"Oh, yeah?"

"Yeah, 25 cents an hour."

"We both got the same raise?" I asked.

{ 323 }

"Well, yeah," he replied, as if no other possibility never crossed his mind.

I went in and I asked to Edd, "What's the deal with the raises?"

"What do you mean? I gave you 25 cents."

"You gave Hank 25 cents, too. Are you thinking we work the same? Is that what you see? That I and he are putting out the same kind of effort here?"

"Well..."

"Do you want me to come down to his level? I can sure do that. Or do you want him to have an incentive to come up? If he wants a raise he needs to put out a little more work."

"For the next raise, we'll reevaluate."

And he did. For the next raise, I got 50 cents, and Hank got nothing.

"I didn't get a raise this time," Hank said to me, an accusing tone in his voice, like it was my fault, "but I hear you did."

"Yeah, well, I worked pretty hard to get it," I said, poorly concealing my irritation.

"I'll work harder when they pay me more."

That's not how it works, man.

Customers from the whole valley knew me, seeking me for help. I'd help with windows, help with doors, anything that required understanding details. Hank was helpful on sheetrock deliveries. He could carry two sheets of five-eighths 4 x 8 at once, even two sheets of half-inch 4 x 12.

⊄⊅

"Shing, shing, shing." Sleigh bells. It was Christmas Eve, 1986.

"Jacob, did you hear that?"

Jacob looked at the radio. It was off. He looked at me, confused. *Where did that sound come from?*

{ 37 }

A KNOCK ON THE DOOR. A man's voice: "Ho, ho, ho! Merry Christmas!"

I opened the door, and it was Santa Claus—red suit, white beard, the real deal. The boys' mouths fell open.

"Ho, ho, ho! I hear you've been good little boys."

They were speechless, eyes wide, hands limp at their sides, staring. Santa handed a pair of gloves to Jacob, and a pair to Luke. They could barely raise their hands to accept the gloves.

Santa said, "Now I have other places to go, but I wanted to make a special appearance to meet you boys, because I heard you've been so good." He left as quickly as he'd come.

The boys stood frozen in place.

I said, "Let's go outside and see where his sleigh is. Maybe we can see him leave in the sleigh." They moved like robots, and when we reached the door to peek outside in the darkness, he was already gone.

They were meager, those first Christmases. We did get some toys given to us to give to the boys, and we tried to make the holidays special. We were just happy to be alive.

છાસ્૦

Jacob and I found rooster George with a broken leg one morning in January while we were feeding the chickens and horses. I told Thea when I came back to the house.

"His leg is broken?" Her face showed alarm. "How did that happen? Where is he now?"

"I think a horse stepped on him. Maybe he was hanging out under a grain bucket?"

"Well, he'll live, right? If we take care of him?"

"Yes, I think he should heal up just fine. I nestled him into a bed in the hay, and gave him some food and water in a bowl. We'll check on him when we get home from work."

Thea bolted for the hay shed as soon as we came home that evening. It had been a cold day, and George's water bowl had frozen. She brought it back to the house, knocked the ice out, and added fresh water for him.

Thea maintained her vigil for six weeks, keeping George fed and watered. I think she enjoyed being able to get so close to the little red bird. His leg healed with a funny bend, but it was okay, and he lived for many more years, much to Thea's delight.

While Thea tended to her special charge, Jacob and I each had ours. I gave the horses hay in the morning and hay and grain in the evenings. Jacob came out with me in the mornings and filled a nine-by-nine pan with layer crumble. One chicken used to jump to the pan's edge, pecking the food before Jacob dumped it out. One morning the chicken jumped to the pan, then to Jacob's face, scratching him with her nasty claws.

I grabbed the chicken and drop kicked it. It went sailing over the top of a small tree, squalling and flapping. *Don't ever do that again, you dang chicken!* Attacking my kid? Animals need to have some respect.

I didn't want my boy to be afraid of chickens, either, so he continued feeding them, but kept them off the pan. It all worked out.

෫෫෫

It was time to frame the upstairs rooms. I established the boys' rooms with an eight foot-high wall along the centerline of the north side. I framed the hall wall with door openings, making the rooms twelve feet square, including closets. The hall wall on the south side enclosed the master bedroom, twelve by twenty. I installed a ceiling over the boys' rooms and the hall, which made the attic floor. The attic opened to the master bedroom, which was left open to the peak—spacious.

A lumberyard customer, a log home contractor, always ordered more finish boards than necessary to be able to choose the best. He'd bring back the unused boards for a refund. For one project, he'd ordered some pricey 1 x 4 tongue-and-groove cedar. He returned a bunch, and since we couldn't send it back, I asked Edd to buy it at a reduced price. He agreed, so I loaded it up and took it home. I used the cedar to build the three bedroom doors, and finish the bedroom walls and stairwell. I used black wrought iron acorn-style hinges and door pulls through-out the house.

I wanted the wall boards, where they formed a corner at the log wall, to fit the logs' every unique curve. I placed fifty short copper welding rods parallel to each other and clamped them perpendicular between two 1 x 2 boards lined with a felt strip. By pressing the rod ends against the logs, letting them slide through the board clamp, a perfect pattern was formed. I transferred the pattern to the cedar, and made the cuts—a clean, tight fit. It was really coming together.

୦୫୫

In January, Jackie and Paul Volkman came up on snowmobiles to visit. Thea worked with Paul at the clinic, he was the pharmacist. We talked and laughed. They were impressed with what we'd accomplished. As they were saying goodbye, I could see Thea was distressed.

"Are you okay? What's going on?"

"My vision split. I could only see the bottom half of their faces. It's a migraine—I haven't had one for years."

The next day Thea said, "I talked to God last night for the first time since the baby died. That migraine was God saying He'd had enough of my rebellion. So I asked him to forgive me, but said I'd probably never stop asking why. I said I would accept He was the King, He was in control and knew best, but there would always be a sad little hole in my heart."

I hugged her tight.

{ 330 }

{ 38 }

PROFESSIONAL MUSICIANS JOINED US from as far away as New York for Bach Fest 1987. They were family and friends of performers who lived in Chelan. Jerry Smith lived in Chelan, his brother Karl directed music for a massive New York City church. Their dad was a music director at Pacific Lutheran, so Jerry and Karl grew up with music. Karl came to Chelan for the Bach Fest, and brought a bunch of his New York singer friends.

We lined up for rehearsal, two rows of three tenors in the back, two rows of three basses, then altos and sopranos. I was hitting a note, and Karl said, "I can't believe what I'm hearing. How long have you been singing? I've near heard of you."

"This is my third Bach Fest, and I sang in *A Christmas Carol* and the *Fiddler on the Roof.*"

"Where—New York? Seattle?"

"Ha! No, just here in Chelan."

"Seriously? You're not a professional singer?"

"No—too nervous. I'm just learning to read music."

"You're kidding!"

"Well, I need to hear you sing it once, then I can sing it, too."

"Unbelievable. You should come to New York. You could get a job tomorrow."

"Really?!"

"Oh, yeah. Absolutely. Right guys?"

His friends nodded, agreeing.

"As a matter of fact, come do Summer Stock with us. It's a series of performances in upstate New York all through the summer."

"What?!"

Anne, who reminded me of Bette Midler and had been a principal on Broadway, said, "We could keep you busy— you could make some *moneeeey*!"

"Really?"

"Oh, yeah, honey."

I just wasn't aware. I'd been singing like that my whole life. The cool part is I was having fun—I wasn't so nervous anymore.

I talked to Thea about being invited to sing in New York, and she said, "Let's go! Let's go for a summer, for two summers, whatever."

"But I don't want that life. I'm right in the middle of my log house project. I don't want to just up and leave. Rehearsing takes so much time. I'd never see you guys. I'd be on the road all the time. That's not what I want to do with my life. We're staying here. I'll sing in the Bach Fest because I'm really having fun, but when it's over, I'm still going to be building my log house."

 CSSO

I was riding Cricket way out on the east side of Sawmill, past Nelly Springs, back over the ridge, almost looking down on Washington Creek. I'd been out there hunting all day long, and saw tracks, but never any game. The light faded as the sun settled down behind the highest peaks—another hour and it'd be dark.

Doggone it, I never saw a dang critter all day long... there's one right there!

I kept riding over the little hill to be out of the deer's sight. I tied Cricket off to a bush, grabbed my .30-30 and snuck back to the crest of the hill. I saw the deer—a beautiful four-point, a young buck. He wasn't a big old man, but a good-sized four-by-four mule deer, just as pretty as he could be. He was moving cautiously, stopping to look around and make sure it was all cool before he took his next step.

This is it!

So I aimed my gun and pulled the trigger.

Boom!

The deer was standing where I left him. He looked left, looked right, looked ahead.

Where did the dang bullet go? I was shooting right at him. I was probably sixty yards away is all.

Boom!

He kept searching.

I was so close, and he was at the business end of the muzzle—it had to have been loud, but he didn't spook and run off.

Well, this is cool, at least he's not running off, but where am I hitting? I don't even know where the bullets are going!

Boom!

I saw a puff of dust at least fifteen feet to his left. I looked down at my rifle, and my sight was rolled way over to the side, probably a quarter of an inch off. I think I'm aiming right at him, but the rifle is really pointing way off to the side.

I can't believe it.

I pushed it back, just eyeballed it to the middle of the rifle barrel, and shot again.

Boom!

The bullet hit the ground right between his front legs, and that's when he jumped and ran. He had been quartering away from me slightly. I had one more round, but he was out of sight and gone. He got away. But he was pretty. It was just cool to be so near such a fine animal.

I looked down the hill to Cricket after I made the four shots, and she was just standing there eating grass as if nothing were going on. An excellent horse, nothing freaked her out. She taught me a ton, because at first I didn't know what I was doing.

{ 39 }

OZ WOLFBERG WAS ANOTHER INTERESTING person I met at the lumberyard. He was a retired clock maker to the stars from Malibu, California. He fixed clocks for all the famous people you could talk about. He knew them well. Little grey-haired guy. His wife's name was Zoe.

Oz took a shine to me right away. He'd come into the lumberyard because he knew Edd. In fact, he was instrumental in getting Edd the True Value franchise—he knew somebody who knew somebody, some big shot.

When Oz and Zoe moved to Chelan for retirement, Zoe got involved with the community right away, and Oz wanted a hobby. He was going to make little wooden trinkets to sell at local gift shops. He had been an artistic bricklayer. He made patterned, curving sidewalks or walks that turned to form a wall. As he got older, he just wanted to stay busy.

He bought a teeny little table saw, a teeny little bandsaw, and a teeny little drill press. He said to me, "I don't know how to set 'em up. Can you come help me? At lunch time maybe, or after work sometime?"

"Of course." So I helped him set them up, made sure they were cutting square, and showed him how to work the height and the angles. He often showed up at lunch and said, "Let's get lunch. I'm buying." He'd talk about life in Malibu, and being a bricklayer and clock maker.

"Now don't tell my wife. I'm having some bacon and eggs. I got cholesterol real bad."

"So you're not supposed to eat that?"

"Just don't tell her. She's not going to find out otherwise. So if she finds out, I'll know who told her."

"Oz, I will not say a word to her about it. I can keep a secret."

Many times we didn't go out to lunch. He'd say, "Come to the house. Zoe will be home, we'll feed you lunch, and you can show me some more stuff on my little machines." I parked at the bottom of their driveway the first couple of times I came to visit. The second time I pulled in, Zoe came out. "Could you not park right there? I'm going to have to leave before you do. Could you just pull ahead, pull past our driveway?"

"Sure thing."

I had lunch with Oz a few more times, on occasional Wednesdays or Thursdays. We'd sit around and chat, fiddle with his machines, or I'd help him move some heavier items. I think he just wanted company.

My lunch was about an hour long, from noon to 1:00 PM. Edd and Sharon liked Oz, too, so if I was a little late, I'd explain: "I was out to lunch with Oz." It was never a problem.

"Psst! Come here." Sandy Gruenberg worked at the lumberyard, and she called me over one day.

"What's up?"

"Are you having an affair with Renee?"

"Renee who?"

"Your Toyota has been seen in Renee's driveway a lot lately, around noon."

"No. Who told you that? I've been at Oz's house, that's where Oz lives."

"Well, Pam, the girl who lives below Oz saw your car there several times at lunch time."

"Oh, did she?"

"Renee has a reputation, you know."

"I didn't. I've been at Oz's house. You can ask him. This is just blowing me away this even came up."

"Well, Pam just keeps saying she's seeing your car at Renee's driveway."

"So Renee's house is the one straight ahead? I park a hundred and fifty feet from her house."

"How did you know about Renee's Hawaiian vacation?"

"What?"

"You came in and told us about her vacation to Hawaii a couple weeks ago."

What is she even talking about?...Oh. yeah!

"Oh, jeez. We were at the grocery store, and Renee was in front of us, and she was bragging about her holiday."

I could see a look of recognition cross Sandy's face.

"Look," I said. "You can believe what you want, but there's nothing to it. It's just absolutely not true at all. I wasn't even near Renee's house, I was at Oz's house, helping him with his woodworking."

That night, lying in bed with Thea, talking, I said, "Oh, I have something to tell you before you hear it from somebody else."

Thea said, "What's that?"

"Word around town is I'm having an affair with Renee Petersen."

"Right. When do you have time to have an affair with Renee Petersen?"

"Thank you! Well, the rumor is going around, so let me tell you what's going on."

I kept visiting Oz, and I parked in the same place I'd been parking before. They could stick their rumors.

ଔଓ

Hank said to me one day, "I'm not coming in to work tomorrow. I'm going to go talk to Peebles about getting on with the police."

I came in to work and Edd was waiting. "I wonder where Hank is..."

I said, "He told me last night he's not coming in today."

"Why not? What do you mean," asked Edd.

I gave him a look—I wasn't going to lie.

"He's in town, talking to Peebles. He wants to be a police officer for Chelan."

Edd called the police. "This is Edd Lamar, can I talk to Peebles?...Hi. Is Hank there?...Can I talk to him?...Hank, this is Edd. You're fired."

Hank never talked to me again. Nor did he get the police job.

Then it was all on me at the lumberyard. It's not like I noticed much difference. There was no Hank to load sheetrock, but I managed it all by myself. I helped customers, took their orders, loaded their trucks, and made the deliveries. I came back and did it again, four or five loads a day, by myself.

{ 40 }

THE LAND CRUISER BECAME the Union Valley School Bus—the school district paid our mileage. We fit six kids in the back: Jacob and Luke, the two Forest girls, and the Caravue brother and sister. I'd drop Thea off at the clinic, and the kids would jump out too, trotting to school across the street. I'd go on to the lumberyard in Manson, eight miles up lake.

One muddy morning we slipped and slid down the hill to town, and everyone piled out at the clinic. I backed away, rolling the steering wheel left so I'd swing out right. The rig backed straight. I turned the steering wheel the other way and drove forward—straight back into the parking spot. *What's going on here? This thing won't steer!*

I climbed out and looked under the front end. The drag link was just hanging there with a broken pitman arm still attached. *If that had happened earlier, we would have driven off the road, maybe at a steep spot. Thank you, God!*

I had some tools, and removed the separated pieces of the pitman arm. I'd modified it years earlier, installing a power steering unit from a Chevy. I had torch welded the steering gear half of the Chevy pitman arm to the drag link half of the Toyota pitman arm. The weld had finally failed. The guy at the welding shop was surprised when he saw the pieces that it had lasted at all. The welding I'd done barely penetrated either piece, yet I'd been driving it like that for years. He ground a deep bevel on each piece and did it right. I believe God protected us that day.

෪෩

Thea, working as the clinic's receptionist, met people from every walk of life. One lady boasted about having five kids and no husband. Thea wondered how she made ends meet.

"I'm on welfare. I have more kids and get more money," she said. "This medical stuff is free, and we get food stamps, too."

"None of 'this medical stuff' is free," Thea said. "People like me, who work and pay taxes—we're the one who pay for your free stuff. I work all day and send my kids to a sitter. Most of my paycheck goes to child care."

The girl seemed not to care. Thea said some things she shouldn't have. Her supervisor said they couldn't allow language like that, so she'd need to find another job. It was June, and Jacob was out of school. Thea took off the rest of the summer, stopped paying a sitter, and regularly took the boys to the lake. They swam like fish and tanned chocolate brown, the sun bleaching a blonde halo in Jacob's hair.

Summer faded, the boys returned to school, and Thea pursued a job. A friend mentioned the Manson dentist was seeking an assistant. Thea applied, and her attitude impressed him. She explained about her departure from the clinic. It didn't bother him—she got the job. Her lack of dentistry experience was a plus—he could teach *his* methods.

Thea thrived at the dentist's office. She loved the work and learned quickly. She got along well with patients muted by rubber dams, instruments, Novocain, and cotton balls. The doc was hard to get along with, but she was a month older and used it to her advantage. She loved the surgeries the most and came home with gory stories and a gleam in her eye.

Our jobs put us in contact with so many Chelan Valley locals. *I know every person I pass these eight miles along the lake to work.* They knew me too, and we always waved. I liked the close-knit community.

ᚳᚱᛋᚩ

Jacob had entered fourth grade that fall. His teacher called about him one afternoon—he had written his name in permanent marker on the wall during recess. "The principal would like to meet with you about your son."

We asked Jacob about it. He said he was bored, school was too easy. We met with the principal and asked to know Jacob's test scores. The principal seemed surprised to find they were exceptional.

Thea asked, "Can we move him up a grade? Those scores are in the gifted classes. He needs more of a challenge."

"No...we wouldn't recommend that."

{ 343 }

"We'll take him out of public school, then, and enroll him in the private Baptist school."

"You wouldn't do that."

Jacob started the Baptist school's ACE program the following Monday. The curriculum allowed him to advance at his own pace, and he flourished. The program also integrated the Bible, which Jacob found strange at first, but it helped shape his character. It was the right choice. We moved Luke to the ACE school, too.

The students wore uniforms—boys in navy pants and red shirts, girls in navy skirts and red blouses. School clothes shopping was a cinch, and no one knew who had money or didn't—no one was harassed for wearing the wrong clothes. We didn't have enough electricity for an iron, so Thea laid the clothes out flat to dry. They dried with no wrinkles.

08&90

In October we drove our Webelos Scouts to Leavenworth for a weekend camping trip. Webelos are boys just one year shy of entering Boy Scouts. The National Fish Hatchery there had been abandoned, so the containment ponds were full of silt and weeds and garbage. The US Fish and Wildlife Service invited several local troops of Boy Scouts to clean up the fish hatchery, and they called us too, even though our boys were all younger. They offered us a special patch, so we jumped at the chance.

When we arrived at the site, Thea gave the boys a pep talk. "Gather 'round guys, we're going to talk about this quick, so don't run off. Everybody has something to do. We're going to camp over there against that bank, across this big field, so take your tents and backpacks and sleeping bags over there. We'll get set up for the night, and then you can play.

They fidgeted.

"Listen up, guys, we're here to help clean up, and this is your mission: Pick up every cigarette butt, every candy wrapper, gum wrapper, paper, plastic anything that is not natural, not supposed to be in the forest, and put it in the garbage bags we'll have out. Okay?"

I added, "If it didn't grow here, pick it up and throw it away."

She continued. "You guys are going to be the best Scouts here. We're the youngest, but we're going to show all the other Boy Scouts what a good troop we are. Okay?"

"Okay!" they shouted. They grabbed their gear and tore off across the field.

Johnny Youngblood approached Thea as we set up camp. "Mrs. Beaty?" he whispered. "I've never slept outside before."

"Really?"

"I want to sleep in the tent with you and Mr. Beaty."

"The other boys are all going to be sleeping outside, but if you want to do that, it's okay."

He relaxed a little, and walked away, but didn't seem satisfied.

Thea called to the boys, "Please bring your cans of food for hobo stew. I'm going to cook dinner."

We'd told the boys to bring a can of anything, and we'd throw it all together in one big pot.

Jacob murmured, "This is going to be disgusting."

Thea cut up an onion, fried it with two pounds of hamburger, opened the cans and dumped them in. She added chicken noodle soup, chili, green beans, diced tomatoes, peas, peaches, and more.

It wasn't pretty when she finished.

Lance took one look. "I'm not eating that."

"Oh, but you're going to be hungry," I said.

"I don't care. I'm not eating that."

I watched Jacob take his first tentative bite. His eyes widened in surprise.

"Is it good?" I asked.

"Yeah!"

The other boys seemed to feel the same way, because they came back for seconds and more until the big pot was empty. Lance never took a bite.

"Mrs. Beaty?" Johnny came back to Thea after dinner.

"Yes?"

"Where are you going to have your heads in the tent?"

"We're going to be against this wall."

"If I put my head right next to you, out here, will that be okay? And I could still talk to you? And you could put your hand underneath and I'd be okay."

"That'd be fine, Johnny."

The boys settled in to sleep, and pretty soon they were out. They slept through the night without drama and were up with the sun the next morning to start cleaning up the fish hatchery.

At the end of the day, one of the troop leaders came over to us and said, "You gave those boys a pep talk when you got out of your truck, and I heard it. I wish I'd thought to talk to my boys like you did. Your boys did what you told them they were going to do. You said they were going to be the best, and they were."

"They really did well."

"This was just so great. Nice working with your troop."

Everybody got along, ate Hobo Stew, worked hard, played hard, and made a difference. Several of the kids had new experiences—all of them positive.

{ 41 }

JACOB AND I WERE ON HORSEBACK to go hunting. We rode a path I'd ridden many times. It was Jacob's first time. He was riding Ebony and I was on Cricket. He was ten years old, so I let him ride with an unloaded rifle in his scabbard, just to get a feel for it.

We were a long way out, and Jacob said, "I think this saddle feels loose."

I glanced back. It looked fine. We switched back and forth down a steep path. We reached the valley floor—flash! I watched Jacob face planting into the pine needles, his feet in the stirrups, his hands gripping the saddle horn. Ebony's head was pinned down. The saddle, still cinched, had slid to her ears, holding her head and front feet together.

She's going to freak out! Jacob's going to get hurt!

I bailed off Cricket, tied her to a tree, and talked to Ebony the whole time: "Settle down, settle, settle down..." She never did freak out, just stood there patiently while I extracted Jacob, rolled him away, and freed Ebony. She raised her head, shook herself. She bent down, sniffed the saddle, and bit a stray sprig of grass.

What a great horse!

I put the saddle back on Ebony, cinched it a little tighter, and Jacob climbed back on.

We rode north and then east into no-man's land, so far out we could see Azwell Dam up the Columbia River. In some places the hills were so steep it felt dangerous even to ride side hill. We worked our way south above the Columbia River towards Howard Flats and the Switchback hills.

We were headed for the backside of the Bowl when we saw a herd of mule deer, maybe fifteen or twenty of them. We were in the middle of nowhere, and popped over a ridge to see them all spread out before us. They caught our wind, and the whole herd together trotted away. *Wow, look at that!* I was grinning from ear to ear. I was hunting on horseback in the middle of nowhere with my boy.

The last day of the season we rode toward the Bowl on a more direct path, dropping down into Church Camp and then curving along a trail up around the face. We rode through the Bowl, and circled back around along the rim, looking down onto the angling path we had taken into the Bowl.

We came around the corner to see a big, huge buck. Massive. Huge rump, a big old rack, a big, thick neck.

I looked at the deer. He looked at us. I looked at Ebony carrying my son. We were on the edge of long steep hill.

I can shoot from the saddle if Cricket will stand still.

I looked at Jacob on Ebony again.

I don't want Ebony to jump, and Jacob get his foot stuck in the stirrup, and get hurt real bad, or worse.

I looked at the deer. He was still staring at us.

{ 350 }

I whispered, "Jacob, c'mon, get off, get off, get off." Jacob just looked at me. The wheels were spinning too fast to get any traction. He didn't move. I had been tense, ready to grab my rifle and fire and get that big, beautiful mule deer, but I relaxed. *No, I'm not shooting. The deer is not worth it, I don't even care. I'm not going to shoot until my boy is safe on the ground.*

Jacob finally started moving, and made it down to the ground. I pulled out my rifle.

Boing, the deer bounced. *You had your chance, pal!* He disappeared.

Jacob climbed back on and we tried to catch him, but that deer had vanished.

Well, maybe next year.

∽≀∾

I met a young contractor who came into the lumberyard often. Our kids were the same age, and we got along great. He mentioned he and his black powder muzzleloading group were greeting the Centennial Train at the Chelan Falls train station. They'd be wearing their fur trapper garb, helping celebrate the event. I'd made a trade blanket fur trapper Capote years earlier from plans in *Wildwood Wisdom*. He said our whole family was welcome to share the fun.

Greeting the old steam train celebrating Washington's hundredth year as a state began our family's involvement with the muzzle loading group. We shot targets near Lake Antilon, began making authentic pre-1840 clothing

{ 351 }

for the boys, and even Thea joined in. We camped in a wall tent at first, the boys excited about throwing tomahawks and knives and making their own moccasins. We eventually bought a nineteen foot teepee and made complete outfits of buckskin leggings and breechcloths. Thea made period-correct dresses for herself and enjoyed the beauty and process of beadwork and quillwork. It was great family fun and started with one contact at the lumberyard.

❧

That fall, Edd and Sharon switched me to salary at the lumberyard. It was a fair wage for averaging forty hours a week, a slight bump from my hourly rate. *Okay, well, salary works.*

But it didn't, really. We were still just barely getting by, not getting ahead. The faintest doubts began to take shape unrecognized in the back of my mind.

{ 42 }

WE WENT TO CHURCH with a man named Leonard Cohrane. Thea had worked with his wife at the clinic. Leonard found out I was a machinist. "You should apply to work at the dam. Oh, you would be so good there."

That would be working for the County—good pay, good benefits.

"There's an opening at Azwell," Leonard said. "I've worked there a long, long time."

Ooh, sweet! Douglas County. That's north out of Chelan.

So I applied and was invited for an interview. I drove to Wenatchee and it went well until the interviewer asked where I was from.

"We live in Chelan. I'd be coming from Union Valley."

Long pause.

"Hmm. Well if you were from Seattle, we probably would hire you."

"Well, I live in Chelan now, but I'm from North Seattle. I worked in Seattle at Belshaw. And ELDEC. I'm a machinist from Seattle."

"Well... I don't know. We need to look at some other applicants. Thanks for your time today."

What? Just like that? But I'm the one they're looking for!

{ 353 }

I followed up in person. I wrote a letter explaining my skills and experiences. I dropped all the names I knew. Still they said no.

I have to provide something better than this for my family. Salary was not working out well at the lumberyard. They didn't pay extra for extra work, but they *did* pay less for less work.

I was singing in a production called *The Conspirators.* Marita, playing my girlfriend, and I sang teasers at lunch for various community organizations, promoting the show. Sometimes I'd get back ten or twenty minutes late, and Sharon would dock my pay.

"I thought you said I was salary? You know what I'm doing—I'm singing—with Marita. This is for the valley." My voice was high from the tension I felt.

"Well, we're not going to pay you if you're not here."

"So salary means I work all the overtime you can squeeze out of me with no extra pay, but as soon as I'm ten minutes late, you dock me?"

"That's how we do it here."

That night I talked to Thea about the feed store in Cashmere.

"We could move out there, maybe? I've heard rumors it's for sale."

Thea was always supportive. She'd follow me wherever I suggested.

"Sure, let's check it out," she said.

The feed store in Cashmere was selling blue sky. He proved he made money, but he was including his fencing

{ 354 }

business. He wouldn't separate the feed store from the fencing business. He wouldn't show us the papers.

I said, "I'm going to need a loan. I can't just go to the bank and say, 'Yeah, they're doing really good.' I gotta have some numbers."

He said, "Well, I really can't separate them because I'm running two businesses on the same set of books."

"Okay. Well, we can't buy your business."

Then we looked into ice distribution. The ice was made and bagged in Manson for delivery to the coolers at the grocery stores in the region. Safeway, Apple Market, Pat and Mikes. Manson to Chelan, Pateros, and Brewster.

The owner said, "You do really good in the summer. You do sell ice in the winter, but not nearly as much. It's pretty much a summer business. But my trucks aren't that good anymore. You'd need new trucks."

"Man, this isn't going to work!"

Next we looked into buying the feed store in Chelan. We talked to the owners, and they were making most of their money by selling plants and gardening gear. The feed store itself had one bag of this and two cans of that— it looked like the last day of the final sale.

"How do people get their feed?" Thea asked.

"People come in, order what they want, and come back to pick it up two or three days later." *Well, there's an opportunity for improvement right off the bat.*

"Can you show us your Form C?"

"No, we don't have it. My mom is paying for this right now."

"Well, we have to know what you're making, income and expenses, so the bank will give us a loan."

"Oh, well, it doesn't make any difference, because our mom is paying for it."

"Well, my mom is not going to pay for this for me, and I bet neither is your mom."

"Does your mom have the Form C?"

"I don't think so. It probably wouldn't be very accurate anyway. When we need a bag of grain, we just take it home."

"You don't write that down?"

"No. It's our grain."

"Really? So this is how you run a business? You don't keep track of anything, you don't keep shelves stocked. I've come by a few times in the middle of the day, and you're locked up and nobody is here. How can you possibly run a business when you're not even here?"

I discovered a Manson gas station for sale—a large lot, a big three-bay building—perfect for a farm and feed store. The area needed a functioning feed store closer than Wenatchee. I'd made drawings of how it would all look. I was excited.

Then we learned about extra requirements for using the gas station as a feed store. The EPA said since it had been a gas station, the next owner had to dig out the tanks and leave the ground airing out for two years. I couldn't do a thing with the building for that time. Buy a building to sit and watch it? I don't think so.

Now the doubts were hard to ignore.

Scout camp was a few months away in the summer, and I asked for the time off work to be with my boys at the camp.

"That's a real busy time of year, but you can have the time off. You won't be getting any vacation pay, though."

"What? I've been here almost three years, and no vacation?"

"No vacation."

I walked out. *I'm getting nowhere here. I've been here three years and I'm still struggling. I've been doing a good job for them, I know I have. I know Edd appreciates it, but he's not calling the shots.*

I told Thea when I got home, "You know what? I've had enough. I'm calling a friend from ELDEC. I was a machinist before I left, and they were sad to see me go. I enjoyed that work. Maybe there's an opening."

"Okay," she said.

I called one evening in early May. "Hey, Bruce, this is Jim Beaty."

"Are you looking for work?" He didn't even say hello!

I said, "Well. Yeah."

"If you show up Monday, you got a job." It was Tuesday.

"Really? Where?"

"I'm working at Westwood Precision, by the Paine Field airport. It's a job shop, but we do some production, too. It's a good place to work."

"Really. Wow. Okay. I'll see you next Monday."

I went to Edd the next day and said, "I'm quitting. I got a job in Seattle. I can't do this anymore. I'm getting nowhere. No raises. No vacation. No retirement. You don't—obviously—think I'm that valuable. I don't want to live above a convenience store in a one room apartment. And that's where we'll end up without a decent job. So I quit."

Edd said, "Okay, okay, I understand."

"I can't give you two weeks' notice because they need me on Monday. So I'm gone."

"I understand."

I worked through Friday. On Sunday I drove over the mountains to my mom's house, and I showed up for work on the west side Monday morning.

{ Epilogue }

MY MOM STARTED LOOKING FOR A HOUSE for us right away. She found a place on Mother's Day, May 14th, 1989, and we went for a visit.

"It looks like a wonderful house, Mom," I said. "But we can't afford to put any money down. I don't want to sell our log house."

My mom said, "No, no, no. Don't sell the log house. I'll buy this, and you rent it from me. You make the payment, I'll get the deductions."

Luke said, "I don't think we should move here."

Thea said, "Why don't you think we should move here?"

"Well, first off, when it snows, we're going to freeze to death because there's no fireplace. And there's no wood cookstove."

She walked him around the house. "See this little thing?" It was the thermostat. "This is like at Grampa and Gramma's house. This turns on the heat, and there's a furnace downstairs, and the heat comes up through these vents on the floor."

"Oh."

"And see the stove—it's just like at Grampa and Gramma's and Gramma Gay's house. It's electric, so we don't need the wood."

"Okay."

"Now here's the bad news, Luke. It usually doesn't snow here."

"What!"

"If it does snow, it's just a little teeny bit. There's not a lot of snow here."

ⷢⷪ

Thea was driving across the trestle between Lake Stevens and Everett one day in the fall. The Cascades formed a line to the east in the clear blue sky. Bright white snow blanketed the peaks. *Oh, they're beautiful! And I don't have to worry about snow suits, or if the boots fit, or if we have gloves. Oh, this is wonderful, living here!*

ⷢⷪ

We stayed involved in Boy Scouts, and I became the Scout Master of a Troop in Machias, Washington. We camped and hiked or canoed every year until Jacob became an Eagle Scout and Luke reached Star Rank. Luke pursued Tae Kwon Do and qualified for first degree black belt. We joined a muzzle loading group on the west side, and participated for years in authentic pre-1840's fur trade era events.

We continued to visit the cabin in summer and winter. The three day President's Day weekend trip was a family favorite. We'd leave the west side after work on Friday and arrive after midnight. No one lived near the cabin, so the roads weren't plowed. We'd snowshoe the half mile or so to the house under a shining moon, the snow sparkling, bright as day, hauling our gear on a sled I'd built. Many times Luke or Jake would bring friends, and we'd spend the long weekend sledding and enjoying the quiet.

More recently we've gone over for the New Year, shooting fireworks bought on the reservation. It was quite a show for the neighbors, more of whom live in the area now, who mentioned they liked it. We've gone over for Christmas, too.

We will never sell as long as I'm alive and both our sons think of it as home. It's where they grew up. I think it will stay in the family for many more years.

∽§∾

Leaving was bittersweet. We hadn't failed, we'd really *done* it. We'd built a log house and made a living for six years. We didn't end up supporting ourselves with the land, but I never thought we would. I thought I'd be a more successful hunter, but it wasn't the challenges of cabin living that drove us back to the west side.

There was no future for us in Chelan. Thea and I both had the best jobs available to us. We couldn't get ahead. We couldn't get raises. We didn't have a family business. We didn't have the right last name, and we'd hit an invisible ceiling.

I came to the realization that those little second floor windows above the stores downtown are little one room apartments, and that's where we'd retire. The time would come when we couldn't handle winter anymore, so we'd have to live someplace easier—those places downtown. *I don't want that, I don't want to end there.*

It wasn't a disappointment as much as a realization. We'd done it. We'd built the log house, lived in it year-round, just like I wanted. I didn't have to say, "I wish I had." And I got to keep it.

ɔʒຣɔ

Luke married his high school sweetheart, and they have three terrific boys who love going to the cabin. Their youngest endearingly calls it "The Cavin." Luke became a fire fighter, and is now a paramedic.

Jacob was appointed by Congressman Metcalf to the U.S. Merchant Marine Academy in Kings Point, New York, where he graduated with a Third Mate's license and a U.S. Navy Ensign reserve commission. Five years after graduating, he had the sea time and test scores to advance his license to Master, Any Gross Tons Upon Oceans. In 2006, just twenty-eight years old, he sailed as captain for a disaster relief ministry. The all-volunteer crew took a World War II cargo ship to Israel shortly after the Lebanon War.

Jacob moved back to the cabin in 2007. He reclaimed the house from the moths and the mice and made it his home. He plumbed the house with PEX, added a tankless propane water heater, and installed a solar power system. He mounted the windmill on a tall pole in the middle of a field. It makes electricity when the wind blows hard. He wired the house with outlets and switches—just like downtown!

For wildfire safety in the summer, Jacob pulled up acres of bitterbrush with a special hand tool I made. He gathered firewood for the winter, and learned to plow snow. He loved every minute of life at the cabin, even the hard ones.

Jacob had a great job at the hospital downtown, but he never could find his lady there. She was running the orphanage she'd started in South America. He met her while traveling in Bolivia, but that's a story for another time.

{ Afterword & Acknowledgements}

I WAS FOUR YEARS OLD, MY BROTHER NOT YET ONE, when my dad moved our family to the woods—1983. We traded suburban Seattle for building an off-grid log cabin in the Union Valley of north central Washington. I grew up thinking it was normal to retrieve spring water with gallon milk jugs, and illuminate our home with kerosene lamps.

I returned to the cabin from some years of sea voyaging at the age of twenty-nine. We'd left our cabin home eighteen years before. Cleaning the house, I filled five vacuum bags with moth wings and mouse droppings. Living at the cabin provoked many questions.

"What was the story of the windmill?" I asked my dad around the time living without electricity started to cramp my style. "How long before the house had plumbing from the well?" I asked when I tired of bathing from large stainless steel bowls. "What about the time mom drove off the road?"..."And when Luke fell down the well?"..."What about the cougar that stalked us to the spring?"

I'd heard snippets growing up, and even lived through some of the experiences myself, though with a kid's perspective. Dad and mom answered my questions one story at a time, but I wanted more. I wanted to know the *whole story*.

"Dad, I know what I want for my birthday," I said in the spring of 2011. "I want you to write *Winter's Comin'.*" This had long been the working title of the book we imagined writing about our Union Valley experience.

"But I don't have the calendars with our notes anymore," Dad protested. "I gave them to my sister, and they were lost when she moved back east."

My birthday came and went. No book. I pressed for the story as a Christmas gift. My dad made a large pencil sketch of my cat, and taped to the back the pages containing his first 18,000 words. I was thrilled.

I moved from the cabin to Bolivia in July 2012. Dad had made little progress on the book, despite my asking for more of the story. Jennifer and I married in Bolivia on November 30th, the same day my parents had married thirty-eight years before. Our first daughter was born in October 2013, and the three boys we adopted, ages nine, ten and ten, came to live with us that December.

I taught high school science in Bolivia for two years. I did not renew my contract, but decided to become an author instead. The trouble was, I couldn't create the cabin stories myself. I needed Dad to give me the raw material which I could then polish, sort, and format. Dad had only given me 7,000 more words by June 2014. Mom had written about 4,000 when she came to Bolivia for Sophia's birth. I would not be paying any bills with an unwritten book. Life was less expensive in Bolivia. But not free.

I signed up on a freelance job website and was offered a job in Search Engine Optimization. I knew nothing about SEO, but I was a quick study and lapped up everything my kind boss taught me. This paid the bills, but I kept pressing my dad for more stories.

Our family traveled to the States in the fall of 2014, and I brought my voice recorder. *If Dad won't type, I know I can get him to talk*...And talk he did! My brother Luke asked some great questions, as did Jennifer. Mom and dad both answered at length, quarreling only occasionally about details or sequence—their memories were thirty years old.

All told, I recorded forty hours of recollections, including a few rabbit trails. Back in Bolivia, I began transcribing—one minute of talking took about four minutes to type. Mom and dad often talked over one another, making it difficult to discern what they were saying. Even when only one was speaking, I couldn't keep up. The process dragged.

Once all the stories were transcribed, I had to organize them. The stories hadn't been told in chronological order. Winter stories and hunting stories and kid stories came lumped together, even if they happened years apart. I created codes for the individual stories and filled a massive spreadsheet, organized by month and year. The spreadsheet guided me to cut and paste big chunks of transcribed text into the manuscript.

I set to work polishing and formatting, still regularly asking mom and dad for clarification or more information. Lydia was born in April 2015, and we moved back to the States in September.

Finally, I submitted the manuscript to our editor on January 30th, 2016—still with a few holes Dad needed to fill. The edit motivated my dad to generate 10,000 more words and fill in the last gaps. Bradley Harris has helped us trim the fat and keep the book a reasonable length.

I am grateful to my dad for setting my life's adventurous tone, for loving his family, and for always serving as a great provider and guide. Thanks, Dad, for living an experience worth writing about and sharing the story with us. I am grateful to my mother for supporting my dad and his crazy plans, for loving her family, and always caring for us. Thanks, Mom, for enduring the hardships and being the mom Luke and I needed. I am grateful to my brother for his questions and encouragement throughout this writing process.

My wife Jennifer deserves my gratitude for her encouragement and support and steadfastness. She reviewed the book and asked for more of the story from my mom's perspective. Much of the human interest component story is thanks to my wife's guiding questions. Thank you, dear.

I am grateful to my friends and extended family who have provided encouragement and declared their interest in reading the whole story. I am grateful to Brad for tightening the final product.

Finally, I am grateful to you, reader, for taking a risk on an unknown author—I hope you have enjoyed our story and been encouraged to persevere and live a life without regrets.

ABOUT THE AUTHOR

Jake & Jennifer on their first date

Jake Beaty is co-author with his dad, Jim Beaty, of *Winter's Comin'*. They built a log cabin in the woods, lived without electricity or running water, and survived bitter cold winters. Jake grew up in the cabin, and still considers the place home.

Jake graduated from the US Merchant Marine Academy, and sailed as ship's captain by the age of 28. He volunteered with Friend Ships and sailed to Haiti, to New Orleans after Hurricane Katrina, and to Israel during the Lebanon War in a WWII ship. These adventures will be the subject of Jake's next book.

Jake met his wife Jennifer in Bolivia. He was visiting a child he sponsors through Compassion International. She was directing the orphanage she had founded eight years before. They have five children: Joel, Michael, Samuel, Sophia, and Lydia. These adventures will be the subject of Jake's third book.

ABOUT THE AUTHOR

Jim & Thea on their first date

Jim Beaty is co-author with his son, Jake Beaty, of *Winter's Comin'*. Jim's desires and future plans were shaped by Bonanza, Davey Crocket, and Saturday morning westerns. He pictured living with his family in a log house he'd built with his own hands. Jim's wife Thea was willing to share his dream.

Jim built on his mechanical aptitude as a kid by taking apart everyday items to see how they worked. He worked as a commercial artist, managed a bicycle shop, and logged giant first growth trees along the Washington coast. The experiences of using chain saws and rigging would come in handy while building the cabin.

Winter's Comin' recounts the hardships and victories in Jim's pursuit of his childhood dreams. Be encouraged as you read Jim's story of his lifelong dream fulfilled, and start working toward fulfilling yours.

{ 370 }

61883834R00205